Social Media Tribes

Social Media Tribes

Jordan's Bedouin and the Margins of the State

GEOFFREY F. HUGHES

University of Texas Press *Austin*

First edition, 2026

♾ The paper used in this book meets the minimum requirements of ANSI/NISO Z39.48–1992 (R1997) (Permanence of Paper).

Cataloging-in-Publication Data is available from the Library of Congress

ISBN 978-1-4773-3471-3 (hardcover)
ISBN 978-1-4773-3472-0 (paperback)
ISBN 978-1-4773-3473-7 (PDF)
ISBN 978-1-4773-3474-4 (ePub)

doi:10.7560/334713

To Isaac

Contents

Illustrations

Note on Transliteration

Pronunciation is political and of course so is transcription and transliteration. As elsewhere, how a Jordanian speaks Arabic says a lot about them: their origins, alliances, commitments, and aspirations. At the same time, Arabic is very much a *written* language—and the correct spelling and pronunciation of the formal register of the language as revealed in the *Qur'ān* (known as *faṣḥa*) has been highly standardized for well over a thousand years. Jordan is also a small country in which almost everyone has been required to devote years of their life to learning the formal register of Arabic thanks to compulsory schooling. The resulting linguistic shibboleths are consequently so subtle and specific that they would probably be more accurately described as "registers of locale" despite a thriving local language ideology that tries to parse the differences between tribal, Palestinian, Bedouin, urban, Jordanian, rural, and peasant "dialects" of Arabic (Doughan 2017). For instance, pronouncing the *qāf* as a glottal stop, rendered as ['] in this text (and not to be confused with the pharyngeal fricative or *'ayn* [']) is a common way to mark oneself as urban and possibly of Palestinian, Egyptian, Syrian, or Lebanese descent. Other decidedly urban and thus usually non-Bedouin and nontribal variants include a tendency to pronounce the letter *thā'* as a [t] and a tendency to pronounce the letter *dhāl,* as a [z]. Meanwhile, pronouncing the letter *kāf* as [ch] is associated with certain rural and tribal communities, especially around the town of Karak (though it is also common in parts of Iraq and elsewhere). Pronouncing the *qaf* as a [g] or pronouncing it correctly are both associated with rural, Bedouin, and tribal groups. In fact, there is a long history in the region of treating Arabia's Bedouin tribes as the custodians of "correct" Arabic and even of urban intellectuals turning to them for linguistic guidance (though it was mostly premised on treating the Bedouin as living fossils). For the purposes of this book, I merely note some of this by means of introduction to the fractiousness of Jordanian identity categories and attendant ideologies—even as the performance of these subtle distinctions is also complex, situated, and uneven. Because almost everyone I interviewed would agree more or less about how the Arabic words I render in Latin script in this book should be spelled in Arabic, I have opted to mostly sidestep this layer of ethnographic richness in verbal performance by relying on the transliteration system of the *International Journal of Middle East Studies*. However, in a few places where I refer to a specific verbal utterance, I let the original [g] shine through instead of "correcting" it to a *qāf*. I also defer to local pronunciation in the case of certain colloquialisms. For instance, tribute (literally "brotherhood") is rendered as *khāwa* and not *khuwwa* (as it is pronounced in many parts of Syria and the Arabian peninsula). In cases of place names, personal names, and words like "sheikh" that have been assimilated into English, I generally defer to the standard English spelling.

Social Media Tribes

INTRODUCTION

Tribalism and the Politics of an Accusation

Is social media making us tribal? Many important people certainly seem to think so. From heads of state like former US president Barack Obama and Australia's former premier Scott Morrison on down to academic superstars and rank-and-file school disciplinarians, a growing chorus of authority figures warns that liberal democracy—even public order—are threatened by social media–inspired "tribalism." For instance, weeks before Donald Trump's victory in the 2016 presidential election, Obama took the occasion of his final address to the United Nations as president to caution against tribalism in a speech that was widely interpreted as an oblique attack on Trumpian populism.[1] In the speech, Obama warned that despite the promises of globalization and technological innovation, "technology now allows any person with a smartphone to see how the most privileged among us live and the contrast between their own lives and others." While this might lead to resentments, Obama warned, "if we discriminate on the basis of race or tribe or ethnicity, then the fragile bonds of civilization will fray. We see this mindset too often in the Middle East" (White House 2016).[2] Echoing and expanding upon these themes in the aftermath of a deadly 2019 terrorist attack by an Australian white supremacist against Muslim worshippers in neighboring New Zealand, Morrison spoke of how "as debate becomes more fierce, the retreat to tribalism is increasingly taking over, and for some, extremism takes hold. Reading only news that we agree with, interacting with people only we agree with, and having less understanding and grace towards others . . . simply because we disagree with them."[3] Morrison then likened the act of anti-immigrant violence against Muslims to the specter of Islamic terrorism, echoing Obama in treating social media as something sinister, other, and vaguely oriental that threatened to sow division, degrade democratic debate, and promote violence.

However, my research as an anthropologist living and working with highly networked, self-styled Bedouin tribespeople in the Middle East offers an ironic counterpoint to the warnings of these elder statesmen. When I say "self-styled," I mean that my Bedouin interlocutors consciously fashioned themselves and their communities as tribes. Openly contemptuous of modernity and cosmopolitanism, they grounded their ethics and politics in what they took to be their customary obligations to kin in marriage, care, and collective defense. Working as a Peace Corps volunteer from 2006 to 2008 (a high-modernist *mission civilatrice* if there ever was one), it did not take long for me to realize that references to things as "civilized" (*ḥaḍari*) were generally condescending at best. Long before I set out to study how the uptake of social media was shaping (and being shaped by) the region's politics and society, I had grown accustomed to hearing elegiac monologues (usually from older men) about the deleterious impact of new communications technologies on society. A common refrain went that, "These days, the youth don't sit and learn [in tribal gatherings] the way they used to. They're always on their phones!" These senior males were not worried about an upsurge in tribalism, though. To the contrary, they fretted that social media was leading to democracy (*dīmukrātiyya*), which to them meant chaos and insubordination, and represented an assault on their tribal customs and traditions. Yet the claim that the traditional tribal order was disappearing, so often repeated by Jordan's gerontocracy, became increasingly incongruous as time went on and the Arab Spring erupted in 2011. There was instead a marked uptick in what the new online press and those who commented on their stories on social media referred to as *ishtibākāt 'ashā'iriyya* in Arabic and "tribal clashes" in English. In fact, this was precisely why these self-appointed guardians of the social order increasingly counseled me not to confuse the village youths' violent tribal clashes with Jordan's venerable "customs and traditions."

I want to take a step back, though, from somewhat tired debates about whether social media is democratizing or anti-democratic, progressive or regressive, and focus instead on the social function of these wider problematics. Of course, if the dangers of social media were only invoked by political leaders in an attempt to dodge accountability for their failures amidst a wider crisis of legitimacy, these concerns might be dismissed easily enough. One could even be forgiven for seeing similarities in the parallel anti-social media jeremiads of Western politicians and Jordan's tribal elders. Especially against the background of the tumult of the "Arab Spring," it was common until recently for people to see revolutionary potential in social media. This networked protest movement emerged in Tunisia in 2010 and spread to Egypt and the entire region, sweeping away entrenched dictatorships and directly influencing Occupy Wall Street, Black Lives Matter, and other protest movements in the process (Juris 2012; Tufekci 2017). In the early 2010s, there were widespread, often downright euphoric predictions about social media's potential, with Facebook and Twitter receiving top billing. In a column that was derided even at the time (Fernández 2011, 234–236),[4] *New York Times* columnist Thomas Friedman—pointedly ignoring the agency of the protesters themselves—even urged his readers not to overlook the effects of Google Maps, which he claimed had allowed the masses to catch a glimpse of how their rulers were living in luxury even as they wallowed in poverty.[5] At the time, paranoia about the corrosive effects of extreme levels of political and economic inequality seemed justified—especially when coupled with the idea that a new technology could either bring the whole edifice down or serve as its salvation.

Yet this folk sociological analysis emphasizing the transformative impact of social media, so apparently *of the zeitgeist* from the halls of power to the streets of major world cities and even sleepy Jordanian villages, also deserves some suspicion. For one thing, social media (or *tawāṣul ijtimāʿī* as it has come to be known in Arabic) is a slippery concept with porous boundaries that clearly incorporates dramatic social, political, economic, and legal transformations that both precede social media's arrival on the scene and also seem to feed off of it. Social media denotes a nexus where financialization, low-cost computing power, the retreat of the state, and new forms of authorship and cultural production come together. Social media also has affinities with related concepts like "digital media," which focuses less on the interactive dimension and more on the mode of dissemination, especially computers, cell phones, and other devices that encode and decode information as a series of ones and zeroes (Coleman 2010). Social media is also sometimes conflated with the phenomenon of user-generated content—though this phenomenon of course long predates the arrival of the internet.[6] Then there is "the platform economy" (Kenney and Zysman 2016), exemplified by companies like Uber, Google, and Amazon. While heavily reliant on variations of the peer-to-peer dynamics and algorithmic trust systems of social media, such platform economy companies are usually considered distinct insofar as social media is typically seen as entertainment. Part of the confusion is strategic: like other "platforms," social media operations claim many prerogatives enjoyed by existing companies in state-regulated industries but also claim to be something wholly different when convenient. My use of the term "social media" here (like my use of "tribalism") is therefore intended less as a context-free theoretical concept and more as an appropriation of a local, "emic" concept that my interlocutors deploy to make sense of the world around them. In both cases, the usefulness of terms like "tribe" and "social media" is due in no small part to their ability to shift meaning strategically as social actors alternately highlight their connections to the state and disown them as convenient.

For my part, I could sense that some sort of global sociotechnical shift was afoot as soon as I set foot in Jordan in 2006, even if I lacked the vocabulary to grasp it. I quickly abandoned any romantic ideas I had entertained about joining the Peace Corps and shedding my technological attachments. Mobile phones that could handle text messages and voice calls were ubiquitous, and while it would take another five to ten years before most Jordanians had internet access through their phones, there was a lively trade in music and video files with people in the immediate vicinity via Bluetooth. Accordingly, I quickly bought a cheap Chinese-made model to join in. Especially among the younger generations, Jordan has been at the forefront of adopting these technologies, much like other parts of the global South that skipped over the landline and immediately embraced digital, cellular alternatives.[7] The nearby university town in Irbid where I was initially based boasted of holding the record for the most internet cafes in the Guinness Book of World Records at the time.[8] When I joined Facebook in 2008 as I was finishing my service in Jordan, many of my friends and colleagues in the village where I taught English already had accounts, and as I went off to begin studying for my PhD, the emerging phenomenon of "social media" became vital to keeping in touch. As a result, I have never completely "left" Jordan in the way that traditional anthropologists did: it was easy to keep up with weddings, funerals, and other important community events from afar, engaging in what my colleague Anna-Maria Walter and I have termed practices of "staying tuned" (2021). Far from seeing Jordan romantically as a sort of technological backwater, as I had assumed in my ignorance prior to my arrival, I quickly came to experience it as a laboratory on the technological cutting edge.

Yet as the fieldwork for my first book on changing marriage practices unfolded amidst what many commentators have come to call the Arab Spring, I quickly became dissatisfied with how the idea of an "Arab Spring" and the attendant technological triumphalism were being mobilized to describe what was happening around me. While 2011 was certainly more of an inflection point in countries like Egypt, Tunisia, Syria, and Libya, there were also important continuities with previous protest movements in those countries, including the long-standing political ambitions of the Muslim Brotherhood and leftist and trade unionist groups. In fact, in a report from the Carnegie Endowment published in the early and heady days of 2011, seasoned activists from "labour unions and leftist political parties" were already presciently arguing that "the use of social media creates short-lived coalitions but not lasting structures and organizations" (Ottaway and Hamzawy 2011, 9). Unsurprisingly, though, the report went on to note that activists, especially the younger ones, who had been drawn to the flexibility of these new organizing methods were already sick of hearing these critiques, foreshadowing many later controversies.

My concern with the image of the Arab Spring that I was reading about in the Arabic- and English-language press as I was conducting my fieldwork was therefore not merely a concern about periodization, but also about the wider social dynamics that were at stake. Here, my perspective was profoundly shaped by the fact that I was living in a rural community where some of the most overt expressions of the Arab Spring were couched in a tribal idiom: between 2011 and 2012, my ostensibly unrelated research on marriage brought me face-to-face with five separate incidents of these so-called "tribal clashes." They were all organized online through Facebook and WhatsApp, with the outcome later disseminated there as well. Some involved the tribe I was living with, while others broke out in the markets of Madaba (where I was doing fieldwork at the local Sharia Courts) and at Jordan University in the capital city of Amman (where I was doing some archival research). These clashes were politically ambiguous. In some cases, more marginalized tribes rose up against tribes with deep connections to the state security apparatus, as in the case where members of a tribe of Palestinian refugees attacked another local tribe's market stalls in retaliation for a murder while I sheltered with surprised fellow patrons. In fact, as Sean Yom (2014) has detailed, some of the most tenacious critics of the regime to emerge in 2011–2012 were the Ḥirāk, a largely tribally based opposition movement rooted in some of rural Jordan's most marginalized communities. Yet in other cases the clashes seemed like yet another way that certain well-connected families could, perhaps more than ever, practically get away with murder.

All these experiences led me to see tribes (alongside the Arab Spring and social media) as morally and politically ambiguous. They could help mobilize support either in favor of the state or against it. To a degree, they could help the weak and the poor to organize, but they could also do so much more when the powerful mobilized their substantial resources and privileges to take advantage of a given situation or controversy. These experiences sensitized me to the fact that the uptake of social media was not just transforming tribal dynamics in Jordan. Rather, tribal dynamics were profoundly shaping how social media was being taken up in Jordan. In fact, to the degree that the tribe had long served to mediate between individual identity and the state, it suddenly seemed perfectly suited to the social media era in Jordan. Moreover, the more anglophone commentators evoked the specter of social media tribalism, the more I began to appreciate how social media was not merely some sort of exogenous technical intervention into society, but rather something always already highly social—and politicized. In that spirit, this book is not merely concerned with how "social media" came to transform tribal politics in Jordan, but also with how ideas about tribalism have profoundly shaped the uptake of social media in Jordan and beyond.

Social Media, "Tribalism," and the Specter of Primordial Ties

In this book, I will argue that the popular anglophone discourse of tribalism that has proliferated in recent years is fundamentally projective and othering, exaggerating many of the worst excesses of now-discredited anthropological approaches. While there is a sense in which tribalism is taken to be a human foible that anyone can fall prey to, the whole conceit of the framing is fundamentally polemical because it positions the speaker and those in the audience who agree as savvier and more sophisticated than those being diagnosed with tribal tendencies (who are therefore delegitimated as political actors). The accusation of tribalism implies that the accused's arguments are fundamentally given in bad faith and can thus be readily dismissed because they are too self-interested, subjective and readily influenced by the immediate peer group. Paradoxically, this suggests (as I will explore at some length in the coming pages) that the most "tribal" thing one can do is to accuse those with whom one disagrees of tribalism. I will argue that the only path out of this aporia is to recognize tribalism (at least as anthropologists today encounter it) not as something primordial and other, but rather as a historical byproduct of the state that can emerge under specific political conditions where centralizing authorities struggle to manage their hinterlands.[9]

The discourse of tribalism that has become a mainstay of political commentary and futurology in the mass media finds its counterpart in a growing academic literature that seeks to diagnose, map, and explain the phenomenon of tribalism in various ways. There is a pronounced interest in political science, for instance, in mapping out and defining the so-called political "tribes" that define our contemporary moment.[10] There is also a revival of interest in moral psychology that has leveraged the concept of tribalism to analyze human behavior more generally, exemplified by Joshua Greene's *Moral Tribes* and Jonathan Haidt's *The Righteous Mind.* Finding a puzzle in how opinions about seemingly unrelated "culture war" issues tend to cluster together, these authors argue that the explanation is that group belonging is producing moral and political judgments (rather than the other way around). What these analyses have in common is a tendency to see in this "tribalism" a sort of return of liberal cosmopolitanism's repressed, posing a challenge to the ideal of a public sphere in which the issues of the day and political alliances are determined by individuals engaged in rational deliberation. As I will argue, despite the occasional claim that tribalism is a human universal, there is also a markedly self-exonerating tendency to treat it as distinctly Middle Eastern and foreign to more "Western" ways of thinking.

It is also notable how vague and amorphous the term "tribe" becomes in much of the contemporary popular commentary on tribalism. At least in traditional anthropological jargon, the word "tribe" had a rather specific meaning. It described an essentialist form of group identity and social organization grounded in idioms of blood and soil, where direct descent from a common ancestor was not just an ideological conceit but also subject to a modicum of genealogical precision. This is distinct from the more self-consciously artificial notion of "clan" in which the identification is more abstract, potentially even involving a myth of common descent from an animal in the case of so-called "totemism" (Durkheim [1912] 1995; Fields and Fields 2012, 200–212; Levi-Strauss 1962). In contrast, one of the hallmarks of tribespeople (for both anthropologists and tribespeople themselves) is that they care deeply about the specifics of their ancestry, usually the male line of descent in particular. In fact, my inability to say much of anything about my ancestors more than a few generations back often surprised my Jordanian interlocutors and rendered me (to them at least) distinctively nontribal. Moreover, at least from the perspective of Middle Eastern anthropology and history, sectarian religious identity is not just a variation on the theme of group-feeling—though it is that too, most famously as expressed in the fourteenth-century historian ibn Khaldun's ([1377] 2015) notion of *'aṣabiyya* or "group feeling." Even as kinship and sect are repeatedly conflated in practice (Kaminer 2024; Mikdashi 2022), religion continues to be held out as precisely the force that can transcend the situational morality and politics privileging kin-based, tribal identities with a notionally universal morality and politics. In fact, Islam's initial appeal is often explained by both believers and scholars of the tradition as a rejection of the tribalism of the pre-Islamic "Age of Ignorance" or *jāhiliyya* (Aslan 2011, 29–32).

The standard response among anthropologists with specialist cultural knowledge in recent decades has been to avoid engaging with commentary on tribalism that is so terminologically imprecise and often deeply riven with orientalist conceits. Yet this has had the effect of ceding the field to those using the term's academic credibility for their own polemics. To be clear, I am not calling for a return to a use of the term "tribe" as an allegedly culture-free analytic concept. In fact, as the slipperiness and analytic imprecision above implies, there are excellent reasons why anthropologists have long worked to banish the term from their analytic vocabularies. However, as the frequent resort to the term "tribe" (and the concept of tribalism) by ethnographic interlocutors and Western public intellectuals implies, ignoring the phenomenon will not make it go away. In fact, I would argue it is a part of anthropology's legacy that, embarrassing as it may be, anthropologists have a professional obligation to confront.

In that spirit, it is worth considering some of the key critiques of the concept of "tribe" that first led anthropologists to abandon it. I have already made reference to its imprecision, connotations of primitivity, and the barely covert normative assumptions about how "we" live now. For Edward Said, tribalism today means "fracturing societies, separating peoples, promoting greed, bloody conflict, and uninteresting assertions of minor ethnic or group particularity" (1994, 20). Echoing the liberation movements that inspired them, African and Arab postcolonial scholars like Said, Joseph Massad (2001), and Mahmood Mamdani (1996) argued for a greater emphasis on how tribes had been "invented" (Said 1994, 264) by colonial officials and orientalist writers—if not merely "lingered over and caricatured" (1994, 275–276).[11] Anthropologists could hardly ignore that there was some truth to this—or that there was growing impatience among many in the postcolonial world to treat tribalism as a sort of *Colonial Effect* (as Massad titled his history of Jordan and its tribes) and consign it to the dustbin of history even where it had been taken up "antagonistically" by "liberation movements" (Said 1994, 193).

Amidst the postcolonial backlash against tribalism, even the tradition of anthropologists writing of tribalism positively started to seem sinister.[12] As Lila Abu Lughod noted in her critique of how tribalism has traditionally been handled in the anthropology of the Arab world:

> A certain admiration tinges descriptions of the fierce independence attributed to those in segmentary societies, including Middle Eastern tribesmen. These are real men, free from the emasculating authority of the state and polite society. Furthermore, for many writers, these tribesmen represent romantic political ideals of freedom from authority and loyalty to democracy. (1989, 286)[13]

I will have a lot more to say about how the anarchic dimensions of tribalism sit awkwardly with its hierarchical and patriarchal underpinnings in the chapters on **Tribalism** and **Mercy**—as well as how early anthropologists were often blinded to these inequalities due to their own masculinist and elitist biases. However, as Abu Lughod goes on to note in drawing on the work of Michelle Rosaldo, this can also easily serve as "a rhetorical assertion of anthropologists' freedom from the projects of domination in which they participate" (Abu Lughod 1989, 287). In this way, identifying with such tribesmen allows anthropologists to preserve what Gloria Wekker (2016) has called "white innocence," abrogating to themselves the benefits of colonial systems of domination without any of the moral responsibility. Given my own positionality as not only a white male anthropologist but also a former employee of the US government (and sometimes-beneficiary of its largesse in the form of grants and fellowships), I must be especially wary of falling into this trap.

Yet it is not merely the implicit normativity of the concept of tribe that needs critiquing, but also how it has traditionally been used to construct a certain impression of time and historical development. To borrow a turn of phrase from Michel Rolph Trouillot, the tribesperson has traditionally filled what he called anthropology's "savage slot" (2003, 7–28). Abu Lughod's critique likewise sensitizes us to how *both* the romantic and modernist constructions of the tribe help to mystify the contemporaneity of the ethnographic encounters that produce anthropological knowledge about tribalism by abstracting them from their (post)-colonial context. In this regard, there is a real danger that the uncritical use of language like "tribe" and "tribalism" can participate in what Johannes Fabian (1983) has called "the denial of coevalness." As Fabian notes, ethnography often derives much of its authority from the intersubjective sharing of time in the ethnographic encounter, only to reject that shared time or "coevalness" in the final written account in favor of a detached and allegedly "objective" representation of ethnography's object of study existing in some other time.

Thanks to these critiques, a more recent review of the literature on the anthropology of the Middle East by Lara Deeb and Jessica Winegar notes positively that "tribal social organization has practically vanished as a topic of concern for scholars," though they continue less optimistically, "not for policy makers, right-wing analysts, and anthropologists embedded with the US military, many of whom persist in using stereotyped notions of tribal structures to explain political violence" (2012, 540). However, the tide appears to be shifting yet again. A recent roundtable in the *International Journal of Middle East Studies* framed the phenomenon as an "enigma" of the modern world in need of explanation: "The tribe seems to be all that the modern state is not: it defies positive law, rational administrative structures, equal citizenship based on individual rights and duties, and, still, in some cases, sovereignty based on fixed territorial boundaries." Yet as the conference call went on to note, tribalism has not merely endured. If anything, tribalism "seems even more pronounced in today's period of state disintegration and instability" (Wien 2021, 471). This represents a step forward in problematizing many of the tired binaries that have kept the study of tribalism so marginal for decades (between stasis and change, past and present, society and state in particular), and I am especially interested in taking up the implicit invitation here to go further in exploring how tribes can thrive not just in spite of the state but *because of* the state.

The tendency to oppose tribe and state deserves special scrutiny here because it can easily reproduce now-discredited hierarchies of political and cultural "development" in a more subtle form. On the one hand, as Seraje Assi notes in *The History and Politics of the Bedouin*, there is an agrarian, territorializing, sedentarizing, and ultimately statist bias uniting modern colonial and anticolonial movements in which "tribal and nomadic elements become no longer imaginable under colonial and national institutions, but are either erased . . . largely excluded . . . or modified and integrated" (2018, 12). Tribespeople themselves may even agree with this determination. As Yazan Doughan has noted, there has been a recent surge of interest in Jordan in a revisionist historiography rejecting universalizing and modernizing state narratives in favor of hyper-local histories of their own ancestors' long histories of tribal resistance (2019). On the other hand, the fact that states and tribes often find themselves in antagonistic relationships itself implies a deep and abiding relationship forged precisely amidst those antagonisms (its own sort of coevalness). This insight was central to the mid-twentieth-century political anthropology of scholars like Edmund Leach (1954), Morton Fried (1967), and Fredrik Barth (1968), who detailed how tribes enabled their putative constituents to cross political, ethnic, and ecological frontiers in search of autonomy, fortune, prestige, and other goods. While tribespeople might frustrate the aims of nearby states, they might also be instrumentalized to extend state power further than had previously been thought possible (Sneath 2007; 2009). The attempt to render tribes as a fundamentally "pre-state" phenomenon (even if their stubborn persistence increasingly became the thing to be explained) risks obscuring the ongoing vibrant traffic between tribes and states in personnel, ideas, and even organizational forms.

At the same time, if anthropologists have been guilty of invoking tribalism to deny coevalness with their interlocutors (in more or less subtle ways), then the discipline must also recognize how those interlocutors often invoke tribalism to *refuse* coevalness with anthropologists and the ideological projects with which they are associated. Acknowledging the historicity of tribes does not mean that anthropologists are in a position to force tribespeople to submit to a certain version of history. In fact, tribespeople often insist on their status as tribespeople precisely so that they can insist on alternative histories, which often critique the progressive developmental teleologies of nearby states and the anthropologists they employ. Anthropology risks naively parroting imperial discourses of self-legitimation if it is too assiduous in erasing what Andrew Shryock (1997) has called the "genealogical imagination," which negotiates present-day relations between individuals and groups through stories of their common ancestors.[14] Abu Lughod was certainly correct when she wrote that the Middle East had become a "prestige zone" for what she called "Homo Segmentarius," but the solution is not to deny tribalism's ongoing relevance but rather to reground it in the context of both its local *and* global imperial histories. However, doing so requires some rethinking of what the anthropological project was all about in the first place.

Reverse Anthropology: Methodological Reflections on Working with Jordan's Tribal Publics

The most exciting trend in anthropology in recent decades has been the increasing ability of those who were once silenced by the institutional structures of anthropological knowledge production to talk back and inform research agendas. This has taken the form of straightforward diversification of the field as jobs are distributed more equitably (if only haltingly so far). Yet there has also been a more general epistemological shift in how anthropologists approach their subject matter. Instead of objectifying their interlocutors, anthropologists today prefer to highlight the role of this dialogism in the production of anthropological knowledge, often emphasizing the power dynamics that exist between the researcher and the interviewees, and how this should inform how readers analyze the evidence that they are being presented with. However, the commitment to dialogism also requires a refusal to reduce ethnographic interlocutors to mere evidence, which has led anthropologists to increasingly rely upon those they encounter during fieldwork as not only "informants" (as they were once called) but also sources of anthropological insights that might contribute to philosophical and political debates within the discipline itself.

Of course, the often indigenous and marginalized communities that anthropologists have traditionally disproportionately studied are under no obligation to solve anthropologists' problems for them. Yet as it happens, human beings tend to be self-reflexive about their lot in ways that are mutually intelligible—even across wide cultural gulfs. These sorts of encounters can even lead to what Roy Wagner has called "reverse anthropology," critical attempts to understand anthropology from the perspective of those traditionally studied by it. Wagner developed this term in response to the abuse of anthropology to render people exotic and primitive in places like New Guinea, where he conducted fieldwork. For instance, he took issue with the concept of the so-called "cargo cult," made famous in images of Melanesians building mocked-up air strips in anticipation of cargo-bearing planes that never arrive. The term, with its connotations of overawed magical thinking, has since gone on to have a second life in computer programming, where so-called "cargo cult code" is reverently reproduced from iteration to iteration out of a fear that removing it might break something, despite the fact that it is no longer operative.

Wagner was especially contemptuous of what he calls the "Sunday-supplement view of cargo cult, a counterpart of mission ideology about saving the 'lost' heathens, or the sentimentality that perceives tribal peoples as impoverished relatives begging for a transistorized handout" (1975, 31). Wagner was unsparing in his criticism of this interpretation, noting that for those who are deeply engaged in these religious movements, cargo (or *kago*) is not really about the material objects at all—it is the social relationships and their promise of redemption that are really at stake. Wagner observes, "'Cargo' is practically a parody, a reduction of Western notions like profit, wage-labor, and production for its own sake to the terms of tribal society" (1975, 31). As Wagner goes on to note, "Cargo cult can be thought of as a pragmatic sort of anthropology that invents in anticipation of the future, in a manner reminiscent of Melanesian magic, rather than reconstructing the past or present out of shards of evidence" (1975, 32–33). Thus the common interpretation of the cargo cult reveals far more about "us" (the observers) than "them" (the observed) and—more intriguingly—suggests practices that might initially seem irrational could later prove to be a source of great insight in their own right.

This tendency of Western observers to project their own proclivities for mystified materialism onto others is long-standing, of course. It was parodied famously by Marx (1867) in his memorable passage in *Das Kapital*, "On the Fetishism of Commodities."[15] If European adventurers felt comfortable mocking those they encountered for being in the thrall of idols and other fetish-objects, then they had only to see how their own social order rested upon the notion that value (a social relation) inhered in the commodities themselves. We can see a similar tendency toward an over-awed relation to the power of technology in the guise of "technological determinism," like Marshall McLuhan's (1964) oft-quoted dictum that "The Medium Is the Message."[16] In fact, Jordanians themselves are often keen to note that a tendency to invest too much agency in technology is characteristically American and Western. For instance, the Jordanian sociologist and public intellectual Hussein Taha Mahadeen has written extensively of what he terms "technology as ideology" (*tiknūlūjiyyā ka-idīūlūjiyya*), critiquing a Western tendency to overestimate especially the benefits of introducing new technologies like social media. In doing so, he highlights the urgency of developing robust means for distinguishing between people's ideological beliefs *about* media and the workings of media itself.

To borrow from the anthropologist Ilana Gershon (2010), we need to be especially careful about distinguishing between social media itself and what she has called "media ideologies." Just as interview data in general is best approached as a variant of behavior rather than *necessarily* offering privileged insight into deeply felt beliefs (Briggs 1986), so must analysts work to avoid the category error of confusing popular talk *about* social media with the phenomenon itself. This is not to say that the two have nothing to do with one another or merely exist in some sort of abstracted, map-territory relationship. Rather, folk theories about social media may inform actual use dynamics in ways that can be self-reinforcing, unconnected, or even *counterperformative*. For instance, in her work on how university students used social media to navigate their romantic attachments, Gershon found that while there was widespread agreement that texting was too informal for breakups, threatening to break up via a message could be either dismissed as unserious or serve as all the more reason to see the relationship as finished. As Gershon notes, "It is not just how you think about a medium, it is how you reflexively engage with the medium given what you think about it" (2010, 34). Gershon's insight here is a call to understand how technologies like social media are deeply embedded in wider normative frameworks and folk theories about humans and their emotions and motivations that condition their uptake and use.

There is wisdom in Gershon's statement for the aspiring ethnographer, whether they hope to study emerging digital worlds or any other social dynamic, which these days will inevitably have some "digital" component or other—even if their work is primarily focused on those living on the other side of the "digital divide." Whether it is making contacts, networking, collecting data, or disseminating findings, social media increasingly informs all ethnographic practice. For one thing, ethnographers increasingly arrive in the field with a social media footprint that precedes them and will likely find that people have already googled them and categorized them on that basis. This is why, to return to an earlier theme, my colleague Anna-Maria Walter (2021) and I have recently highlighted the blurring of the boundaries of the traditional ethnographic "field" and the potentially profound implications for everything from fieldwork's status as a professional "rite of passage" to the authority of the ethnographer.

In what follows, I draw on over a decade of online and offline research on the impact of social media on Jordan. This includes nine months of intensive, dedicated fieldwork focused on social media on the ground in Jordan between 2016 and 2022. The fieldwork, almost all of which was conducted in Arabic, involved hundreds of informal face-to-face conversations with dozens of Jordanians from all walks of life about their use of social media, as well as over sixty more structured face-to-face interviews with intellectuals, journalists, activists, government-recognized "tribal judges," members of the security apparatus, and other important actors. I made a point of interviewing at least one editor or journalist from all of Jordan's leading online and offline publications, from the partially state-owned newspapers *Al-Ra'i* and *Al-Dustoor* to the Muslim Brotherhood–aligned *Assabeel* and a host of online-only publications including *Khabernī*, *Saraya News*, and *Jo24*. My fieldwork also involved spending time in person observing newsrooms and various tribal truces, negotiations, and reconciliations. One of the most productive sites for fieldwork, though, was Amman's lively nighttime café culture, where journalists and other intellectuals gathered to smoke, drink coffee, gossip, and play card games and chess.

Of course, a significant portion of my research involved observing these sorts of events online—both by myself and with Jordanians. Watching such content has become a common pastime for those more or less directly involved and the merely curious or nosy. I visited with tribal judges who sat with me for hours replaying the greatest hits from their career for me, all faithfully captured on camera for posterity. I also frequently encountered family members involved in various disputes who wanted me to see a particular insult or *coup de grace* for myself to better understand their feelings about those conflicts. Yet often people were primarily interested for the human drama of it and the opportunity to see unfiltered videos of riots, dead bodies, lamentations, and heated arguments. The online nature of the phenomenon I was studying pushed my methodological assumptions to their very limits: the whole idea of a "site" so usefully developed by George Marcus in his proposal for "multi-sited ethnography" (1995) felt like it was in danger of slipping through my fingers if I tried to grasp too hard. Yet at the same time, I was often surprised to find that not only friends but even complete strangers like shopkeepers and barbers would without prompting reference the events I was following online. While I often fretted that my work did not resemble the sort of traditional "village ethnography" for which anthropology is so famous, I had to admit that adopting the style of "patchwork ethnography" (Günel et al. 2020) was actually well-suited to answering my research questions. First my growing personal and professional obligations and then the pandemic made it impossible to maintain the traditional relationship between "home" and "field," which in turn forced me to rethink fieldwork itself.

Indeed, as the boundaries of the ethnographic field become blurred, so too do the boundaries between researcher and researched, with ethnographic interlocutors increasingly becoming media-savvy auteurs in their own right. Perhaps nothing better captures the shifting dynamics of (self-)objectification in ethnographic practice better than an experience that unfolded less than a week after my return home from my fieldwork in the summer of 2017. One of my interlocutors, himself an anthropologist, began frantically messaging me on WhatsApp as I was sitting in my living room in England. He told me that rumors were circulating online that I was a spy, backed up by photos that someone had taken of us without our knowledge. Over one image from the series of off-center, strangely angled, furtive-looking photographs taken of us walking outside the library at Jordan University, bold lettering accused me of being a "zionized agent" and him of being one of the "devils of the Ḥirāk." He gave me strict instructions: I was to contact the US embassy and the FBI to inform them that rogue elements of Jordanian intelligence allied with Jordan's queen were inciting violence against an American citizen.[17]

He was unmoved by my protestations that I had no ability to contact high-ranking US officials—and that in any event the spread of nasty rumors about me was hardly a US government priority. After all, isn't that exactly what a spy *would* say? In fact, I had come to suspect that he might have been spreading rumors that I was a spy himself—the better to burnish his own image as an important person with powerful connections. Suddenly, his propensity for "joking" about me being a spy in front of people took on a different cast. Questioning my own sanity slightly, I even entertained the idea that he had set me up by arranging this meeting to achieve just this end. Whatever the motivations of those who spread these rumors, though, the controversy drove home how social media has become a powerful tool not just for research and self-expression but also for their repression, with profound ethical implications for researchers like myself. Ultimately, I had to content myself with letting the controversy stand as an example of how Western anthropologists can no longer dictate the terms of engagement as they once had—and of how the so called "field" can intrude into the researcher's life, even from thousands of miles away.

To be clear, most of the fieldwork for this book did not have quite this level of cloak-and-dagger intrigue, yet there were serious ethical, methodological, and logistical challenges nonetheless, especially when dealing with those who lacked the power, platform, and connections to defend themselves or fight back. My own positionality as a white, male, American researcher obviously had a profound impact upon how I was perceived and the sorts of answers people provided me. I also had to be extremely transparent about my funding, whether it was my university, or government agencies like the National Science Foundation, National Endowment for the Humanities, or British Academy. My clear passion for the local language and culture was often taken to be flattering, but it could also provoke discomfort. I had to respect boundaries of "cultural intimacy" (Herzfeld 1996; Shryock 2004) by making sure my attempts to fit in did not veer into the realm of cultural appropriation. For instance, while some of my interlocutors were more than happy to view me as one of a long line of adventurers like Lawrence of Arabia who have taken up roles in local politics, I was never comfortable adopting traditional garb (much to the confusion of some and the relief of others). I even had to negotiate these issues in my use of language: while much of my Arabic was learned through immersion in rural Jordan, I had to be careful to balance between the local dialect (which could help build rapport or be polarizing) and the more formal register found in schools, newspapers, and satellite TV broadcasts. Unlike those early orientalists like William Lane who tried to blend in by pretending to be Arab or Muslim, I was more apt to introduce myself with a handout approved by my university research ethics committee describing my research. Even when I was just going about my day, though, people would often try to "place" me, which offered an opportunity to explain that I was an American from a Christian background with no family ties to Jordan who was being funded by some British or American institution to conduct social research. At this point, I might introduce my research questions and gauge whether they would like to participate in my research if they seemed interested.

My status as a privileged outsider afforded me access that the vast majority of Jordanians could not expect—something that people would sometimes comment upon, lest I misunderstand the gracious hospitality I was receiving. I was also afforded generous leeway to ask stupid questions and to surface what might otherwise be unspoken norms. I take seriously my responsibility to use these privileges that I was afforded to conduct the most socially beneficial research possible, and part of that means acknowledging the inequalities that put me in the unique position to "study up" (Nader 1969) in my research. My apparent connections to distant, inscrutable sources of authority allowed me to slide into these somewhat seedy worlds of power and influence and report back to a wider audience on what was happening while trying to protect the anonymity and safety of those who spoke to me. As I was often told, "You can say things we can't." This included critical views on what many journalists referred to as "the three d's" seen as "red lines" for the state: *al-dīwān wa al-da'irāt wa al-dīn*, or the [royal] court, the offices [of the security services], and religion. However, I can also defend Jordanian, Arab, and Bedouin culture in ways many of my more thoughtful and self-critical interlocutors would find vaguely embarrassing—precisely by demonstrating how thoughtfully self-critical many of their avatars actually are. This is not to say that I will not find plenty to criticize or that I promote a crude relativism, but rather that I am keen to draw attention to what I see as most perceptive and thoughtful in contemporary Jordanian discourse on the politics of social media.

Most anthropologists would like to think they have learned from the errors of their Victorian forebears, perhaps especially since such work continues to have an outsized influence on perceptions of the field and its subject matter to this day. In the classical formulation of early anthropologists like E. B. Tylor and Lewis Henry Morgan, "tribes" were placed within an evolutionary teleology that inevitably ranked the anthropologist's own "civilization" as more advanced and knowledgeable than its "tribal" other. This approach was, as Matthew Engelke has put it, "moral philosophy masquerading as science" because it began from the premise that the "man in the top hat" was not merely "more culturally evolved" than the so-called "savage" but actually *better* (2017, 43). In contrast, this study treats tribalism as not only a vibrant and at least potentially contemporary discourse but also one which might yet teach metropolitan theory a thing or two in regard to its own unexamined assumptions about the social world. While placing one's ethnographic interlocutors on such an equal footing might once have seemed like a magnanimous gesture, I would argue that, increasingly, it simply reflects the shifting power relationships that characterize the relationship between researcher and those being studied in an increasingly postcolonial and mass-mediated world.

Laboratories of Democracy (and Authoritarianism)

If tribalism was once (as Abu Lughod put it) "the only issue in the anthropology of the Arab world that relates to a classical anthropological debate actually transcending the region" (1989, 285), then there are good reasons why later anthropologists grew weary of it. Yet I will argue that there are compelling reasons to revisit these themes in an era when anthropologists and other scholars are increasingly being challenged to decolonize their knowledge practices and assumptions about the social world and to rebalance the relationship between researcher and researched. If many Jordanians insist on the relevance of tribal identities in their lives, it would be foolish for me to tell them otherwise. In fact, these ideas resonate far more widely than is usually appreciated. This might have something to do with the fact that tribalism touches on something inherent to the human condition, but it might also be a function of the technopolitical assemblages in which we all increasingly find ourselves enmeshed.

For one thing, Silicon Valley is itself increasingly dependent on financial support from the Arab world. The sovereign wealth funds of major oil producers like Saudi Arabia have become deeply fascinated by the potential uses of new communications technologies like social media—especially at a time when questionable promises of astronomical profits are offered up as a means of helping to curb the region's "addiction" to oil (Nagarajan 2020). Then there are individual investors with close ties to the Saudi royal family like Al-Waleed bin Talal, for instance, who have long been major stakeholders in companies like Twitter (Durot 2022). There is also, however, a political interest in these technologies, which have shown some potential as a threat to authoritarian rule, but also involve unprecedented opportunities for surveillance, misinformation, intimidation, and what Marc Owen Jones has called digital authoritarianism (2022). In his profile of the ongoing conflict between Qatar's ruling family and rival dynasties in Saudi Arabia and the United Arab Emirates, [social] media becomes one of (if not the most) important battlefields on which the conflict is prosecuted. I will return to this conflict, which many of my Jordanian interlocutors viewed as fundamentally tribal (rather than national) in nature, several times in the course of this book. The very centrality of Qatar's *Al-Jazeera* network to that conflict (and the demands of its adversaries that it be shut down) merely underlines the far-reaching implications of the media for the region (at least as far as some of the most powerful political actors are concerned). It also underlines that tribalism shapes the uptake of social media even as it is itself transformed through the uptake of social media. Yet despite this important work, current accounts of the development of the internet remain far too Euro- and America-centric. Even when they do acknowledge the contributions of those living beyond what has traditionally been perceived as the imperial core, they tend to ignore especially the imaginative labors of those living in the contemporary Middle East.

The modes of political and cultural production that are being pioneered in the Arabic-language public sphere today are no mere recapitulation of the familiar sorts of nationalism described by scholars like Eugene Weber (1976), Benedict Anderson (1983), and Partha Chatterjee (1993). Compulsory schooling and mass literacy continue to play a pivotal role, but the forms of media they support are no longer the novel and the newspaper, or even the national news broadcast. While state boundaries remain important, social media now allows cultural production to operate at both subnational and supranational scales. While the shared lingua franca of Arabic has allowed channels like Qatar's *Al-Jazeera* to become a popular news source from Morocco to Iraq, it has also allowed for a proliferation of subcultural publics or "counterpublics" (Warner 2002). This fragmentation of the Arabic cultural scene has, in turn, created an opening for activists and entrepreneurs working at subnational scales (often in more peripheral areas like Jordan) to challenge established incumbents by foregrounding new forms of identification. While this book will focus primarily on tribal identification, the internet has also been a powerful organizing tool for a host of minority groups, including religious, linguistic, ethnic, and sexual minorities.

Yet even as the internet has allowed all sorts of minorities across the Middle East to push back against a stultifying conformism that defined an earlier era of media centralization and regulation, it has simultaneously enabled a backlash (Mahadeen 2021; Rachdi 2024). This backlash emerges in particularly vivid detail in the literary theorist Tarek El Ariss's *Leaks, Hacks and Scandals*. In a perceptive analysis of how social media is transforming Arab intellectual life, he contrasts the bounded subjects of high-modernist media like the novel with the sorts of "leaking subjects" that social media seems to promote. On the one hand, there is subversive potential to the media that he identifies with what is known in Arabic as *faḍḥ* or "making a scene." He writes, "The leak exposes fictions of power, making a scene of their porousness and spills. Acts of hacking and revelation, 'releases' and 'leaks' form multiple trajectories: trickles and tsunamis, flash floods and flash mobs" (2019, 21). On the other hand, forces of conservatism and conformity can leverage the virality of new media to attack those who resist their hegemony using "a model of tribal warfare that erupts through a portal into the archaic in cyberspace." Here, El-Ariss advocates a model of subjectivation downplaying "discourse, power and the state" and their literary genre par excellence (the novel) in favor of pre-Islamic "*Jahiliyya*-like rituals that herald new forms of community, public and political order" (2019, 29). I will have more to say about the chrono-politics of El-Ariss's characterization of these trends later, but what I want to stress here is the idea that social media seems to involve a rethinking of basic assumptions about the nature of subjectivity, emotions, and human motivation. Understanding how Jordan's tribal publics have increasingly come to mediate between individual identities and the state requires attention not only to more quotidian matters of political economy, but also to local beliefs about human motivation and the nature of highly politicized and emotionally charged phenomena like envy, shame, paranoia, and mercy.

In particular, the notion of the bounded, individual subject with a rich interior life so beautifully rendered in so many works of art produced in the wake of the Enlightenment gives way to more agonistic, relational notions of personhood and subjectivity that are also reflected in the prestige media of their respective eras. Rather than assuming that this shift is some technologically driven misunderstanding to be corrected (through better education or possibly even state regulation), I want to consider the possibility that this might be a more anthropologically defensible approach to subjectivity—at least right now (Strathern 2018). As I hope to show, the Bedouin tribespeople I have worked with to produce this book have a rich tradition to draw on when it comes to arguing that people are deeply entangled with one another and indeed primarily exist *through* each other. I will show how Bedouin folk sociological categories like tribalism, envy, face, the deep state, and mercy can shed new light on not just social media but also the contemporary human condition more generally. My goal here is to reevaluate and hopefully recuperate concepts I will argue have been too readily stigmatized and discarded. My Bedouin interlocutors have convinced me that even I have good reason to worry about things like envy, losing face, the deep state, and the prospect of a society with no room for mercy. Perhaps you, reader, do as well.

Yet first I need to introduce Jordan: a relatively small monarchy that tries to project an image as a progressive, pro-business country while playing host to millions of refugees and struggling with unemployment and housing shortages. In "The Many Faces of the State," I focus on the development of the state apparatus and in particular the role of three figures in helping to materialize that apparatus: the journalist, the police officer, and the sheikh. The description will mix a broader institutional history of their respective occupations (focusing on the relationship between press regulation, political repression, and the cooptation of the leaders of Jordan's most powerful and well-organized patrilineal kin groups) with ethnographic sketches of the sort of personnel who tend to occupy these positions and shape their work. In particular, I will argue that the emergence of social media is best understood as a form of privatization characteristic of the shrinking of certain ideological facets of the state apparatus at the turn of the millennium. This is not to say, however, that those responsible are themselves liberal—or that their aims have been liberal. Rather, I seek to show how those tasked with regulating media have come to see the sorts of state centralization that defined much of the twentieth century as needlessly complex and have merely opted to devolve many of these control functions to what is sometimes called "civil society"—though not necessarily with any intention of fostering democracy, the rule of law, or other liberal values. Having situated this more general shift in global political practice within a specifically Jordanian context, I then turn to a series of local concepts that Jordanians have used to make sense of their world: Tribalism, Envy, Face, the Deep State, and Mercy.

Taking up the concept of **Tribalism**, or *'ashā'iriyya*, I note that dominant discourses on tribalism rarely treat it as a neutral description of social behavior. Rather, they fashion a normative framework for legitimating certain perspectives (usually of those making the accusation of tribalism) at the expense of others (usually the accusation's targets). My starting point for this critique is the fact that, unlike most places where the term is deployed today, Jordan is actually home to many proudly self-identified tribespeople, who consciously reject the cosmopolitanism and progressive futurities that many academic commentators hold dear, *refusing coevalness* and asserting their own past-oriented temporalities as more authentic and vital. Drawing on a particular blood feud that became a social media cause célèbre because it coincided with the holy month of Ramadan, I show how Jordan hosts a range of opinions on tribalism—from liberal, leftist, and Islamist voices who use "tribalism" as an epithet to proponents of tribalism who see it as a counterweight to the state that defends important social norms and even an informal safety net. What many of these views hold in common, though, and what I want to highlight, is a recognition of tribalism's contemporary appeal and, in fact, an assumption that tribal behavior is the height of political rationality in many contexts (whatever their normative judgment of it). Such conceptions of tribalism figure attempts to transcend it as an act of faith or gratuity. Rather than rejecting the concept of tribalism due to the impossibility of using it in a politically neutral way, I seek to recuperate it precisely for its sober recognition of the impossibility of political neutrality.

Having introduced the concept of tribalism, the next chapter turns to a discussion of **Envy** (*ḥasad*). As I was often told, envy is at the heart of tribalism: just as any individual of any worth wants to be the best, so that ambition is extended to their family and so on, bringing them into inevitable conflict with neighboring kin groups who want the same things. The idea that there is something invidious about social media is hardly unique to Jordan, but its alleged invidiousness was believed to take on a special significance against this tribal backdrop. Against a widespread tendency to treat envy as "unjustified and critically effete," as the critical theorist Sianne Ngai has put it (2005, 21), most Jordanians viewed envy as a social and moral force of the utmost significance. The chapter begins in the offices of one of Jordan's leading Islamist publications, with the staff explaining how envy is at the heart of everything from neighborhood street fights to the rivalry between Qatar and the United Arab Emirates, emphasizing how their tribal and Emirati rivals were especially motivated by envy. While some (especially the powerful) are quick to paint envy as a property of the poor and marginalized who resent their betters, the more subversively minded flip this on its head. These commentators argue that the elite are often the most envious: they jealously guard their privileges and see any benefit accruing to others as impinging on their positional advantage within a hierarchy. Following these discourses online and offline, I argue that for many Jordanians, envy is a powerful social force transcending mere subjective emotional states with profound political and cosmological significance—and that there is actually something to this. At the same time, I suggest that envy's illusiveness should give us pause about the frequent recourse to "emotions" as an explanation for human behavior on social media and in the wider social field.

Having begun to show how Jordanians parse subjectivity and personhood in interesting and subtle ways and what is at stake in these struggles, I turn to another concept that has historically been viewed with condescension, despite my interlocutors' continued embrace of it: **Face** (*wajh*). The concept of "face" as developed first by Hsien-chin Hu's (1944) work on the Chinese concepts of *liǎn* or *miànzi* and then generalized in Erving Goffman's discussions of "facework" (1967) has often been treated as vaguely orientalist, but it offers yet another example of how local concepts can inform metropolitan theory. Here, I begin with the concept of "cutting the face"—the practice of purposefully violating tribal truces and thereby humiliating the guarantor or "face" of the group who has negotiated the settlement, forcing him to pay a surety while being shown up as unable to speak on behalf of the wider group. Drawing on interviews with elders and youths, I show how the arrival of Facebook and other social media fed off local ideas of "face" and simultaneously opened new opportunities for divide and rule from below. By heightening the vulnerabilities of those who had previously been able to use state patronage to act as the "face" of wider collectivities unchallenged, social media required existing power structures to quickly adapt in their wake.

The discussion of how Jordan's repressive apparatus has responded to social media leads inexorably to the concept of the **Deep State** (*al-dawla al-ʿamīqa*), a concept that originated in the region yet increasingly serves as an object of fascination for many around the world, with US president Donald Trump serving as a particularly notable exemplar. While there has been a lot of discussion of how social media might be leading to an upsurge in conspiracist thinking and paranoia by mainstreaming previously marginal ideas, I am particularly concerned here with how social media seems to be making elites more receptive to conspiratorial discourses—sometimes to great effect. As the chapter will show, theories of the deep state can be generative of social movements in their own right—especially in one case I highlight where a Jordanian soldier's murder trial became a cause célèbre far beyond his tribe, transforming him into the alleged victim of a deep state plot after a fatal encounter with four US military trainers. Then, taking up Jordan's response to an alleged coup by a former crown prince, I show how theories of the deep state can also be mobilized by the state itself to justify repressive measures. Instead of dismissing the deep state as mere "conspiracy theory," the chapter asks why so many at the heart of the state apparatus itself are now so taken with the idea (Trump being merely an extreme example). Moving between Trump's invocation of the deep state as his chief political foil at home and his administration's alleged involvement in the attempt to overthrow Jordan's king, I argue that at least in the absence of broad-based democracy, theories of the deep state become completely plausible and—more importantly—efficacious. The only problem is that (as many have learned too late), it is not always so easy to differentiate between the deep state and its many impersonators.

The final Bedouin concept I explore is **Mercy** (*raḥma*). I analyze how mercy challenges not just a number of cherished assumptions about the nature of personhood and subjectivity but also the nature of the state, law, and indeed justice itself. I begin by considering whether Jordan's traditions of tribal dispute resolution might offer a useful model of restorative justice at a time when social media has been presented as an attractive (if often chimerical) solution to problems of elite impunity that a growing carceral archipelago seems unable—or perhaps merely unwilling—to deal with. Shifting away from matters of "high policing" (Brodeur 1982) around subversion, insurrection, and murder, I consider the more mundane work of low policing: dealing with interpersonal conflicts like domestic violence and car crashes. Tracing negotiations online and offline, on-stage and off-stage, I emphasize the darker side of this form of restorative justice, not least its patriarchal and gerontocratic underpinnings. However, this darker side also includes the often self-interested motives of would-be mediators, the wide-ranging effects of the immense financial burden of paying the blood money, the constant (sometimes menacing) phone calls, and the creative use of the criminal justice system and insurance regulations to compel a resolution. Against a tendency to see mercy as antithetical to revenge, I argue that at least for many of my Jordanian interlocutors, the ability to make one's enemies beg for mercy (and then grant it on one's own terms) was one of the sweetest types of revenge imaginable—especially after the initial shock of a transgression had passed. In this regard, Jordanian tribespeople's sensibilities about mercy resonate deeply with their ideas about tribalism, envy, face, honor, and a more abstract sense that one's being is fundamentally tied up with how one is perceived by various others. In doing so, the chapter offers an unvarnished depiction of existing restorative justice that just might be more convincing as a model of justice for its studied anti-utopianism.

In the epilogue, "Locking Down," I take the narrative forward to the COVID-19 pandemic and its aftermath, offering some retrospective conclusions on how the state's attempts to police its emerging digital frontiers recall deeper histories of state boundary-fashioning. In particular, I focus on the recent proliferation of practices of blockade, quarantine, and embargo (*ḥiṣār*) in Jordan and the wider region. This is a time of retro-futurism, with a return of a whole range of practices rolling back previous liberalizing tendencies toward increasing freedom of movement, from siege warfare to sprawling censorship regimes, tariffs on trade, and quarantine. Against this backdrop, social media tribes are redolent of older attempts by states to police their more physical frontiers—and such initiatives may well prove likewise logistically challenging and hence fleeting. That does not necessarily mean the social experiments that emerge in these frontiers will be liberatory. In fact, such zones have often been equally amenable to rearguard actions in which hierarchical centralizing schemes are further perfected. If the tribe has long offered people living with states in the region an opportunity to think about (and beyond) the state, then I suggest it can continue to serve that role despite rapid technological change, even as so many eagerly try to consign the tribe to the dustbin of history.

Social media has been implicated in a number of notable shifts in the relationship between individual identity and the state in Jordan and far beyond its borders. As elsewhere, this has led to a widespread sense that social media is leading to a resurgence of "tribalism"—though, as I will argue, what that means can vary markedly depending on the broader social context. In Jordan, the uptake of social media has itself been shaped by existing tribal dynamics as well as associated beliefs about human motivations and emotions, from fears of the invidious comparisons that social media may enable to concerns about its ability to shame individual tribal "faces" or the collective "face" of various tribes. Similarly, the appeal of social media (especially the gossipy preoccupation with leaks, often of online interactions) feeds off folk beliefs about the "deep state" and simultaneously transforms vernacular experiences of this chimerical figure. Meanwhile, social media has insinuated itself deeply into the practice of tribal justice in ways that make the performance of mercy more mediated than ever before. Yet as the case of Jordan should make clear, this is not a simple story of technological determinism, but rather a more complex set of interactions in which political, social, cultural, and economic developments that often preceded the emergence of social media have been able to feed off new media in ways that can be quite locally specific. That being said, one of the initial promises of the internet was that there was real value in engaging with faraway people because they might have profound insights to offer. My hope is that this book might still make good on some of that promise.

CHAPTER 1

The Many Faces of the State—the Sheikh, the Policeman, and the Journalist

If Jordan's Bedouin have interesting things to say about the politics of social media uptake, then it might be at least in part because their positionality gives them something of a privileged vantage point from which to view these developments. After all, Bedouin have long situated themselves ingeniously in the interstices of competing imperial systems, and, as I will show, Jordan may be a particularly artful construct even as the notoriously artificial nation-state goes.[1] However, in various ways, the Hashemite Kingdom of Jordan is surely both typical and atypical of early twenty-first-century nation-states, both within the Middle East and globally. The aim of this chapter is to contextualize rather than normalize or exceptionalize. If one recognizes something of their own country in a self-styled liberal monarchy that holds occasional, largely indecisive exercises in representative democracy that amplify economically marginal but politically and culturally dominant rural areas at the expense of urban population centers, then all the better. The same goes for Jordan's problems with housing shortages and unemployment alongside the rapid embrace of the internet by its disproportionately young citizenry, which is typical of much of the global South and beyond. At the same time, other aspects of Jordan may put its social media dynamics in sharper relief and require contextualization as I describe how the peculiarities of my research allowed me a very specific kind of access to Jordan's distinctive discourse around social media.

Having spent much of their postcolonial history in a legal state of emergency, Jordanians can hardly fall back on liberal-democratic bromides that depend on a scaffolding of hard-won rights that are increasingly under attack globally. To the degree that the liberal ideal of an independent "public sphere" within "civil society" determining the direction of the state through rational deliberation might have ever seemed plausible (Habermas 1989; Calhoun

1992),[2] this is certainly not the case in Jordan: like many of its neighbors, the kingdom's first publication was an official gazette, and state censorship was not far behind.[3] In fact, as Ayish and Mellor observe, this pattern continues today: "Arab journalism in the twenty-first century continues to embrace much of the traditional values of nationalism and mobilization, despite recent upheavals and liberal market developments" (2015, 10). If anything, they argue, this tendency to see the media as a key vehicle of national mobilization has only been accentuated as journalism has come to be couched increasingly in a pro-regime/opposition binary since the uprisings of 2011.

In fact, I would argue that this fixation on journalism and "media" in general as an important wellspring of political power in the interstices between state and society is itself in need of explanation. Just because the media have become a popular explanation for social dynamics does not mean that they are a good one. As I suggested in the introduction, perhaps especially in a context where "media" is seen increasingly as a source of power, "media ideologies" (Gershon 2010) should be taken both seriously *and* critically as they become the ideologies par excellence for an era of liberalization and privatization. As I hope to show in this chapter, media ideologies increasingly represent a vernacular idiom that in some ways prefigures and in other ways simply extends the arguments of theorists like Timothy Mitchell, who argue that the constant drawing and redrawing of the state-society boundary itself can be "a mechanism that generates resources of power" (1991, 90). By advancing claims about the power of "the media," social actors develop a discursive and imaginative space for this work of drawing and redrawing state/society boundaries ideal for the era of Public-Private Partnerships (PPPs), Government-Organized Nongovernmental Organizations (GONGOs), and of course media liberalization.

Reflecting the fluid politics found in many authoritarian regimes, and lending urgency to their quest to make sense of shifting political alliances, Jordanians cannot count on much of anything but themselves and the political alliances they forge on their own. Even Jordan as a construct (nation-state or otherwise) remains profoundly contingent—and contested. With the establishment and expansion of the state of Israel, Jordan's entire political and demographic center of gravity has shifted markedly since the kingdom's independence from the British Empire in 1946. While Jordan was able to claim the West Bank following the establishment of the state of Israel in 1948 and through much of the 1950s and 1960s, it would (from the government's perspective at least) lose that territory in the Six-Day War of 1967 and finally formally disengage in 1988 before signing a peace treaty with Israel in 1994. Meanwhile, hundreds of thousands of Palestinian refugees would make their way east amidst the violence to a newly diminished Hashemite Kingdom, especially during and after the 1967 war. The ensuing economic and political turmoil in turn inspired an expansion of the country's security services, which would increasingly devote themselves to suppressing Palestinian national sentiment throughout the late twentieth century. Jordan's rapidly shifting borders and demography have thus accentuated fundamental political questions about the nature of the state and its relationship to identity and legitimate political discourse more generally (Layne 1994; Lynch 1999; Massad 2001).

At the same time, Jordan cannot merely be contextualized through a short political history, since these histories are lived in everyday practice and embodied in institutions, professions, and quotidian rituals of sociality. To keep the discussion grounded in the everyday rhythms that formed the basis of my fieldwork data, I weave in three figures or "faces" of the state drawn from my interviews with members of key professions that I worked with during my research: the sheikh (exemplifying pre-Hashemite Ottoman rule), the policeman (exemplifying the Hashemite state-building project), and the journalist (exemplifying the country's neoliberal turn since the 1990s). Because they represent some of the main professions I engaged with during my research, these three *dramatis personae* are convenient narrative tools that have the added advantage of illustrating how I negotiated access with different social gatekeepers and the limitations these negotiations imposed on my research. If Philip Abrams once argued that the state is not the "reality that lies behind the mask of political practice" but rather "the mask which prevents us from seeing political practice as it truly is" (1977, 58), then it is worth inquiring how the state comes to take on such personas in particular eras, and how the Jordanian state has in turn profoundly shaped the lives of my various interlocutors.

The Sheikh: The Ottoman Roots of Modern Jordanian Politics

To place Jordan in its proper context, I follow other scholars—including historians like Eugene Rogan (2002) and Yoav Alon (2007), and political scientists like Jillian Schwedler (2022)—in tracing many important contemporary dynamics to the middle of the nineteenth century, when what is now Jordan was coming under intensifying Ottoman imperial administration. As Nora Barakat argues in *Bedouin Bureaucrats*, the sheikh and the tribe began to take on a new importance in the mid-nineteenth century in an emerging Ottoman "agrarian imaginary" (2023, 90–100), increasingly serving as one of the primary tools through which imperial rule was maintained. Even before Jordan emerged as a promising frontier zone for new development, the empire had long cultivated sheikhs as an alternative to an independent state administration. Sheikhs were typically drawn from local subject populations, and those populations often had a degree of say in who would serve as their point of contact with the Ottoman state. Depending on the time period, the number of people concerned, and the more urban character of those concerned, the figure might also be called a *mukhtār*, but the pattern was similar: they would be given certain trappings of authority (like a seal for notarizing documents), but if there was any trouble or taxes went uncollected, then the onus would be on them to prove their continued loyalty—and usefulness.

I primarily worked with fourteen self-styled sheikhs during my research, all of whom were also government-recognized tribal judges, lending some official sanction to their often-contested attempts to speak on behalf of their kin. Each was unique—in fact sheikhs are sometimes referred to as "personalities" (*shakhsiyyāt*) or "faces" (*wujūh*) as a result of their penchant for individual assertion—but the role itself came with pronounced obligations that these often quite domineering men could not easily shirk. After a while, their answers became extremely repetitive and the sorts of social dynamics they generated grew all too familiar. Here as with my other two *dramatis personae*, I want to emphasize how these histories are lived, embodied, and passed on from one generation to another (or not). I will call the sheikh I focus on here "Sheikh Salim" (here as elsewhere, the names have been changed to protect the innocent and guilty alike).

Like many sheikhs I interviewed, Sheikh Salim was a diminutive older man with a keen mind, enjoying a comfortable retirement from his role as an influential member of the security services, surrounded by his sons, whose beautiful newer houses encircled his much older home. They were relatively well off, but not necessarily the richest in the area. I first met him because his kinsmen were eager to introduce us. His sons made clear to me that they were not so simple as to take me for a spy or someone with close connections to the embassy. There was nothing I could do for them, they assured me (not that it stopped them from proceeding to inquire about my "connections" anyway, of course). They replied to my protestations that they would not benefit at all from participating in my research by noting that since I was writing about the area, they still had to consider their good name. They fretted that I would get the wrong idea if I only spoke with other local notables, who might give me the wrong impression about local politics. I was only too happy to oblige them. Whenever I am in the area now, I make a point of stopping by to call on Sheikh Salim, a demonstration of my respect for him and his wider importance in the world, and of course an opportunity for me to learn from him and be honored by his hospitality.

Like most sheikhs—though certainly not all—he was circumspect in his communication, always clear in his support for the pillars of the status quo that undergird his own claims to authority in the community: "God, King, and Country." The sheikh had a lot to say about social media for a man who (like most men in their sixties and seventies in the mid-2010s) primarily taught himself how to read, did not have a Facebook account, and still used a simple mobile phone whose most distinctive selling point was the flashlight. As he often complained of his younger kinsmen, "They bring me phones from far away!" He continued, "Us in the old times, we didn't have phones in our customs." He groused that his suggestion to "throw away the phones" was always ignored and summed up his sense that he and others of his generation were losing a battle with the phones for the respect and obedience of the youth by saying: "It used to be the people would listen to the elderly. Now no one listens to the old." Bemoaning the decline of the prerogative of the eldest brother to regulate the violence of his younger brothers' descendants, he continued, "The fights are getting stronger, and with some of them the uncle can't keep [his own kinsmen] out of the fight." For this sheikh and most like him, it was inconceivable that tribes could survive without the gerontocratic power structures whose heights they commanded.

Yet of course such eulogistic treatments of the tribes and confident predictions that they were disappearing have been common for well over a century. As scholars like Eugene Rogan (2002) have detailed, by the mid-nineteenth century, inter-imperial competition was driving Ottoman elites to abandon their policies of indirect rule via sheikhs and tribes by mimicking the modernizing policies of European competitor states. Incursions by the French, the British, and the Russians into Ottoman lands had served as a wakeup call. The result has come to be known as the *Tanzimat* or "reorganization" and involved a massive extension of what Rogan has called (following Mann 1984) Ottoman "infrastructural power": roads, telegraph cables, and rail lines, all of which were intended to facilitate the state's increasing penetration of society in support of more efficient taxation that could fund ever-larger military expenditures (Rogan 2002, 1–3). As such, universal conscription and wide-ranging attempts to register land more precisely were key to the reform agenda. In 1857 a censorship office was established to enforce a new press law modeled like so many other aspects of the reforms on French law (Ayalon 1995, 21–22), which would remain in effect despite multiple regime changes until it was superseded by Jordan's 1953 constitution (Ayalon 1995, 102).

However, *Tanzimat* had other, more subtle dimensions to it. As I have written elsewhere (Hughes 2015b; Hughes 2021), another enduring facet of the *Tanzimat* was the introduction of a new family law that drew liberally on the Napoleonic code, fomenting new notions of the individual, the family, and society in the process. Thus, by the time the Ottoman Empire had decisively collapsed following World War I, the British and French colonial administrations could only intensify the sorts of transformations in land tenure, personal status, administrative structures, and the built environment that had already been underway for decades.

Despite all of this Ottoman enthusiasm for state-building and modernization on its frontiers, Jordan remained a relative backwater on the eve of British colonial rule. The Ottoman administration had by that point built the Hijaz Railway through Jordan to facilitate the annual pilgrimage to Mecca. The first Sharia court in what is now Jordan began operations in the town of Salt in 1869 (Barakat 2023, 124). It also resettled Chechen and Circassian refugees retreating from Russian advances in the north of the empire to new settlements in Salt, Wadi Sir, and a small agricultural community called "Amman," near some ruins, that would one day become Jordan's capital and largest city (Hamed-Troyansky 2024; Rogan 2002, 74–75). However, unlike in Palestine, where land registration and the increasing penetration of Sharia courts (and especially secular, *niẓāmī* courts) was much more intensive, Ottoman influence remained relatively weak to the east of the Jordan River. Instead, the area remained dominated by tribal confederations with shifting leaderships and loyalties. The 'Adwan projected power from their control of the Jordan Valley (Shryock 1997), while the Huwaytat did much the same from Aqaba (both low-lying areas that served as prime places for wintering livestock, which allowed them to extract their own tribute or *khāwa* from subordinate tribes). Meanwhile, the Sukhur enjoyed a key role as protectors of the annual pilgrimage, for which the tribe's leadership was richly rewarded (Barakat 2023). Like modern nation-states, these tribal confederations wielded power through a mix of violence and ideological justification (mostly expressed in poetry)—though, as Andrew Shryock notes, with the exception of the poet Nimr Al-'Adwan, much of this poetry was produced by slave-poets and other dependents (1997, 188).

For his part, Sheikh Salim (like most who are acknowledged by their neighbors and kinsmen as such) also served as an intermediary between his tribe and the state, and while tax collection has long been outsourced to a sophisticated professional bureaucracy, he could still potentially exercise considerable influence over communal affairs through his role as a tribal judge. This meant that he had long enjoyed government recognition of his role in solving certain kinds of conflicts that the authorities deemed to be inextricably linked to tribal "customs and traditions." The sheikh reckoned he had seen a thousand cases in his life, at least sixty per year. These officially included the three crimes of "blood" (homicide), "honor" (sexual crimes), and "cutting the face" (the breaking of truces).[4] In practice, a much wider range of disputes came under his ambit than the three acknowledged by the government. He explained, "Lots of people decide not to go to the courts at all and they just bring it to the tribal judge and he solves it right there. [For instance] there's a [civil] law against slander here and in Britain, but a tribal judge will solve it too." Car accidents were another source of endless controversy that would keep him busy and his mediation skills sharp. But, he said, "It's mostly fights." Sixty cases per year would be over one per week, and while one might take this as clear embellishment, I think it more represents the sheikh's primary mode of engagement with the world around him, which he saw as a series of conflicts to be mediated (preferably by him).

The most serious cases of blood, honor, and cutting the face involved a carefully choreographed progression in which the sheikh would work hand-in-hand with the state, conforming to—but also transforming—the stateless modes of authority that had been at the heart of tribal dispute resolution prior to its reorganization under British rule. Banishment (*jalwa*), once forced upon the perpetrator and his kin by the enraged defenders of the victim under threat of violence, has come to involve the perpetrator and those listed in his government-issued "family notebook" facing banishment at the hands of the governor—ostensibly for reasons of public order. The "truce of the boiling blood," which lasted three and a third days, has become a "security truce" imposed by the governor for the same duration. The respective sides continue to select their own judges and guarantors (who promise to pay a large surety should their kinsmen break the truce), but now their prerogatives have come to be backed by the state, which will step in to assist in cases of "cutting the face" to enforce truces and reconciliations. Through a series of longer, less-exacting truces, judges still try to engineer a state of forgiveness, mercy, and, ultimately, reconciliation among the antagonists through a blood money payment and the ritual pageantry of the meetings themselves. Yet ideologically at least, the state now holds that this side of the case, which is for the "victim," can only lead to a sentence reduction. The sheikh, echoing most others I spoke with, said, "A homicide is fifteen years [in prison], but the state will cut it in half if there is reconciliation: seven and a half years for the victim and seven and a half for the state (*dawla*)."

Like most (but certainly not all) of the tribal judges I interviewed, Sheikh Salim, while eager to criticize [social] media, went to some lengths to avoid openly questioning the state. Nonetheless, his frustrations still came through at times—especially when I began to question him about the post–Arab Spring rise in tribal clashes. As he often complained, "All the young men are on their phones—even in gatherings. Even the men around us aren't understanding [listening to] us." He would sometimes continue, "The role of the sheikh is gone. Now there are people making Facebook pages for sheikhs. How can a Facebook page take the place of a sheikh?" Speaking of the Arab Spring in particular, he suddenly became more guarded and chose his words carefully, saying, "There's a political interpretation." Mixing speculation with the recollection of widely circulated images of the first protests for reform in Jordan in 2011, when the police initially welcomed protest before later cracking down, he eyed me before continuing: "The Jordanian regime was dealing with a lot of protests and giving [the protesters] room to blow off steam and [the police were] giving them water and juice."[5] He complained, however, that the failure to use a "strong hand" had allowed things to spiral out of control as young people saw what they could get away with and incited each other to greater violence: "Now there's a weakening of the security situation and they've started committing crimes with theft and stealing cars and everything. It's an indirect effect of the Arab Spring weakening the security situation." As he moved rapidly between the state, media, and talk of young delinquents, it was hard to ascertain who exactly "they" might be and how these actors were related, and I sensed he was not in the mood to be interrogated.

Even if state prerogatives often proved impossible to exercise in practice (whether in individual cases of interpersonal conflict or even against massive protests at various points in Jordan's history), the concept of state authority has inarguably come to suffuse a system of dispute mediation that once styled itself as far more stateless. Indeed, at the time of research it was clear that many conflicts that could be resolved by the courts never make it to court, that victims' families in many cases continued to try to raze the homes of the perpetrators' families, and that there was a pronounced fear that the well-connected could get away with murder. To the degree that social media promoted these challenges to the state-backed status quo, they provided a *raison d'être* for men like Sheikh Salim. Yet social media also left men like him in the unenviable position of bearing the same responsibility for the actions of their kin while offering those kinsmen novel avenues to undermine them through new forms of mediated political activity. Backing away from the implication that the government was deliberately undermining sheikhs like him to move to the safer ground of complaining about a much-alleged—though hard to verify[6]—post–Arab Spring crime wave, he said, "Tribalism is what protects the security of the country. . . . The tribes listen to each other more than they listen to the state. . . . The central family is the Hashemite family and God forbid that anything change that!" To understand how the Hashemite family and the Jordanian state have institutionalized themselves in this peculiar manner requires a turn to the second of my *dramatis personae*: the policeman.

The Policeman: The Hashemite State-Building Project

A good deal of commentary on the Hashemite state-building project inevitably focuses on one of the main aims of the Hashemites and their British patrons: to build a viable army and police force. If the Sykes-Picot Agreement had divided the Ottoman Empire between France and Britain and set the stage for the series of mandates that would become the basis for the region's current borders, then British military advisers would have to work with the Hashemites to transform that "line in the sand" (Barr 2011) into facts on the ground. Fortunately, those who were pivotal in establishing these forces, like Frederick Peake (1934; 1942) and John Glubb (1948), also paid future historians the favor of writing extensively about their exploits, motivations, and self-justifications. As Joseph Massad has demonstrated, state consolidation proceeded apace during this period through "coercion and cooptation of local elites" (2001, 16–17), not unlike Sheikh Salim. Those who could not be bought off were simply killed or imprisoned when they rose up. Even after independence, Jordan's army continued to be led by Glubb until 1956 (Massad 2001, 104–105). While one might think that it would be difficult to study police officers and other members of the security apparatus, many were already accustomed to having professional relationships with Americans and saw nothing strange about my work. Plenty of people even drew explicit parallels between my work and that of Glubb and T. E. "Lawrence of Arabia." Moreover, given the number of outsourced trainers, consultants, and researchers who circulated in Jordan as independent contractors, many were interested to learn more about my trade as an anthropologist, which struck many as an exciting and potentially appealing line of work in its own right.

Here I center on someone who was relatively advanced in the police force hierarchy, with a special focus on youth crime, giving him more professional training than most on the influence of new technologies like social media. Perhaps twenty years junior to the sheikh, a college graduate, and much more comfortable with technology, a policeman I will call Major Ahmed nevertheless shared the sheikh's dim view of recent developments and his pessimistic prognosis for Jordan's future. Like the sheikh, he saw the confluence of new media, a breakdown of patriarchal authority, and dissident politics as a perfect storm of self-reinforcing dynamics that threatened to send Jordan careening into chaos. His work on youth crime put these issues front and center in his mind, and he sought to balance a certain nostalgic appreciation for the old ways of doing things with a commitment to professionalism that involved keeping up with the latest best practices in progressive policing methodologies. As with the sheikh, Major Ahmed and I both spoke with an appreciation for the need for circumspection, with me often having to avoid pushing too hard on a particular line of questioning that would put him in an awkward position. In this regard, our conversation followed patterns and conventions that date back over a hundred years.

The British victory in World War I had entailed a number of local alliances, and, in the case of Jordan, one alliance of particularly lasting significance had been with Jordan's future rulers: the Hashemite family hailing from the north of what is now Saudi Arabia. Dispatching various adventurers like Lawrence, British officials sought to induce the local Bedouin to rebel. As the tide of the war turned against the Ottomans, they found a growing number of willing volunteers, most famously 'Audeh Abu Tayeh of the Huwaytat tribe, whose largely opportunistic role in "the Great Arab Revolt" would come to be central to the narrative of Lawrence's experiment in belletrism, *The Seven Pillars of Wisdom* (1922).[7] While Hashemite rulers would also be installed in Iraq and Syria, only Jordan's Hashemite monarchy would survive. Following a brief attempt to establish a capital in the prominent Ottoman-era market town of Salt after Abdullah I was declared Emir of Jordan in 1921, the Hashemite court would decamp to Amman, an area with less of a local sense of autonomy due to an influx of settlers from other parts of the empire under Ottoman tutelage. In the ruins of past kingdoms and empires and a burgeoning new colony, a new capital would emerge for a new state that would eventually come to collect millions of refugees from the shards of surrounding communities: first from Palestine, but later Iraq, Syria, and beyond (Tobin 2016, 23–31; Schwedler 2022).

Yet despite their impressive British-backed military and police forces, Jordan's Hashemite rulers could not completely operate as they wished: while they had little trouble killing their most obvious rivals with British-supplied armored vehicles and air support,[8] they could not really control how those around them perceived their actions. As Marc Lynch (1999) has argued, Jordan and its rulers were and are profoundly constrained by their deep entanglement in a wider Arabic-language public sphere to provide the context for their political project. Not only were most media of note produced outside of Jordan, but the whole ambition of the Hashemite political project itself was to use its small territory as a "launching pad" (Lynch 1999, 24) for building a much larger state in the future. Such considerations rendered Jordan's rulers uniquely vulnerable to opinions that circulated via a growing industry in print, radio, and eventually television that was initially based in historic Palestine and the major regional metropoles of Cairo, Beirut, and Baghdad under the patronage of wealthier and more sophisticated state and nonstate actors there.

Concerns about the inability of the Jordanian state to control the media and wider public sphere persist today. Major Ahmed would often say that there should only be one source of media controlled by the state or, otherwise, a powerful press syndicate that would only allow reputable journalists publishing reputable sources to operate. To the degree that such structures had weakened in recent decades, the policeman saw members of the security services like himself bearing much of the brunt. He said, "We're still not very developed in the regulation of this new media, unlike you in the West perhaps. So we only have negative effects. There needs to be *kuntrul*," striking the table with his hand and code-switching into English. In his estimation, news sites were motivated solely by their need for attention, followers, and views—to the detriment of social order. Using a recent example from his own village of Sarih (discussed further in the next chapter), he grew impassioned as he described the negative impact of social media. The problems in his village started with a dispute over a parking space but escalated after blows were exchanged. Youths on both sides used tools like WhatsApp and Facebook to coordinate subsequent violence. "Every tribe has its own Facebook group. They say, 'Let's meet here at this time and take revenge.' This is because when someone kills a member of the tribe, they believe they must kill a member of the other tribe to make it even. They do not wait for an investigation, though, and they do not care if the person who dies is the killer."

Furthermore, he argued that social media normalized the violence, sowing fear and encouraging young men to behave even more aggressively than they would otherwise. He said, "They do not go into the fight wanting to kill. They want to look strong and become sheikhs so they take pictures of themselves with guns and knives and put them on the internet." He worried that media might become a means of realizing new, violent forms of self-expression and self-actualization. Even worse, he charged that the media exaggerated the scope of the problem. "If you read the articles and saw the pictures these sites were publishing, you would think the situation [in Sarih] was like [war zones in] Raqqa [Syria] or Mosul [Iraq]. But I was there myself! They just take a small corner of the situation. This adds to the fear of the people, which is another negative. There were people who were afraid to go home because of these reports." Here, media content might lead to anxiety and even panic, creating a host of other policing challenges that must also be confronted. The allure and fear of violence might not be new, but in his mind, to the degree that the media might allow for the wider circulation of such images and behaviors, it necessarily represented a qualitative change in the sort of challenge he was confronting.

Fully aware of the power of new media technologies, Jordan's early Hashemite rulers dutifully set up the rudiments of a media industry to go along with their new government: first an official gazette called the *Arab East*, and then later official radio and television stations. Yet like earlier experiments with Arabic-language mass media in Egypt and Lebanon, they struggled to compete for the attention of the public with for-profit alternatives (cf. Ayalon 1995, 20)—even as Jordan could hardly sustain its own media industry, with many preferring instead to consume radio, print, and television media emanating from neighboring countries. In such a context of rising Palestinian and Arab national sentiment, Jordan's rulers often found it more expedient to suppress unwanted media and protest than to finance more agreeable content. In fact, as Jillian Schwedler demonstrates in *Protesting Jordan* (2022), the very built environment of Jordan's capital of Amman has been profoundly shaped by the state's efforts to control and channel dissent from the moment the Royal Court felt compelled to decamp from the town of Salt.

Jordan would become even more concerned with its own security as Israeli settlers flooded into Palestine to the west of the Jordan River. The kingdom's military would succeed in taking control of the West Bank amidst the chaos surrounding the massacres and mass expulsions of Palestinians known as the *nakba* or catastrophe that led to the formation of the state of Israel in 1948. Abdullah, first in his capacity as emir and then in his capacity as Jordan's first king following independence in 1946, had always viewed the Zionist movement in Palestine as a potential ally despite the strong opposition among emerging Arab publics in Palestine and their extended merchant networks that reached into Jordan. In 1951 this perceived complicity with Israel would be King Abdullah's undoing when he was assassinated by a Palestinian in Jerusalem during prayers at Al Aqsa Mosque (Massad 2001, 130). The following year would see Jordan's new constitution enacted under the brief rule of Abdullah's son Talal before he was declared unfit due to mental illness. Talal's son Hussein took over the throne in 1953, becoming a towering figure in Jordanian politics who would rule for over four decades (Wilson 1987, 209–213).

At the time, there was no reason to think Jordan or its young Hashemite king would last, though. The question of Palestine loomed large, but Jordan was also eclipsed culturally and politically by its other larger and more prosperous neighbors as well: Egypt, Saudi Arabia, Iraq, Syria, and even Lebanon. What Jordan did have and continued to develop were relatively strong internally and externally facing security apparatuses, which allowed the king to pursue a more pro-Israel line than his neighbors in return for support from the West. Under Hussein, the country's General Intelligence Directorate (known colloquially as the *mukhābarāt*) expanded along with the military and uniformed police. Yet there were limits to how far King Hussein could follow this strategy, most notably when he was pulled into the disastrous Arab-Israeli War of 1967 through his alliance with Egypt, which led to Israel's occupation of the West Bank and drove hundreds of thousands more Palestinians to flee east of the Jordan River. As Lynch argues, King Hussein's position was profoundly compromised by the emergence of the Palestine Liberation Organization, which became more entangled with the struggles of his subjects living west of the Jordan (1999, 77–79). However, once Israel had taken that territory, it suddenly became easier to jettison much of the country's pretensions to speak on behalf of the Palestinians. What began as tensions between Palestinian "West Bank" guerrillas and their Jordanian "East Bank" hosts eventually escalated in 1970 to the expulsion of the PLO and their East Bank supporters in a series of events known as Black September, during which thousands were killed by the Jordanian military and loyalist auxiliaries (Massad 2001, 134–137).

Black September marked a turning point in the politics of Jordanian national identity as the country's connections to Palestine became increasingly problematic. In fact, the defeat of the Arab armies at the hands of Israel marked a more general turning to the political right in the region. Like neighboring regimes, Jordan increased its support for Islamic groups like the Muslim Brotherhood during the seventies as a counterweight to leftist and nationalist political movements (Wiktorowicz 1999). The brotherhood's network of social services would eventually fill the vacuum left by the departure of the PLO, especially in the refugee camps. However, as Linda Layne (1989) argues, there was also a conscious decision as part of Jordan's disengagement from the West Bank to increasingly emphasize the country's Bedouin, tribal identity at the expense of its connections to Jerusalem and Al-Aqsa Mosque. Of course, the Jordanian intelligentsia's conception of tribalism is no mere continuation of that older Ottoman agrarian imaginary but builds upon it, incorporating not just developments on the ground but also "Western social scientific concepts" as well as Islamic objections (Layne 1989, 25–26). By the time Jordan officially renounced its territorial claims on the West Bank in 1988, the most prominent supporters of the Palestinian cause had largely been purged from the bureaucracy and the security services (Massad 2001, 137) and the Bedouin identity so predominant already in the security services had been elevated as the privileged Jordanian national identity.

Given how central the institution of the tribe has become to Jordanian national identity, the policeman could hardly fault the institution of the tribe itself for the sorts of social media–fueled tribal clashes that occupied him in his professional capacity. To the contrary, he saw tribes as a solution and argued that they prefigured the principles of "community policing" that he was learning in some of the classes he took from British and American trainers. In particular, he compared the system of tribal law extant in Jordan to the idea of the "social ladder" in community policing, a term of art from criminology that was an important part of his curriculum. Community policing attempts to break down the state-society divide and make members of the community extensions of the security apparatus (Williams 2011). For instance, bar owners, landlords, or universities may be encouraged or required to put pressure on law-breakers where police are unable to achieve their desired results on their own. Likewise, the policeman explained how tribal notables have long been used to control recalcitrant troublemakers. At the same time, though, he mocked some of the other aspects of this model and said they were unrealistic. He observed, "People expect the security apparatus to do everything, but we are just one part of the state. There are more basic problems of poverty and unemployment that we cannot affect. And then they want us to go out into the street and hug people. People don't want to hug us! They say, 'You take my money, arrest me, write me tickets, fine me, and put me in prison and you want to hug me?!'"

Major Ahmed argued that what was admirable in these modern best practices resembled the policing model of the 1970s and 1980s, contending that the Jordanian policing philosophy of that era had been a much more effective version of the community policing he was now being encouraged to practice. Speaking of his work with the juvenile crime division, he related how Jordan's current king Abdullah II was encouraging the police to treat young criminals as victims instead of yelling at them, beating them, and throwing them in jail like they were adults. The policeman underscored that the goal was to identify social causes of crime like poverty, unemployment, family problems, and drug use before they became too serious. Referring to his list of all the sheikhs in his district, he said that the first thing he would do when a youth was apprehended was to call the relevant sheikh in an attempt to release the offender to him in a guarantor capacity. He said, "It's not effective to go out and hug the youth who is smoking in the street because he has no incentive to cooperate. But the shiekhs and 'faces' [leaders] are another matter. They have an interest in order. In fact, they are usually themselves retired from the security apparatus. So you serve twenty years in the police or the army and then you become a sheikh. If there is a problem, the police go to their former colleagues." He argued that both his trainers and those who had devised Jordan's older policing strategies understood the value of making more established community members responsible for more combustible elements of the population—but that really the tribes were the essential component in Jordan's relative stability.

While the policeman believed that the confluence of patriarchal authority, strong centralized control over the media, and political conformity all worked to maintain Jordan as a rare island of stability in a troubled region, he feared how easily this arrangement could unravel. In fact, as I will show in the next section, this sense of a social contract in crisis long predates the advent of social media and includes a range of wider social, economic, and political transformations associated with Jordan's neoliberal turn. Namely, despite their political dominance, Jordan's rural, "East Bank" population (of which both Sheikh Salim and Major Ahmed are proud representatives) began to face a sustained challenge to their way of life as the country was forced to undergo a neoliberal structural adjustment regime beginning in the late 1980s. Ironically, these externally imposed austerity measures would force the state to attack the jobs and other privileges of its own historic backers. In 1989, rural Jordan would see a wave of protests against austerity that were often termed "bread riots" in response to the withdrawal of various state subsidies for basic goods (Ryan 1998). In the ensuing years, Jordan would intensify (if haltingly) various liberal reforms, including holding its first parliamentary elections since 1967, the legalization of political parties, and the fostering of a wider public sphere for debate about the issues of the day through new laws regulating the press.

The Journalist: Jordan's Neoliberal Turn

Having officially ceded the West Bank to Israel in 1988, lacking in fossil fuel reserves, and struggling to integrate Palestinian refugees, Jordan had little choice but to accede to much of the economic and political orthodoxy of the post–Cold War era "Washington consensus," as it would come to be known. This is not to say that Jordan completely lost its autonomy. In fact, Jordan was one of the only countries to side with Saddam Hussein in the first Gulf War, something widely attributed to the deep ties that had developed between Jordanians and Iraqis through the 1970s and 1980s while both were reliable US clients.[9] Yet with Iraq's decisive defeat, the ensuing international ostracism, and further debate, Jordan would increasingly repudiate its ties to Iraq to the point where it would serve as a major US ally in the second Iraq war. To accomplish this transformation in Jordan's domestic and international political economy would require fundamental changes to how the country regulated the media. Journalists would come to represent a new face of the state, perfect for a neoliberal era in which the state-society divide was crumbling and public-private partnerships suddenly abounded.

Like the sheikh and the policeman, the journalist (who I will call "Abdullah") also took a dim view of the effect of new forms of media. Yet where Sheikh Salim and Major Ahmed saw the media gaining power at their expense, the journalist (like most in his profession who I spoke with) was hardly convinced that he and his colleagues were gaining any power. In fact, he argued that new media technologies were making the state and local powerbrokers more powerful than ever. The son of a midlevel officer in the General Intelligence Directorate (more commonly known as the *mukhābarāt*), the journalist had grown up in a tribal neighborhood in the capital, part of an earlier wave of urbanization that brought large numbers of tribesmen employed by the state from rural areas into Amman. Like his father, he was an ardent nationalist with a keen sense of disgust for the rampant corruption he saw around him.

Perhaps my choice to focus on a man literally embodying a generational shift from the intelligence directorate to the newsroom is a bit too perfect, but it should not be too surprising that there are plenty of other examples of this, given the changes in Jordan's political economy over the past thirty years. In *Women and the Media in Jordan*, Ebtihal Mahadeen defines 1989 as a pivotal moment in Jordan, marking a shift from "full state control" to "relative liberalization" and the emergence of new forms of media (2022, 15). As she argues, the Royal Court, the General Intelligence Directorate, and those interests represented in the king's handpicked council of ministers primarily negotiate the structure of the media through two regulatory bodies: the Jordanian Media Commission and the Telecommunications Regulatory Commission. Another key gatekeeper is the Jordanian Press Association: since its establishment in 1953, it is only by joining the state-dominated syndicate that one could legally practice journalism in the country—something that would be officially extended to online publications in 2014 (Mahadeen 2022, 21–22). As Mahadeen observes, these bodies have strengthened and relaxed the rules on various occasions in response to various challenges to the state's legitimacy, serving very consciously as a sort of "pressure valve" (2022, 13).

This was certainly how many journalists saw things: while many could be arrogant and self-aggrandizing, a key aspect of professional comportment was a healthy cynicism (which Abdullah certainly exemplified). As was typical of those with an established place in the industry (and especially in front of an American interloper like me), Abdullah never seemed to fit into the neat pro-regime/opposition binary. He was doing well personally. A fully licensed journalist, his expensive membership to the Jordan Press Association was financed by the online news site he worked for.[10] He was deeply aware of the increasing polarization of Jordanian society and keen to underline that he could see what was happening around him. As he saw it, at one end of the socioeconomic spectrum was the more conservative and devout mass of hard-working yet often underemployed citizens in neighborhoods like his. At the other end of the spectrum was a small elite that mimicked Western mores and allied itself with US foreign policy while benefiting massively from privatization policies. Most of our conversations centered on the intrigues that he attributed to Jordan's colonial and postcolonial sponsors—and the ways in which he believed our encounters were implicated in them. In a sense, we had both come to believe that we could learn about emerging regimes of publicity and secrecy from each other: modes of disclosure and systems of obfuscation.

The journalist, like most of his colleagues, would often counsel me to not be deceived by the people I was meeting. Even those who worked in the online media sector believed it to be a bit seedy: filled with propaganda, incitement, and the politics of personal destruction. Journalists repeatedly told me during my research that most other journalists were working for some intelligence agency or other. Stories were typically dissected with an eye toward what US, Israeli, Iranian, or Jordanian state interests might be advanced by them. This was quite understandable, and hardly novel, perhaps all the more given the history of heavy overt state involvement in the media. Yet Jordan is hardly unique in that a large percentage of the information journalists relied upon came directly from the security services. Jordan is also far from unique in that information from the police is generally treated as authoritative until proven otherwise.[11] The journalist matter-of-factly explained, "Public Security publishes the correct information as a matter of the right of the citizen to information. Of course, if I find extra information, I can publish it—as long as I provide documentation." At times, he was willing to take the blame upon himself and his colleagues for the poor professional standards of Jordanian journalism, arguing, "Most journalists have no professionalism here. They just want it to be easy. They steal videos, pictures, text, and put their own name and logo on it. Then we have to call them and fight about it. . . . Of course, it is also safer to just say what Public Security says, but we can report what we want as well so long as it isn't about the king or the queen." I will have more to say about this practice of relying on government press releases in chapter 4

(**Face**), but for now I want to emphasize that it challenges traditional ideas of how [self]-censorship operates in a context of economic austerity and fierce competition amidst an increasingly fragmented and fractal interplay of what was once a more rigid state-society divide.

Like many neighboring countries, though, Jordan has long struggled not just to regulate its media but simply to develop a sustainable national media in the first place. On the one hand, the state has a clear incentive to fund an apparatus that can disseminate its view of events to the public and (notionally at least) the funds to do so. On the other hand, not only is media costly, but the sort of product on offer from the government is rarely enticing unless it is merely intended that functionaries should read government-provided materials as part of their jobs (cf. Ayalon 1995, 20–23; McFadden 1953, 8–9). Meanwhile, private ventures must contend with low circulation rates that make it difficult to find sufficient advertisers or subscribers to offset costs. As a result, Ayish and Mellor observe that "The media sector . . . has been subjected to increasing waves of market liberalization, paradoxically coupled with rigid media laws" (2015, 9). Again, though, this dynamic has a venerable pedigree: as Ayalon notes, Egypt's Khedive Isma'il Pasha pioneered state manipulation of the domestic and foreign press in the 1860s when he purchased shares in the previously critical French periodical *Les Temps*, bribed papers in the rival power center of Istanbul for favorable coverage, and secretly financed a popular paper that nonetheless billed itself as privately owned (1995, 19). In this environment, government media holdings are moved off the official balance sheet to increase their credibility and compel them to seek a profit, but they are also subject to increasingly intensive scrutiny over their content.

For the journalist, these dynamics could easily take on a more sinister cast. After all, Abdullah's boss had been imprisoned for promoting a video that embarrassed an important foreign dignitary from the Gulf, and one of his journalistic idols (Nahed Hattar) was shot dead by a preacher on the courthouse steps at his trial for sharing an allegedly blasphemous political cartoon on his Facebook page (an event described more fully in the chapter on **Face**).[12] In a moment of particularly acute cynicism, the journalist told me that someone who worked for the intelligence directorate once bragged to him, "The *mukhābarāt* no longer need to bother monitoring demonstrations and documenting the participants for later surveillance." Now, Abdullah noted wryly, they just "sit in the air-conditioning" and let journalists like him do the documenting. These represent but a handful of examples of the sorts of experiences that had pushed him (and many of his colleagues) to cultivate a healthy mistrust of surface appearances.

Even today, as the region becomes an almost universally literate society where a growing middle class has the disposable income to patronize their preferred media, the industry is still far from a straightforward moneymaking proposition. One Egyptian satellite television tycoon could very well have been speaking for many of my interlocutors when he told *Al-Ahram* that such channels were "a new defensive weapon for their owners" (quoted in Abdullah 2013, 65). In fact, when an early version of the material for this book was being vetted by a former member of the intelligence directorate so I could present it to a Jordanian audience, he told me I had avoided the "red lines" well, but thought I had neglected one thing (and indeed I had discounted the claim before he called me on it): that the most straightforward business model for most small media concerns was to find incriminating material on successful businessmen and use it to blackmail them into buying advertising.

Like most people I spoke with, the journalist had as many questions for me as I did for him—many of which I had been hearing since long before Jordanians started talking about social media. What was to be made of the contradiction between the ubiquitous US rhetoric of democracy promotion and the material reality of autocracy in the region? What of the on-again, off-again alliances of the United States and its Arab allies with everyone from Saddam Hussein to bin Laden and the Muslim Brotherhood? It was hard to keep the allegiances straight because motivations were often so nakedly cynical to begin with. Yet the frequency of unsuccessful, highly damaging military adventures on the part of Jordan, the United States, and its other allies made it difficult to attribute clear and coherent interests: could the United States really have been so stupid as to invade Iraq in an attempt to counteract terrorism? How had Jordan seemingly failed not only the Palestinian cause so decisively but even its own putative "national interest" in defending its sovereignty? Clearly, paranoia and the imputation of sinister motives to others is not new and does not require either social media or the privatization of formerly state-owned media. Nor does paranoia necessarily imply that one is not being manipulated. To the contrary, manipulation arguably becomes more effective in an environment where it already seems plausible.

In fact, one of the central points of interest in the political science of Jordan is how its elections have been explicitly designed to bolster independent tribal candidates considered to be more reliable regime loyalists over more ideological formations like the Muslim Brotherhood (Gao 2016; Kao 2023; Yom 2009; 2013). After the Brotherhood's political party, the Islamic Action Front, did well in Jordan's early post-1989 experiments with parliamentary elections that allowed for bloc voting, Jordan switched to single nontransferable voting in 1993 in the hope that limiting people to one vote within a limited geographic area would push them to prioritize voting for family members. As Kristen Kao argues (2012; 2015), this has had the foreseeable effect of limiting the Brotherhood's electoral prospects, but at the cost of empowering a coterie of local powerbrokers who use their seats to exercise a personalistic form of power that tries to maximize state resources for their tribal base at the expense of competing groups.

So when the Muslim Brotherhood did comparatively well in local elections, it was no wonder that Abdullah saw a hidden hand. At the local level, the journalist was disappointed that his own "tribal" candidate had lost out to the Muslim Brotherhood candidate, who had been heavily backed by those living in the neighboring Palestinian refugee camp. Claiming to have seen the vote-buying himself in the barber shop ("the *mukhābarāt* of the neighborhood . . . you tell everything to the one who touches your head"), Abdullah explained, "They went into the camps and bought votes for twenty dinar each. These are really poor people. You have a family with 9 or 10 people . . . that's like 180 or 200 dinar! That's like a month's salary for them . . . I tell you, the day after the elections you could smell the cooking meat wafting from the refugee camp." He assumed that this was orchestrated at higher levels and that it was his job to help his readers puzzle it out through subtle, impeccably sourced pieces of reporting from which they might discern the reality through a layer of censorship.

Speaking of the Muslim Brotherhood's success at the national level, most notably in Zarqa (Jordan's second-largest city), Abdullah reasoned, "The state must be behind this." In doing so, he exemplified how the figure of the state remains potent within contemporary media ideologies despite its ostensibly diminished role. That the state's role was so well effaced was itself evidence of the state's masterful manipulation of the media to disguise its true nature. As he continued, "They allow the Muslim Brotherhood to exist. Without the state there would be no Muslim Brotherhood so they must have a reason for supporting them."[13] Growing more cynical, he suggested, "There are some nightclubs, bars, and liquor stores that need to be approved by the municipality. We will see if the Brotherhood approves them." Unlike others I have profiled—or even Abdullah's own father—who have experience of working for (perhaps even "in") "the state," what is striking here is how the state in the journalist's account appears to be a pure exteriority and otherness.

Certainly, Palestinian and Islamist journalists could—and indeed did—make similar claims if and when the shoe was on the other foot, and my profiling of a Jordanian (or a Palestinian or an Islamist or a tribesman) could easily mask heterogeneity of the profession. I must also emphasize that these sorts of scenarios were often delivered in more informal moments with a mix of deadpan and sardonic detachment—but there is also always truth in jest.

The journalists who liked to weave these scenarios for me and others were, of course, deeply aware of the stereotype that Arabs have a penchant for conspiracy theories. Yet they often gently mocked me as an American for being so credulous about surface appearances—while also distancing themselves from particular popular theories that they knew I would be familiar with, but that they personally found implausible. Indeed, I was always keen to underline my acceptance of the fact that many of the most pivotal events in modern Middle Eastern history have been conspiracies designed to manipulate preexisting social cleavages for the benefit of outsiders, like the Sykes-Picot Agreement that partitioned the region between the British and French amidst the collapse of the Ottoman Empire. What I want to emphasize is the media ideologies involved and how they hinged on shared notions of publicity and secrecy within a broader shared political context.

The same modes of reasoning about media through notions of state, publicity, and secrecy also manifested in explanations for the Jordanian government's indulgence of tribal custom and press coverage of so-called "tribal clashes." For the self-identified Palestinian and Islamist journalists I spoke to, this coverage minimized serious crimes and spoke to the different rules that operated for different communities in Jordan. When clashes exploded on college campuses, such commentators took it as a massive indictment of the failure of the rule of law. In particular, those opposed to tribalism saw in such university violence the subjugation of the meritocratic premise of education to government quotas for its tribal supporters and those entitled to royal sponsorship at university because of their parents' employment in the security apparatus.[14] For critics of tribalism, the media were merely making plain a dirty local secret. Yet for tribally aligned journalists like Abdullah, the terminology was a malicious media attack on the rights to an education for some of Jordan's most patriotic citizens.

What was striking was how something like a riot on a college campus or a particular candidate's success in an election could be explained as a sinister attempt by the US or Jordanian security apparatus to either foment the Arab Spring or thwart it—to bolster the tribes and undermine the Palestinians, or the opposite. What all these modes of explanation had in common was how the media became a tool controlled by some power center for its own ends. This sort of estrangement from "the media" is one thing when it manifests itself among the obviously marginalized and disaffected, and indeed a common folk sociological explanation of conspiracy theory is that it is a psychological response to marginalization. Yet these were the journalists themselves, who in turn were hardly any less conspiratorially minded than local powerbrokers or the police.

Conclusion: Ideology, Media, and the State in a Neoliberal Age

The claims of the sheikh, the policeman, and the journalist as differently situated social actors temper one another's more extreme assertions while valorizing their basic—if somewhat opposed—perspectives on the changing role of media in the construction of authority in contemporary Jordan. On the one hand, the fears of the policeman and the sheikh that Jordan was rapidly spinning out of control following the Arab Spring seem even more unfounded in retrospect: tribal conflict still seems to dissipate tensions as much as it organizes them—and each year, the Arab Spring fades further into the background and seems more and more like a nonevent. The same goes for the more extreme fears of the journalist that he is but a cog in a system of surveillance that he cannot begin to fathom, working to advance interests that might be completely counter to his own. What I found was not a well-oiled apparatus of social control with lavish funding and dedicated cadres of experts collaborating night and day while weaving together intelligence gathering, law enforcement, and propaganda, but rather a decentralized, alienated, and highly ambivalent collection of relatively isolated individuals.

While most online news sites had offices in West Amman and journalists from rival sites often gathered in the evenings at cafés, they were politically divided and fundamentally in competition for readers, advertisers, and exclusive content. Many of the editors and owners had deep grudges against one another. These were people inclined to eye everyone around them as both foe and potential ally—including the foreign ethnographer–interloper. Yet while the reciprocal mistrust and paranoia manifest across the social field might be perceptive and well-founded, the key features of the most prevalent media ideologies that I encountered also helped produce what one might call either stability or paralysis (depending on one's perspective), effectively maintaining the status quo. Here I would argue that it is best to focus less on particular collections of shadowy interests and more on the media ideologies that promote the belief in such shadowy networks of interests, seeking to understand what such ideologies do to a country's politics.

The pervasive cynicism, alienation, and opportunism that represented the condition of possibility for my research was a reflection of the degree to which professional self-preservation required journalists, sheikhs, and police officers alike to be constantly mindful of censorship, surveillance, intimidation, blackmail, and illicit financial inducements. This sort of mindfulness in turn led to an appreciation for the efficacy of conspiracy and a widespread strategy of cultivating a diverse range of informal relationships to hedge against unpredictable developments. Conspiracy, of course, is the basis of most nondemocratic modes of governance, where deliberation happens far from public view because "the people" are not seen as a source of authority but rather as an impediment to its exercise. Yet such a state of affairs also makes it exceedingly difficult to know who is really in charge (a point I will return to in chapter 5, "**The Deep State**"). Rather, the key question becomes one of who (or more precisely *what*) protects the visible symbols of authority while successfully cloaking itself and thereby gaining the power to withdraw that support at will. In contemporary Jordan, at least, it is the "media" that increasingly fulfills this role, helping commentators posit the existence of covert channels that allow for the manipulation of the ostensible sources of authority within society (the state, the monarchy, foreign powers) by shadowy networks with opaque intentions.

Needless to say, in my interactions with the journalist (as with the others), I was deeply aware of my own positionality and, in particular, the constant joking about me being a spy, including mock denunciations, mock attempts to audition for the role of CIA asset, and moments when people suddenly became genuinely suspicious and reticent. Perhaps, much like the anthropologist Katherine Verdery (2018), I was actually the mark. Even if I might recoil at the notion of having Jordanian "informants" (as colonial anthropologists used to call their interlocutors), perhaps my interlocutors were right to see me as a potential informant. Rightfully suspicious of US machinations and struggling to understand what these new technologies were doing and how they could prevent the Americans from turning them against Jordan and its people, I can only hope I did them some good. If anything, it sometimes seemed that the more people were convinced I was a spy, the more eagerly they messaged me, invited me for coffee, and helped arrange meetings with other people. Undoubtedly, the fact that I was American accentuated these dynamics, but the dynamics themselves were also necessarily an extension of organizational logics that pervaded Jordan long before I arrived in ways that, happily, tended to make me irresistible to the kind of people I most needed to interview. While these modes of reasoning long predated the emergence of social media, social media fed into them as older modes of mediation (from the barber shop and the system of tribal dispute resolution to the uniformed intelligence services and official state media) were increasingly supplanted by a globalized, privatized, and unpredictably regulated "information economy."

Censorship is, of course, inherently difficult to study, but Jordan's quasi-regulated media do not seem to suppress social conflict—nor do they seem to concentrate it on the visible centers of power. To the contrary, it seems to refract conflict in a range of unpredictable directions, forcing everyone from local notables to journalists to members of the security apparatus to eye one another warily and be prepared to switch allegiances should the political winds change. The degree to which journalists in particular now play into the publicizing of threats to public order in real time marks a notable departure from decades of accepted practice. Yet it is unclear whether the increasingly widespread dissemination of news about all manner of such threats substantively challenges state authority. This dynamic is consonant with findings elsewhere. For instance, researchers working on China have argued that the statements most likely to be censored on the Chinese internet are not criticisms of the government but collective expression (King et al. 2013), and that large numbers of fabricated posts seem aimed at distraction as opposed to argument (King et al. 2017). Marc Owen Jones's *Digital Authoritarianism* (2022) has much to say about how Saudi Arabia and the United Arab Emirates also seek to instill division and mistrust in their opponents through social media. It is easy to discern similar logics at play behind Jordan's apparent red lines. The media ideologies I have tracked in this chapter all seem to accentuate the difficulty of ever really knowing where genuine political solidarity might emerge if not from the particularity of kinship, patronage, and neighborhood defense.

The emergent socially networked tribal publics that I have documented here are very much at odds with both Jurgen Habermas's rational-deliberative "public sphere" (1989) and even Michael Warner's "counterpublics," which, despite challenging "modernity's social hierarchy of faculties," "do so by projecting a space of discursive circulation among strangers as a social entity, and in doing so fashion their own subjectivities around the requirements of public circulation and stranger sociability" (Warner 2002, 87). In contrast, the attraction of tribal publics seems to be precisely a consequence of their presumed inability to conform to the requirements of true public circulation and stranger sociability, forcing a more irrevocable sort of allegiance onto social actors. It seems as if the very uprootedness and promiscuity of the era of "new media" has come to encourage a valorization of what Geertz (1967) called the "primordial ties" of kinship, ethnicity, and "blood"—primordial not in fact, but because they seem that way. At a moment when people feel increasingly connected to distant sources of power, such conflict is resolutely local, grounded in incontrovertible daily realities of neighborhood, mutual defense, and political patronage. These media ideologies, with their emphasis on media as a tool for affecting power at a distance, may therefore somewhat counterintuitively bolster preexisting structures of authority by pushing people to seek a grounding in the visible, the tangible, and the ready-to-hand—even if a few old men are humiliated in the process.

CHAPTER 2

Tribalism

In May of 2017 my fieldwork in Jordan coincided, as it sometimes does, with the holy month of Ramadan. Given the mixture of fasting and hot weather, I found interviews predictably difficult to organize and gatherings mostly pushed back until after the breaking of the fast at sunset, which made it too easy to justify passing more time than was probably necessary on Jordanian social media. Intrigued by the increasing role of social media in the lives of those I had been working with for over a decade, I had come to Jordan to study how local power structures might be shifting in response to these new technologies. As I have been describing so far, there was certainly a widespread perception that social media was both revitalizing tribal bonds *and* challenging gerontocratic tribal power structures. The most commonly cited evidence here was a marked uptick in the frequency and severity of what Jordanians call *ishtibākāt 'ashā'iriyya*, or, when translated into local English-language press coverage, "tribal clashes." Perhaps especially because my Jordanian friends were primarily Bedouin and rural (including a few from Sarih), my attention was drawn to a series of these tribal clashes in Sarih that had become a national outrage of sorts among many pious Jordanian Facebook users.

A popular genre of Jordanian news item, such "tribal clashes" were always unfortunate, but it was seen as a sure sign of the country's moral predicament for them to coincide with Ramadan—a month ideally devoted to fasting and prayer, when raising one's voice or even *feeling* angry can represent the breaking of the fast. I will have more to say about who these online critics of "tribalism" were and how they mobilized this event to advance their competing ideological visions, but first I want to interrogate what it meant for different Jordanian publics to either act for or against these tribal structures and the ideology of *'ashā'iriyya* or tribalism in general. Most importantly, I hope to explore how my Jordanian interlocutors developed their own anthropology and mobilized it to transform their social realities in various ways, concluding that even if academic anthropologists continue to be wary of how such invocations of tribalism can resurrect now-discredited anthropological theories, they ignore tribalism at their peril. Instead, I ask what similarly stigmatized concepts that my interlocutors mobilized to make sense of tribalism—like envy, face, the deep state, and mercy—might contribute to contemporary anthropological debates as well as wider societal debates about the alleged tendency of social media to encourage tribalism.

In this chapter, I begin by sketching what tribalism means to Jordanians (including both its proponents and detractors). I focus on how some Jordanians style themselves as tribespeople and how they argue with their detractors about tribalism's place in contemporary Jordan. I then show how tribalism has been rendered increasingly invisible to sociocultural anthropology despite its persistence as a powerful organizing force within the contemporary social field in places like Jordan. As tribalism's forthright rejection of so many of anthropology's cosmopolitan pretensions became more embarrassing, I contend that cultural anthropologists have increasingly ceded the field to pop neo-evolutionary approaches and self-styled counterinsurgency experts. I then return to Jordan to illustrate where current approaches tend to fall short (to the detriment of all involved), drawing on the online and offline commentary surrounding Sarih's Ramadan blood feud. While many noted the seeming irrationality of the violence itself as the rest of the nation recoiled in horror at the violation of a taboo on violence during the holy month, critics did not frame tribalism as merely irrational and other, but as something all people were susceptible to that must be surmounted through a sort of leap of faith embodied in a popular refrain among those calling for an end to the violence: "God guide the mind." Critics called upon Jordanians to rise above their invidious differences by embracing the godly attributes of mercy and grace, at turns cajoling and entreating the state security apparatus, powerful "faces" who claimed to speak on behalf of the rival tribes and for the tribes as a whole. I suggest that in tempering their recourse to projective and othering attributions of tribalism by seeking to work with it, these critical voices offer a welcome model of more intellectually curious engagement with the phenomenon of tribalism.

Actually Existing Tribalism

My interest in studying tribalism developed somewhat in spite of myself. When I first arrived in Jordan in 2006 as a Peace Corps volunteer armed with an undergraduate degree in anthropology and ready to teach English in a village in the kingdom's southern desert, I was inclined to view the whole topic of tribes as old-fashioned—if not downright retrograde. Yet as I began discussing with Jordanian friends and colleagues my interest in conducting ethnographic research after my service, many would scoff at my propensity to frame my interests in national terms as a study of "Jordan." Perhaps unsurprisingly, given that I had been embedded among Jordan's southern Bedouin tribes, I was often told that the only worthwhile research I could do would be on the Bedouin and their tribes. These self-styled Bedouin tribespeople reckoned that, while Jordan was merely decades old, the tribes had existed since the dawn of time and would certainly outlast Jordan and its gleaming new cities, much as they had survived all of the previous empires now reduced to ruins strewn across the landscape. Such proud Bedouin tribespeople reasoned that they were the ones who had *ʿadāt wa taqālīd* (customs and traditions) and "culture" (*thaqāfa*—though many adopted the English "culture" as a loan word).

In Jordan, being truly "tribal" has historically meant being "Bedouin," and vice versa. Etymologically and ecologically, Bedouin come from the *bādiyya*: the desert or wilderness beyond the cultivated lands under the rule of the state. Thus the opposite of being tribal or Bedouin is being "civilized" (*ḥaḍari*): those who are sedentary and live under the rule of a state, including not just city folk but even the peasantry. They too may organize themselves into tribes, especially at moments when the state is weak. In fact, the village of Sarih is in Jordan's more arable north and most would consider it a historically peasant community, meaning sedentary, state-governed, and hence civilized. In contrast, it is the desert-dwelling Bedouin who are seen as embodying the essence of tribalism in how their lightweight and adaptive social structure mirrors their material culture—especially as their ceaseless movement gives rise to their alleged antipathy to the state's more *static* designs. One journalist I knew whose family hailed from Sarih spoke vividly of how the Ottoman Empire's conscription of the village's young men often left his peasant ancestors open to attack by Bedouin raiders sweeping out of the desert—not that it stopped him from referring to himself as Bedouin when emphasizing how hospitable he was or explaining his instinctive distrust of the government. Those like the journalist who styled themselves as civilized—even if only contextually—might refer to the Bedouin with derision and often blamed them for the continued importance of tribes in Jordanian politics. As I briefly noted in the introduction, Bedouin for their part returned the favor by imbuing the word "civilized" with a connotation of condescension (implying it was deracinated, decadent, or effete). Engaging with the Bedouin and their culture required accepting that they were proudly atavistic and dismissive of standardized containers like the nation-state that my previous training in the social sciences had taught me to fit them into.

Over the years, I have watched as the rivalry between Bedouin tribespeople and their urban(e) detractors has moved online, birthing a whole genre of videos comparing the stereotypical Bedouin and *ḥaḍarī* child.[1] One particular video that I must have been shown by at least a dozen Bedouin on their phones over the years first shows the "civilized" boy beginning to cry as he stands next to a goat while his father tries to coax him into petting it. Then a "Bedouin" child is shown leaping on a goat with a wide grin and riding it for a few seconds to the tune of a raucous Bedouin song before the video cuts out. With the didacticism so typical of much online cultural production, my interlocutors here articulated Bedouin identity as authentically rooted in enduring tribal kinship structures epitomized by the father-son bond and pastoral modes of livelihood, while "civilization" entailed the dissolution of such certainties, rendering the "civilized" a pathetic spectacle of fearful impotence. Even as they embraced new technologies like the internet and smartphones, such interlocutors refused to accede to evolutionary teleologies that invoked tribalism as an origin point against which humanity's progress was to be measured. Instead, they rejected progressive temporalities, embracing "endurance, if not eternity" (Birth 2008). In doing so, my interlocutors presented a spirited challenge to so many contemporary treatments of tribalism because they at least took tribalism seriously.

Far from viewing tribalism as irrational, even many of its Jordanian detractors had to grant that at least in a Jordanian context where centuries of state policy had formalized tribes and their feuds through the institutions of policing and the media, tribalism often represented the height of political rationality to be overcome (if at all) through a sort of leap of faith. To be clear, as is typical for the era of globalized mass media uptake, Jordanians were often extremely well-informed about the rest of the world and could be as jaded as anyone when they traded barbs about world affairs both offline and online. Cynics were not shy about mocking the idea of being loyal to nation-states, abstract ideals, and even distant and seemingly inaccessible world leaders like Bush, Obama, Biden, or Trump. While Jordanians were often quick to be self-critical of what they saw as their own country's propensities for corruption and poor governance (often in ways I found self-orientalizing), there was also a widespread belief that no matter how venal tribal leaders might be, there were effective, time-honored strategies for extracting concessions from them.[2] After all, these men were known quantities, mired in complex, overlapping obligations of hospitality, debt, labor, marriage, protection, and patronage. Tribal leaders, often known as "faces," had clear vulnerabilities that could be exploited when (as was so often the case in Jordan's brief history) universal human rights proved to be an aspirational slogan rather than a material reality (cf. Arendt 1951). This did not stop many Jordanians from embracing various forms of universalism nonetheless, but what I hope to highlight is how (unlike so many treatments of tribalism in metropolitan theory) Jordanian critics of tribalism resisted the urge for self-congratulation and recognized the real stakes of relinquishing tribal claims in favor of more abstract and universalist claims.

During the fieldwork for my dissertation in 2011–2012, I continued to live with a Bedouin tribe, much as I had during my earlier Peace Corps service—though I moved closer to the capital to facilitate my access to archives. While some Bedouin continue to live in tents for some or all of the year—in fact, this has helped me secure accommodation during fieldwork on occasion—most Bedouin today have accepted a degree of sedentarization and now live in patrilocal family compounds. As the family grows, sons are given plots of land or individual units around their father's home, ensuring the parents will be cared for in old age as succeeding generations reproduce the family tree in concrete and steel rebar on the ground. As I found during my dissertation research on marriage (Hughes 2015a), though, this arrangement also creates tensions—especially for women. Conflict between wives and their mothers-in-law are a mainstay of Arab literature, film, and cultural production more generally. It was taken as a given that women pursued matchmaking strategies designed to help related women cluster together, and even men told me that they liked to facilitate this to obviate the need for strict modesty rules (since everyone was related). More generally, the research and the resulting book (Hughes 2021) focused on how marriage has become a site of struggle where tribal kinship norms are increasingly being contested by liberal, nationalist, and Islamic institutions, which see an opening in tribalism's frequent subordination of the desires and aspirations of individual young people to those of the group.

To be clear on this point: Jordan's tribalism is straightforwardly patriarchal in theory as well as in practice—in the strictest sense of the word. Individual women may have significant power over particular men, but if it has a tribal basis, it will be a function of their relationship to wider male kinship structures: first through their fathers and later through their husbands and then sons. The self-styled tribeswomen I met often derived significant satisfaction from their work as mothers and providers and did not suffer fools lightly. They also boasted of their "expensive blood" and how people feared their brothers, fathers, and uncles, and even the family name itself. Of course, in doing so they underlined how tribalism unapologetically privileges *male* kinship and promotes a model of authority that is profoundly public and masculine (Charrad 2001; Joseph 1987). Individual women have a number of strategies through which they can and do pursue their own personal advancement *as women* within the tribe and society at large, but it usually involves what Deniz Kandiyoti called "bargaining with patriarchy" (1988). A lot of this revolves around their control of their own and other women's procreative powers through the institution of marriage (Delaney 1991; Hasso 2011; Shryock and Howell 2001). While a woman's position after marriage is stereotypically vulnerable and tenuous at first as she moves from living with her tribe to living with her husband's tribe, tribalism promises women that if they submit to its logics, they can amass significant power and notoriety in their own right as they have more children, grow older, and involve themselves in the social life of the community.

If tribal leadership is paradigmatically masculine and public, an alternative modality of power that is more private and feminized coexists as its counterpart and often emerges (for example) in male anxieties about the impossibility of men fully controlling the arranging of marriages and (by extension) paternity (Hughes 2015b). Yet even when tribeswomen have power (after a fashion), it may not be the sort that anyone would ask for. Due to this tribal preoccupation with grounding group identity in shared paternity, even minor sexual transgressions on the part of women (real or perceived) can threaten the reputation of the entire tribe and provoke a violent response. While the stereotypical perpetrator of an "honor" killing is a brother or father, researchers and advocates emphasize that these killings are often carried out with the blessing of the whole family, and that women may be active participants who sincerely believe they are defending their own prerogatives.[3] Fadia Faqir illustrates this dynamic in a bracing account of the murder of a Jordanian woman named Basma who left her husband for another man:

> Her family was ostracised, her eight sisters were deemed unmarriageable, and her brothers were mocked in the streets, even by their close relatives, who argued that they should kill their sister to cleanse their honour. Her mother went looking for Basma to kill her, but could not find her. Her 16-year-old brother's manhood was questioned, so he finally tracked Basma down and killed her. Her 18-year-old sister said, "Now we can walk with our heads held high." (Faqir 2001, 72)

While Jordan has a relatively low murder rate for both genders (on par with Western Europe), such killings need not be common to foster an intense climate of fear around sexuality—especially for women. Given the risk of romanticizing how women in tribal communities can survive and even thrive despite a rigged social order, it is important to underline how women's power must remain a subversive and subordinate sort of power within this tribal paradigm, the province of what one might call "practical representations" (Peletz 1994, 137–138) rather than "official kinship" (Bourdieu 1977). Ultimately, there is a strict, highly gendered division between public and private, and the fact that the work of tribal dispute resolution and politics more generally is a quintessentially public and male activity can only work to women's collective disadvantage (cf. Ortner 1972).

The life in the "village" (*qariya*) as my neighbors called it that grew out of and buttressed this gendered division of labor was structured around maximizing tribal self-sufficiency despite a profound reliance on government jobs. With the exception of the one Palestinian family in the settlement where I conducted fieldwork (historically excluded from politically "sensitive" positions), most of the men worked in the security services until they were middle-aged. Having reached a pensionable age, they could retire and focus their energies on finding positions for their sons, building their houses, and doing more casual work in trade, transportation, or agriculture. Despite being situated on the border of the Greater Amman Municipality and spending more and more of their lives on their phones, villagers lived among chicken, sheep, goats, and fields of wheat, okra, and other crops. The settlement itself was situated on a hilltop, and residents noted with some satisfaction that it was the highest ground between them and Jerusalem, whose suburbs lit up the night, radiating out like a carpet in the distance below. My neighbors had supplemented deep cisterns, likely dating back thousands of years in some cases, with their own dug with modern equipment and lined with concrete for storing water in case of emergencies. Many kept livestock, but there was a general emphasis on agriculture, including cash crops like okra as well as more traditional peasant fare like wheat. While the youths did not seem to take much heed, a number of the elders would talk in somewhat apocalyptic terms about such endeavors. They said the end times must be near when people began to fly and humans again sought to build towers reaching up into heaven (recalling the tower of Babel). Preparations for future strife also involved being heavily armed, to defend their livestock from thieves but also in case of conflict with neighboring tribes or the outbreak of war: over the years I saw pistols, rifles, shotguns, and at least a few automatic weapons.

Here, tribal ties were not metaphorical—nor did they necessarily struggle to manifest themselves through new media, be it the concrete and steel rebar of people's settlement patterns or (as we have seen) Facebook-mediated blood feuds. Even the mobile phone carriers could come to be associated with particular tribes, as in-network discounts led people to pressure their kin to switch networks. From settlement patterns to family dynamics and the wider organization of Jordan's infrastructure, the constant reification of tribal kinship ties formed the strong basis for (and end goal of) a whole host of everyday activities. Yet a whole debate raged among my neighbors about what it meant to be Bedouin in the twenty-first century, which largely centered around different responses to this imperative to maintain the integrity of the tribe. A lot of my friends from the southern Bedouin tribes scoffed at the idea that some of these families in Amman's exurbs were real Bedouin tribespeople. A Bedouin could be a soldier, perhaps, or even work in tourism, they would allow, but to pick okra or grow wheat or run a sprawling plantation of greenhouses growing cucumbers and tomatoes? Such people had become civilized, *fallāḥīn* (peasants) even, the very opposite of Bedouin. For those who viewed the Bedouin as occupying what was effectively an ecological or economic niche, a real Bedouin lived in a tent and his primary livelihood was livestock or—even better—warfare, allowing him to move with his tribe and evade taxation, conscription, and other forms of submission to the state and other temporal authorities. Most tribespeople granted that at least historically there had been a hierarchy among the tribes, with the most elite tribes living deepest in the desert, facilitated by their reliance on camels (as opposed to sheep or goats). Keeping their wealth in camels allowed their tribes to move greater distances without water and hence maintain an even greater degree of autonomy, marking them as a sort of nobility. In fact, given the importance of camels for military logistics and long-distance trade across deserts, such a livelihood could even allow some Bedouin tribes to engage the region's states and empires on more equal footing as trading partners and mercenaries.

Nonetheless, more sedentary and urbanized Bedouin had their own arguments for why they were actually authentic Bedouin—or even the most authentic Bedouin of all. While some urban Bedouin adopted the apocalyptic sensibilities I have already described, many Bedouin tribespeople shared the technological sensibilities of Lila Abu Lughod's Awlad 'Ali Bedouin in that they did not "experience any jarring sense of discontinuity" (1986, 74) at all. Such Bedouin knew perfectly well that their ancestors did not drive trucks, build concrete houses, or work for the government, but this did not impinge on the essence of their identity as Bedouin tribespeople. If being a Bedouin tribesperson was really about being part of a privileged genealogy, then it was about good birth, reputation, and wealth, and any technology that supported those aims was to be embraced. They could easily dismiss those who actually continued to work with livestock as mere "shepherds." The very fact that they still had to do such manual labor itself was all the proof needed that they lacked the proper tribal pedigree. The wealthiest Bedouin families in Amman's suburbs generally preferred to train their children as doctors and engineers under the rationale that then they could always afford to hire a less-successful fellow-tribesman to keep a few livestock on a corner of the property as "heritage" (*turāth*). Armed with advanced degrees, government positions, and—increasingly—social media profiles, they embodied the essence of Bedouin identity by serving as "faces" for their groups at gatherings both personally and virtually.

One of my friends embodied the tension between these two sensibilities particularly well. Despite being a proud Bedouin tribesman, his family had fallen on hard times after he was forced to sell his livestock to pay for a blood money settlement to keep his brother out of prison after he was found responsible for a car crash. Yet despite having to claw himself out of debt by ploughing otherwise inaccessible plots of land for local *ḥaḍarī* landowners with a mule, he insisted that peasants and Bedouin were fundamentally different kinds of people and that there was no continuum allowing—or even forcing—people to shift from one ecological niche to another as their circumstances changed. I found this apparent contradiction fascinating, and I even suggested that his family history was replete with precisely the oscillation in modes of subsistence that his current predicament embodied. After all, even if he felt himself to be more Bedouin than the "Palestinian" family down the road, his family had been banished from Jordan to Palestine because of a blood feud in the early twentieth century to the south not far from where I had been a volunteer, and he grew up working the fields with his family as refugees after they fled during the *nakba* in 1948. Yet he would have none of it.

After offering detailed and often convincing rejoinders about the incommensurability of peasant and Bedouin lifeways that showcased how masterfully he grasped the minutia of both modes of subsistence from long personal experience, my friend ended with a straightforwardly essentialist argument. He said, "Everyone has *usūl* (roots or origins). Everyone has an essence. Just look at people and there is always a *dalīl* (guide or sign). You can see it in their faces. Take the [neighboring tribe] and how they all have that thing with their eyes, you know?" I felt defeated because I had to bashfully admit that I knew exactly what he was talking about. While the idea of indulging in amateur physiognomy had been the furthest thing from my mind when I embarked on my research, I had to grant that I had noticed what I might call (with apologies to Wittgenstein) a "family resemblance" without anyone needing to mention it. As a coda to this friendly back-and-forth, I must add that at the time of writing my friend has again amassed a large herd, allowing him to live off-grid for a number of years now in a tent with his family and suggesting that perhaps he had a point. Despite a century of setbacks, his family was again living the Bedouin lifestyle they had always aspired to on the margins of the state.

There was, however, another side to this debate about the place of Bedouin tribespeople in contemporary Jordan, represented by those Jordanians who found the persistence of the tribes an embarrassment at best, which often manifested itself in the form of disapproving comments (online and offline) in response to reports of corruption and tribal clashes. There was widespread opposition to tribalism across the ideological spectrum, from Islamists to Jordanian nationalists, Baʿthists, Nasserists, liberals, socialists, communists, and anarchists. Even the relatively apolitical were often highly critical of the arbitrariness, violence, favoritism, and corruption so often associated with tribalism. The left-liberal arguments in opposition to tribalism should be clear enough: the patriarchy of it, the inherent tensions with egalitarianism, due process, and procedural fairness. However, even more conservative nationalist and Islamist voices often blamed Jordan's problems on tribalism, especially due to the scourge of what is known as *wāsṭa* (connections) and its corrosive effects on the wider social totalities that they sought to actualize.

While there is a tendency to co-opt discourses of *wāsṭa* and *ʿashāʾiriyya* and transform them from culturally internal discourses of self-criticism into a form of orientalist cultural pathologization (Brown 2008, 448), these discourses clearly do refer to something significant. At times Jordanians were quite open about how they personally used tribal and other unofficial connections or *wāsṭāt* to accomplish various tasks, from obtaining government jobs for family members to receiving priority treatment in government offices. Jordanians would sometimes threaten to use their connections to take revenge on others or brag about how they used connections to enrich themselves—though most preferred to emphasize how they needed to rely on family connections to simply receive what they were entitled to. Here, rather than talking in terms of such *wāsṭāt*, it was more common to speak euphemistically of how one unfortunately had to rely on tribal obligations of acknowledgment, preference, and hospitality just to function in these fallen times. In fact, far more prevalent was a lively debate about how *other people* were responsible for the scourge of *wāsṭa*, and how one's own recourse to what might look to others like *wāsṭa* was purely defensive.[4] In fact, the way the system "made a thief of you" as people were forced to use informal means to secure what should be their rights was often understandably taken to be the crowning insult atop the injury of Jordan's weak institutions.

For those Jordanians who fashioned themselves as ideological (whether that journey had led them to Islamism, liberalism, or communism), becoming "committed" (*multazim*) was often in part expressed in a narrative of breaking with familial and tribal obligations, usually at some personal cost. One leftist journalist likened the tribes to a mafia and spoke of how his father's tribe initially had taken his family in after the father's untimely death, but later disowned his family when they refused to help carry out a revenge killing and even threatened to harm him when he defended his mother's wishes. However, many successful people with liberal and Islamist leanings told less dramatic versions of this narrative, with a similar dynamic: as they progressed higher in their professional worlds, they had to bat away what they saw as annoying and unreasonable requests for help from kin they perceived as lacking in personal initiative and overly fixated on parochial, self-serving concerns.

That being said, Jordanian leftists, liberals, nationalists, and Islamists could not completely reject tribalism given their wider social milieu, and so they also sought to lionize what they saw as its positive qualities to be preserved in pursuit of their more utopian visions. Leftists and some nationalists drew parallels between the traditional tribal "commons" (*mushā'*) and the vision of a future national or humanity-wide commons. In fact, the Arabic for communism (*shuyū'iyya*) shares a root with *mushā'*. For Jordanian and Arab nationalists, hailing from a tribe (also known as *'arab*) was a key precursor to the national project itself, which might replace these older loyalties but was still in many ways modeled upon it. As for Jordan's vibrant Islamic movement, there was a lot of invocation of the Quranic verse 49:13, which reads, "Oh people that we created from male and female and made you nations [*shu'ūb*] and tribes [*qaba'il*] so that you may know one another. The most noble of you according to God is the most faithful." Depending on one's perspective or even the issue at hand, one might emphasize the first part about God placing nations and tribes on an ontological par with male and female—or retort by emphasizing the second part that the only real form of merit was piety.

Even as Jordanians often diagnosed tribalism as exacerbating many of their country's problems (for good reason), it was hard to completely dismiss its political rationality. As I argued in the last chapter, tribalism was not merely a set of deeply held values—it was part of a long-running state project spanning the reigns of numerous empires. As discussed in the previous chapter, today the purest manifestation of tribalism's continued state patronage amidst the alleged triumph of liberal democracy after the Cold War is Jordan's so-called "one person, one vote" electoral reforms, which were designed to empower independent tribal candidates at the expense of ideologically organized political groups like the Muslim Brotherhood (Kao 2012; 2015; Yom 2009; 2013). Andrew Shryock (1999) has called the resulting political formation "dynastic modernism," emphasizing how Jordan is ruled as a patriarchal household writ large, with the monarchy doling out favors to competing subjects it figures as squabbling children. While the model is cynical and patronizing by nature, it seems to have survived the change from one king to another intact, despite consistently being subject to spirited challenge. Yet the sober recognition of entrenched systems of inherited inequality so common in Jordan sits uncomfortably with some of the more triumphalist currents of cosmopolitanism and universalism now favored by metropolitan theory, leaving current theoretical fashions ill-equipped to deal with these dynamics.

The Embarrassment of Tribalism

The tribe's fall from anthropological grace took off in the mid-twentieth century as decolonization spurred a more critical appraisal of older evolutionary and structural-functionalist approaches. As Morton Fried noted in *The Evolution of Political Society* (1967), the anthropological concept of tribe was derived from the Latin *tribus*. Yet even in the Roman case, where tribes served as the largest segment dividing the Patriciate for military, legal, and voting purposes, these groups were neither politically autonomous nor of homogenous descent as the standard definition of tribe would have it. As a result, Fried argued that the anthropological concept of tribe "carries confusion back to its origins" and "lacked sociological rigor from its inception" (Fried 1967, 160). Nonetheless, despite the persistent empirical problems, the concept of tribe seemed to offer a profoundly useful tool of frontier pacification and (counter) insurgency, meaning that it was often central to the dynamics that colonial anthropologists encountered—and were tasked with explaining. When these so-called "tribal societies" were presented as a sort of missing link between humanity's postulated Edenic, small-scale origins and the sprawling states of today, the study of tribalism promised an enticing synergy between evolutionarily informed social science and the practical needs of empire. As decolonization picked up steam in the second half of the twentieth century, however, there was a backlash against the concept of tribe, both in nascent postcolonies and then in anthropology and related disciplines as tribes became emblematic of detested practices of imperial divide and rule. Nonetheless, the salience of tribes has never fully dissipated—if for no other reason because the imperial dynamics that the discourse of tribalism embodies and attempts to fix ideologically within a broader civilizational narrative never dissipated either. Yet as a new generation of anthropological work on tribalism is beginning to show, it is not just a tool of empire, but a contested terrain where bottom-up, vernacular forms of politics continue to struggle with the great powers of our time. Contemporary anthropology dismisses tribalism at its peril.

One major reason why colonial anthropology was so engrossed in the study of tribes was that they seemed to be a key to effective colonial administration—which also accounts for some of the subsequent backlash. After all, as I noted in the previous chapter, Frederick Peake used his knowledge of tribal dynamics to supplement his modern weapons and help put down the ʻAdwan revolt. Similarly, John Glubb made an entire career for himself administering Jordan's armed forces as a tribal "patriarchy" (Glubb 1948, 166, quoted in Hughes 2022, 365), outlasting his original British employers in Jordan by nearly a decade. The concept of tribe migrated into anthropology in the nineteenth century via colonial lawyers like Lewis Henry Morgan (1877), who had been trained in Latin and sought to both understand indigenous political organization and the historical fortunes of monarchical and democratic rule more generally in human societies. Especially once Morgan's ideas were taken up by Marx and especially Engels (1884) and became central to Marxist conceptions of human developmental stages, it became common to see tribes as a transitional stage between family-level social organization and the emergence of states on both the political right and left. For anthropologists, though, the figure who best embodies the marriage of soldiering and scholarship would be E. E. Evans-Pritchard, whose work on tribes predated and outlasted his World War II military service. His historical work *The Sanusi of Cyrenaica* (1949) was a product of his wartime efforts to organize irregular forces drawn from the local tribes there to wage guerrilla war against Axis forces and built on his earlier work on the Nuer for the British colonial administration in Sudan.

In his classic book *The Nuer*, Evans-Pritchard presented the titular ethnic group as a strongly egalitarian "acephalous" society existing in a state of "ordered anarchy" (1940, 6) and organized into tribes. Writing under the patronage of the government of the Anglo-Egyptian Sudan, Evans-Pritchard promised an account of Nuer "oecology" and politics for "the student and administrator" (1940, 7) with later promised volumes on kinship and religion pitched to more academic audiences. Among other things, he would argue that attempts to resettle the Nuer and break them of their nomadic pastoralist lifeways were likely to disrupt preexisting tribal dynamics and thus further destabilize the situation. Instead, Evans-Pritchard sought to model the Nuer as a sort of homeostatic superorganism that maintained a delicate political balance through institutionalized feuding. In a series of widely reproduced diagrams, Evans-Pritchard depicted Nuer political structures as a recursive set of nesting oppositions expressed in the idiom of a forking family tree that embodies itself in the division of territory between sons in successive generations (or at least myths of such divisions). Through the lineage system, conflicts were portrayed as being channeled into particular sets of nested binary oppositions at different scales: A is opposed to B as A1 is opposed to A2, and so forth. This tribal subsection and that tribal subsection will unite if challenged by this rival tribe, but others will refrain from intervening when they fight among themselves. Evans-Pritchard reported that this structure further mapped onto the increasing strictness of the norms around combat and exchange of blood money at more local scales that did not hold when these groups combined to attack neighboring Nuer tribes or the neighboring Dinka people.

Much of the subsequent debate about "segmentation" as it came to be known would hang on the ambiguity in Evans-Pritchard's writing between what Paul Dresch called "history as cause" and "history as image" (1988, 55).[5] For Evans-Pritchard in *The Nuer*, it is obvious that "every small tribal segment" is actually a messy agglomeration of adoption, marriage, and outright genealogical fiction, but he claims nonetheless that "the structure of the dominant clan is to the political system like the anatomical structure to the system of an organism" (1940, 228). Later commentators like Susan McKinnon (2000) and Kathleen Gough (1971) were inspired by feminism, Marxism, and other critical approaches to note how Evans-Pritchard's political anthropology depended on artificially amputating his masculinized, politicized world of feuding and tribal politics from a feminized domestic space of reproductive kin relations. As McKinnon (2000, 38) reminds us, Evans-Pritchard's "agnatic" principle conveniently allowed him to relegate other social and familial ties (especially those involving women) to later specialist volumes. With the benefit of Sharon Hutchinson's (1996) restudy of the Nuer (which focused on women), scholars like McKinnon further challenged whether there had ever been anything "stable" or egalitarian about Nuer kinship dynamics at all. In fact, with a greater focus on women, non-aristocrats, and other hangers-on in the cattle camp, it became clear that Nuer kinship could not be governed by a simple principle of agnation (the primacy of male kinship legitimated through marriage). Instead, Nuer kinship involved an inherent push-and-pull between different ways of making kin—in highly unequal terms—as individual leaders known as "bulls" attempted to gather others around them using their control of grazing lands and cattle as an enticement. The latter were used not only for sustenance but also as bridewealth payments that could be gifted to prospective clients to more securely legitimize their children's land claims.

Evans-Pritchard did not develop his ideas about tribalism sui generis, though, which is partly what makes him a useful exemplar of a wider approach and school of thought.[6] Evans-Pritchard himself attributed the idea of segmentation to the earlier work of the orientalist William Robertson Smith, who wrote on it in his 1885 work *Kinship and Marriage in Early Arabia* (1938, 123). As Smith notes there, it was the pension system of the early Islamic state that "afforded a direct stimulus to genealogical research and also, it must be added, genealogical fiction" (1885, 6). In the debate about whether segmentation and tribalism refer to a social structure or an ideology of nonstate societies, it should be clear by now that it was always intended to be a bit of both—and hardly distinct from the dynamics of state formation itself.[7] Evans-Pritchard's *The Nuer* is neither a straightforward factual account of some primitive survival offering a window on humanity's past, nor a racist fabrication of one. The book should be understood alongside its subject matter as a particular reaction to wider imperial dynamics, both in the ways that Evans-Pritchard acknowledged openly and in ways he could only accept slowly and haltingly due to his own deep involvement in projects of imperial knowledge-production with far wider and deeper histories.

As Edmund Leach demonstrated at length in *Political Systems of Highland Burma* (1954), groups that were liable to be termed "tribes" were often suspiciously messy in practice, and while many anthropologists were willing to accept that things had been less muddled in the past, there was no principled reason to assume this was true.[8] All of this would lead Fried to suggest that anthropologists had been getting things the wrong way around: tribes did not lead to the evolution of states or social complexity. To the contrary, Fried suggested that what anthropologists called tribes were a "secondary phenomenon" that was in fact a "reaction to the formation of complex political structures [like states] rather than a necessary preliminary stage" (1967, 170). In fact, continuing on with this evolutionary logic in which the state is associated with complexity and taken to be the implicit goal of political evolution, Fried suggested that tribes were in fact best understood as an "evolutionary cul-de-sac" and of a piece with a "spasmodic cycle" lacking the "institutional raw materials" to lead to the greater "complexity" embodied in the modern state (1967, 173).

However, while Fried's implicitly statist evolutionary teleology fit well with the moment in which he was writing, there is no reason to assume that tribes could not lead to greater "complexity" or that the sorts of "spasmodic cycles" that tribal organization often seems to promote might not be of a piece with all sorts of as-yet unimagined developments. Or, perhaps, "development" was never the point at all: what if greater "complexity" was the real evolutionary cul-de-sac, inevitably waiting to be swept away by more nimble and robust competitors? What if simpler was better? As the anarchist and anthropologist Pierre Clastres quipped, compared to "Western ethnocentrism . . . the savage belonging to some Indian or Australian tribe deems his culture superior to all others without feeling obliged to deliver a scientific discourse about them" (1974, 17). Placing self-congratulatory talk of social progress in more scientific garb and using euphemisms like "complexity" does not make it any less of a chauvinistic myth. There was always a strain of cynicism in anthropology toward the statist narrative of progress. For instance, A. R. "anarchy" Radcliffe-Brown (as he was known during his university days at Cambridge) and other structural-functionalists who prioritized the study of tribes existing in what they called "organized anarchy" (Goody 1999, 6) had long warned against the conflation of evolution and progress (Radcliffe-Brown 1947, 78–79). However, even as the critique of colonial anthropology led to a more positive reappraisal of what had been called "tribal" societies, part of that shift involved jettisoning the word "tribal" in favor of a host of euphemisms (small-scale societies, simple societies, stateless societies, kin-based societies, and of course "so called . . .").

Yet for some of those skeptical of centralized power like Clastres, tribes came to seem like an intriguing leveling mechanism and tool of resistance, which led him to term such societies, *societies against the state*. After all, what was the role of the tribal leader in the Amazonian regions where he had conducted fieldwork? The chief was supposed to gratify the people with regular oratory. He (and it usually was a he) was also usually engaged in polygynous relationships with important families in the community, which, crucially, allowed them to make demands on the chief for labor and other resources (Clastres 1974, 36). Clastres argued that this was no exchange, however, but the very "rejection of reciprocity," which represented "the ejection of the political function from society" as "the very means of reducing it to impotence" (1974, 42). For Clastres, these institutions represent a "veritable defense mechanism": "via the women [the chief] is in a sense the group's prisoner" (1974, 46). Whether or not one accepts Clastres' characterization, though, it became increasingly common to reexamine the practices of what James Scott called those "often mistakenly called tribes" (2009, 13). From an anti-statist perspective, those who gathered like flotsam and jetsam in those areas that states found logistically or even just socially inaccessible (such as deserts, mountains, and swamplands) were not benighted, *stateless* peoples but innovators and practical political philosophers. Their practices could suddenly be reanalyzed for their "escape value" (Scott 2009, xi), from multilingualism and illiteracy to nomadic, "escape agriculture" and even an "escape social structure" (Scott 2009, 23) that could be easily remade to the needs of the moment.

In *The Scandal of Continuity*, Judith Scheele and Andrew Shryock note how tribalism is part of a whole cluster of themes and topics that have become stigmatized in the anthropology of the Middle East since the late twentieth century. If anthropology in the era of Claude Levi-Strauss was content to divide the world into "hot" and "cold" societies and reserve for itself those allegedly unchanging, homeostatic "cold" societies, Scheele and Shryock note sardonically that "today, all human societies are supposedly 'hot.' They are also open, fluid, and connected" (Scheele and Shryock 2019, 7)—even if it must be in spite of local protestations to the contrary. A recent roundtable in the *International Journal of Middle East Studies* captures the frustration and befuddlement that the persistence of tribalism seems to provoke among social scientists when it asks of tribalism, "How can what is seemingly an atavism of pre-modern times still have currency in today's world?" (Wien 2021, 471). In such a context, the conferral of anthropology's overwhelmingly progressive modern temporality onto its interlocutors can become increasingly fraught. As Scheele and Shryock put it, such a conferral of what Johannes Fabian called "coevalness" or "shared time" onto one's interlocutors can start to feel like a "dubious privilege" from "a long list of imperial gifts" (2019, 7). As I suggested in the introduction, when ethnographic interlocutors *refuse* these offers of coevalness, they may not merely challenge anthropologists' own moral and political commitments but even anthropology's ability to make authoritative knowledge claims grounded in having shared both space and time with particular others.

Many anthropologists would like to think they have simply progressed beyond all of this, but as David Price shows at length in *Weaponizing Anthropology* (2011), the discipline remains a tool of imperialism today, and its supposed expertise on tribes remains in high demand.[9] With a focus on the US military's development of a Human Terrain System staffed by anthropologists using anthropological jargon to aid the US occupation of Iraq and Afghanistan, Price shows how the history of anthropology is less a straightforward story of progressive decolonization and more one of an ongoing political struggle. While those who participated in these military crossover collaborations have largely failed to earn academic respect, they have played a role in legitimizing disastrous policies using shoddy reasoning, bad social science, and unethical research practices. In a prescient 2009 piece on US attempts to leverage tribal dynamics as a tool of counterinsurgency, Roberto González warned that selectively bribing local leaders and playing them off one another as a tool of pacification risked creating a "dangerous situation resembling the Lebanese civil war" (2009a, 105). Fears of intensified sectarian violence were borne out as the insurgency continued through the

US withdrawal and eventually gave birth to the Islamic State, which in turn would eventually be dismantled through yet another tribal "awakening" consisting largely of what González would call the "tribes and bribes" model.

Anthropology of course does not usually present itself as a predictive science, and the fact that González was correct that Iraqi and US authorities would go back to fighting the primarily Sunni, ex-Ba'thist Iraqis being paid off and handed weapons once the US tired of supporting them does not necessarily vindicate his entire critique. Nonetheless, it seems notable that González did not need any particular understanding of Iraq or its tribes to diagnose the problem, but rather a solid grounding in the history of empire and counterinsurgency techniques. Such expertise is unfortunately precisely what has been so lacking in recent attempts to co-opt classic anthropology for modern military needs: as Price notes, the anthropological concepts that are borrowed in the resulting counterinsurgency manual are presented haphazardly, with no citation or attention to their subtleties (2011, 137). To give an example that seems especially indicative of the wider problem, González found that Appendix A of the counterinsurgency manual was largely lifted without attribution from the work of T. E. Lawrence (2010, 81). Yet given that Lawrence's brief was to stir up trouble for the ruling Ottoman authorities that would bleed them dry, it does not follow that copying his successful efforts to win "hearts and minds" would lead to a new *Pax Americana*. To the contrary, one might ask whether following Lawrence's advice might be a recipe for permanent employment for counterinsurgency experts with a focus on the Middle East.

The other area where notions of tribe continue to coast along in relatively uncritical form with vague anthropological imprimatur is evolutionary psychology, where there is an increasing interest in the human mind beyond what Joseph Henrich (2010) and his collaborators called "WEIRD" subjects (Western, Educated, Industrialized, Rich, and Democratic). Tribalism presents itself here as an alternative way to be human at a time when it is increasingly untenable to base psychological claims exclusively on what university students will do for Amazon gift cards—or even what can be gleaned from the wider pool of volunteer research subjects in the global North. The greater awareness of the problem of ethnocentrism among psychologists is certainly a welcome development. However, there is also the same temptation to engage in the sort of superficial borrowing of long-discarded anthropological theories that would-be counterinsurgency experts are presented with. Even the acronym of WEIRD and its five descriptors, while self-deprecating on its surface, is certainly still a quite self-laudatory way to describe the traditional subjects of psychological research—and the uncomfortable historical reasons why they could plausibly stand in for all of humanity. From a more critical perspective, one might speak not of WEIRD subjects but rather subjects who were Colonial, Racist, and hence often Industrialized, Rich, and Democratic at others' expense. Nonetheless, thanks to this new permission structure for conducting comparative psychological research and the logistical benefits of globalization, it has never been easier to conduct international collaborative research, and the resulting data has thrown up some stark regularities worth exploring.

In particular, the often-stark contrasts between how much members of different societies report valuing individualism and collectivism has led to an interest in how the idea of tribalism might illuminate the inherent tradeoffs between them. It certainly helps that this contrast is relatively simple to produce consistently through not just ethnography but even more positivistic opinion-soliciting techniques like interviews and questionnaires. However, another key benefit of the individualism-collectivism contrast is that it has proven mutually flattering, especially to American and Asian academic collaborators (Markus and Kitayama 1991; Kitayama et al. 2009). Not only is it easy to develop arguments about how both individualism and collectivism can be beneficial and that there are trade-offs between them, but also there are representatives of several stridently techno-optimist academic cultures eager to take opposing viewpoints on these issues. As experimental psychologists like Markus and Kitayama make clear, while they can produce these contrasts experimentally, there is nothing latent at all about these contrasts—authorities in both societies are quite explicit about how viewing the self as either independent or dependent is a normative ideal in itself. Thus, the production of this sort of knowledge itself becomes part of a wider process of schismogenesis (Bateson 1972; Graeber and Wengrow 2021). Within this increasingly stark mutual (self)-definition, tribalism can help to define a set of mutually agreed-upon excesses of incorrect and transgressive mixtures of individualism and collectivism.

A particularly good example of how tribalism can help broker the relationship between individualism and collectivism comes from Jonathan Haidt's *The Righteous Mind*, in which "tribalism" is used as a slightly more negative synonym for the more neutral-positive human evolved tendency to *groupishness*. In Haidt's evolutionary narrative, such groupishness is part of the more general process of *self-domestication*, whereby humans (like pigs, dogs, and other domestic animals) became increasingly characterized by "smaller teeth, smaller body, reduced aggression, and greater playfulness, carried on even into adulthood . . . tribal instincts are a kind of overlay, a set of groupish emotions and mental mechanisms laid down over our older and more selfish primate nature" (Haidt 2012, 228–229). For Haidt, such "proto-tribalism" served as a powerful evolutionary selector against more self-serving manifestations of aggression, but it had other less desirable implications, namely conformism and an overinvestment in a particular notion of the group, often itself aggressive and essentialist.

However, in Haidt's version of tribalism, there is no room for the subtlety of nested oppositions and the myriad tactics for fragmenting and suturing this tangle of relations into political alliances that have long fascinated anthropologists. Instead, for Haidt, bumper stickers are "tribal badges" because they epitomize what he sees as the glibness of the tribal mentality. Writing for the *Wall Street Journal* about "How to Get Beyond our Tribal Politics," Haidt argues that "mean tweets" are "darts" meant to "publicly shame" and "display tribal loyalties." He accuses social media companies of having "passed out roughly 1 billion dart guns globally" (2022). Haidt claims, "Our tribal minds are equipped with a powerful tool: shameless and clueless hypocrisy" or "motivated reasoning." He laments that "motivated reasoning has interacted with tribalism and new media technologies since the 1990s in unfortunate ways. Social media, hackers and Google searches now help us to find hundreds of specks in our opponents' eyes, but no technology can force us to acknowledge the logs in our own" (2016). Invoking the Bedouin proverb "I against my brother, my brothers and me against my cousins and then my cousins and me against strangers," Haidt worries that "something is broken in American tribalism. It is now 'my brothers and me against my cousins' all the time, even when we are threatened by strangers and even when there is no threat at all" (2016). He darkly predicts that America might no longer be able to "come together" as it did following the 2001 attacks on the World Trade Center and Pentagon.

In *The Righteous Mind*, Haidt attempts to illustrate his notion of tribalism by describing in depth how America's emerging "political tribes" exploit evolved cognitive modules in the human mind to win adherents. As an exercise, he picks two cars and claims that he can use his theories to identify the owners' respective political identifications. He asserts:

> The driver of the "Save Darfur" car is announcing that he or she is on the liberal team. You know that intuitively, but I can give a more formal reason: The moral matrix of liberals, in America and elsewhere, rests more heavily on the Care foundation than do the matrices of conservatives, and this driver has selected three bumper stickers urging people to protect innocent victims. The driver has no relationship to these victims. The driver is trying to get you to connect your thinking about Darfur and meat-eating to the intuitions generated by your Care foundation. (Haidt 2012, 149)

One has to admire Haidt's confidence here: he is not only certain about a stranger's political beliefs from seeing their car, but also about what his readers find intuitive: animals and victims of genocide can only be political props, people can have "no relation" to them, and their only salience is that they key into evolved cognitive modules. In contrast, my own first thought was that the bumper stickers direct viewers to websites (humaneeating.com and savedarfur.org), where people presumably can find more information, letter-writing campaigns, and opportunities to donate to advance these causes. The United States is also home to a large African diaspora, which has been prominent in raising awareness about the crisis and feels a historical connection to it. For anthropologists at least, it is certainly ironic that the American driver is seen as tribal not because they might have a connection to an actual ethnic conflict in Sudan, but precisely because it is assumed that they cannot. Suffice it to say that the author does not seriously consider whether such aporias in his theories might say more about his own efforts to understand how motivated reasoning and tribalism are impacting his ability to understand the shifting political and technological landscape than about those he seeks to diagnose as tribal.

There does, however, seem to be something at least symptomatic in how the orientalist notions of tribalism are (mis)-appropriated in both contemporary counterinsurgency doctrines and evolutionary psychology that is of anthropological interest, indicating a return of the colonial repressed. This is tribalism as a caricature of two extremes: counterinsurgency promises the ability to split groups as needed (the fissiparousness of household division) while evolutionary psychology emphasizes the rigid binarism (the essentialist us-versus-them of the feud). Neither seems particularly interested in engaging with how tribe-as-image and tribe-as-cause interact dynamically in human history to produce particular outcomes in which the very meaning of tribe is contested and remade. In this spirit, I return to the politics of tribalism in contemporary Jordan in an attempt to show how Jordanian discourses of tribalism offer a more subtle account of the phenomenon. Here I hope to build on some exciting recent work at the intersection of anthropology and history exploring how Jordanians are seeking in their tribal past a usable history for contemporary political struggles (Doughan 2019; Wojnarowski 2021; 2023). For most Jordanians, tribalism is not simply something other people are susceptible to (though that self-serving version of tribalism is certainly present). Rather, tribalism is a complex moral and political challenge that must be continually managed both within one's own community and even within one's self.

A Ramadan Feud

As I have argued, the place of tribalism in Jordanian society is hotly contested, and nowhere is it more likely to be critiqued than where Jordan's much-vaunted reputation for "order," so often attributed to the influence of the tribes by tribalism's proponents, gives way to violent flare-ups known as "tribal clashes." On the one hand, the swift justice of burning down someone's house and killing a close relative in response to a murder or an egregious sexual assault is defended as exerting a deterring effect where Jordan's overstretched legal institutions may struggle to assert themselves. Yet the arbitrariness and excessiveness of such a form of justice is also readily apparent. Here I return to explore the reaction on social media to the feud between the Shiyab and the 'Athamneh that raged during Ramadan of 2017, no doubt encouraged by the strong taboos against violence in a month that should be dedicated to fasting, charity, and spiritual reflection. After rehearsing the main events, I focus on how online commentators both developed their own evolutionary narratives about tribalism (often grounded in Islam) while also taking it as an opportunity for individual and collective self-criticism. In particular, I highlight the subtle analytic vocabulary that commentators mobilized, emphasizing the importance of the concepts of envy, face, the deep state, and mercy in making sense of the relationship between social media and tribalism.

The clashes purportedly began around the time of afternoon prayers a few weeks before Ramadan in the village of Sarih in Jordan's northernmost governorate of Irbid. According to subsequent press reports, a dispute over a parking space escalated when one of the belligerents smashed the window of the others' car. The altercation quickly drew in others from the men's respective tribes who felt obliged to defend their kinsmen, ending with a member of the 'Athamneh tribe shooting into a crowd of men from the Shiyab tribe, leaving a man blind in one eye and seriously injuring two others. Then, following a familiar pattern, the dispute moved from the town to the hospital, where the antagonists and their well-wishers again crossed paths. In a fatal moment, a man from the Shiyab tribe was shot and killed in the hospital. To make matters worse, he was an engineer, a "doctor" in fact: a man with education and prestige who represented his family's highest aspirations. Supporters of the family claimed that such a crime demanded *qiṣāṣ* (retribution): the Quranically endorsed prerogative of a homicide victim's kin to have the perpetrator killed. As the days dragged on, the family of the slain man initially refused to bury his body until his killer was executed (a contravention of the Islamic norm that burials not be delayed). While tribal leaders did eventually agree to bury the body as part of a "security truce" brokered by the Public Security Directorate, the governor, and other local notables, outbreaks of violence continued, with scenes from previous clashes on social media "adding fuel to the fire" (as many put it). At one point, members of the tribe published a statement online defending their pursuit of the vendetta into the month of Ramadan in the face of a growing chorus of national opprobrium.

To be clear, aside from the fact that these tribal clashes coincided with Ramadan, many aspects were quite unremarkable. Certainly, there was nothing particularly exceptional in how the clash was heavily mediated by internet news sites, online communiqués, and a veritable chorus of commentators on Facebook and among those writing in more familiar journalistic genres. This particular blood feud was merely a particularly memorable (and, to some, egregious) instance of a wider trend toward increasingly violent tribal clashes during the 2010s. Grudges here were both long-standing (usually predating the advent of social media, in fact) and often deeply rooted in competition over land and other resources. The belief was that such conflicts were already susceptible to being set off over the most seemingly minor interpersonal grievances, leading many to argue that social media made a combustible situation much worse. If anything, what made this conflict so memorable was that, when I asked people in 2019 if they could think of any instances where social media had alleviated tribal conflict, this was the only example they gave, recalling the cavalcade of prayers in the comments to news articles detailing the latest clashes.

Moreover, despite its increasing mediation by social networks, many aspects of the feud drew on patterns that long predated their invention. For instance, the refusal to bury the body was almost a cliché, a move memorably captured in the opening scenes of Michael Gilsenan's *Lords of the Lebanese Marches*, as the anthropologist comes face-to-face with the corpse of the scion of a now-ruined family, whose death was never avenged (1996, 29–37). The site of the killing in a hospital was also not so surprising: a number of medical workers complained to me about how their work often put them at the center of tribal clashes when the injured belligerents left the scene of the hostilities only to encounter each other once more as they sought treatment for their injuries, sometimes leading to renewed fighting. Even the special pleading of the victim's family bordered on stereotype, since they were understandably keen to emphasize how irreplaceable the deceased was in the face of his murder using all available justifications. The tribe's statement defending the Ramadan violence obviously invoked the Quranic injunction to punish murderers. Yet the communiqué also opportunistically invoked everything from nationalist concerns about the killing of a highly skilled "cadre" serving the national cause to humanitarian norms around hospitals as safe havens from violence. It even invoked the king's recent efforts to "lower the crime rate." However, their primary claim was tribal and turned on their prerogative as "guardians of the blood" in keeping with their tribal "customs and traditions" (Miqdadi 2017).

Given the ambience of the holy month, critics of tribalism quickly recognized an opportunity to level their critiques, and it is this backlash that will dominate the remainder of the discussion. Pious Jordanians flooded the comment sections of news articles on social media sites like Facebook to denounce tribalism. Over time, discourse in the comments on the feud was increasingly overwhelmed by a pious chorus intoning prayers for peace. As I noted, when I asked about incidents where people thought social media had led to unity rather than discord (*fitna*) during follow-up research in 2019, this particular feud's resolution was the only example interviewees produced for me, recalling the power of those calls to "guide the mind." Notably, however, much of this commentary was not projective and othering, but rather expressed a feeling of shared culpability. Even the much-repeated phrase "God guide the mind" maintains an ambiguity about which mind is in need of guidance—although one prominent civil society advocate told me I should not be fooled and that all of this pious talk was merely an indirect means of shaming the belligerents as godless. Others, however, were more explicit in transforming the village feud into a moment for national reflection. One commenter said, "We carry the most expensive mobile [phones], wear the most prestigious brands and drive the latest models of cars[.] We're still called Arabs but unfortunately we're never going to advance [–] the backwardness and ignorance will be with us forever." This mention of ignorance or *jāhiliyya* was especially significant because it recalls the so-called "age of ignorance" that predated the coming of Islam (Shepherd 2003), suggesting that Arabs are failing to live up to their professed Islamic ideals.

While contemporary scholars of Islam like Reza Aslan (2011) and Juan Cole (2018) emphasize how traditional Islamic historiography has effaced the existence of a widespread monotheistic milieu in late antique Arabia, Islam presents itself through its sacred texts and later commentaries as a response to a devolution from monotheism into a corrupted and tribalized polytheism. The struggle for Islam's iconic sanctuary in Mecca known as the *ka'ba* serves as perhaps the best crystallization of the fallen spiritual economy into which the prophet Muhammad was born. As the eighth-century Islamic historian Hisham ibn Al-Kalbi argues in the *Book of Idols*, Mecca's sanctuary devolved over time from the sanctuary for Allah built by Abraham and his son Ishmael into a repository for the tribal idols that people came to revere in His stead, with ibn Al-Kalbi organizing his text around the most famous of the idols, stories about their origins and which tribes worshipped them. Muhammad's victorious return to Mecca a decade after his banishment by Mecca's tribal elite and subsequent destruction of the idols is usually interpreted by scholars (Aslan 2011, 29–32; Cole 2018, 167–170) and my Jordanian interlocutors alike as at least a partial rejection of tribal politics and morality. Unlike the proponents of Victorian evolutionary anthropology and its contemporary inheritors who treat the development of religion and evolution in general as a teleological progression through set stages (for example from animism to ancestor worship, polytheism, and finally monotheism), Islam begins from the premise that the first man (Adam) was a monotheist. From there, history unfolds as a series of prophets calling the people back to the worship of Allah as they stray into *jāhiliyya*: polytheism, ancestor worship, idolatry and sorcery, breaking up any inherent connection between the passage of time (which is inexorable) and progress (which is not).

In the aftermath of such violence, Muslim tribespeople will inevitably struggle to balance their Islamic and tribal identities. As Akbar Ahmed argues, on one level the issue is simple: "Tribal codes [call] for revenge, Islam for forgiveness and compassion" (2013, 96). Yet he concedes that even if Islam privileges mercy and treats it as "an act of atonement" for oneself, that same Quranic verse still follows the Bible in endorsing the notion of an "eye for an eye" and a "life for a life" (Ahmed 2013, 99).[10] The *Qur'ān* may prioritize mercy over revenge, but it also recognizes that the tribal valorization of revenge is not so easily dispensed with. At the same time, as we will see, Muslim tribespeople often see Islamic values of forgiveness and mercy as central to their tribal traditions as well. In such a context, the aftermath of killings presents a powerful point of intervention for those disillusioned with tribalism in general or specifically with its penchant for revenge.

Especially in the beginning, there was plenty of idle speculation about the causes of the violence, ranging from the idea that it was about "a girl" to the suggestion that it was about a rivalry involving the local football club. As Ramadan began, however, explanations became more religious and philosophical. Although there is a common Muslim folk saying that the devil is supposed to be locked up during Ramadan, the violence of a blood feud implied instead that the devil was active in the world, sowing *fitna*. There were many calls for God to "drive out the demons." However, one commentator offered an oblique parable of the devil untying a rope to allow a donkey to traipse through a neighbor's fields, enraging the farmer's wife, who shoots the donkey, only to be shot in turn by its owner, who is in turn shot by her husband upon his return. When the farmer asked what Satan had done, he replied, "Nothing, I just let the jackass go." It was a pointed (if not explicit) plea for the importance of individual moral culpability during a month ideally devoted to ethical self-cultivation.

Like other tribal clashes, as the feud in Sarih came to be seen as an example of *jāhiliyya*, it was interpreted through the lens of *fitna* or discord, which in turn led commenters to invoke the role of envy or *ḥasad* in inflaming tensions. As one person wrote on Facebook in response to an article about the ongoing violence:

> It always happens with me that I stop and remember the advice of our lord {opposing the ignorant [*jāhilīn*]}. People are all envy and hatred and no one wishes well on the other to the point where even the brother envies the brother. In this final era the grasp on religion is like the grasp on a hot coal oh lord you protect us and improve our ending and keep us from injury and don't afflict us [and] our loved ones.

Amidst the supplications for God's protection, this comment invoked a common explanation for tribal clashes while figuring it as part and parcel of the classic leitmotif in Islamic history of *jāhiliyya*: tribes were an inherently invidious phenomenon grounded in rivalry and a somewhat paranoid competition among neighboring groups for mastery.

None of this detracted from the belief that there was a logic at work here that could be manipulated for the greater good. As one journalist I interviewed put it, "[Our site] called for the intervention of the big figures and faces and the state to solve the problem . . . when people saw how this was being reported, they were more ready to solve the problem. This is especially true because this happened during Ramadan and they did not want to go against religion." What proved decisive was that those who were involved ultimately had names and faces, and as the attention of the state (including its intelligence apparatus known as "the deep state") and the general public focused more intently upon them, they came under immense pressure to reach a settlement.

Reconciliation came soon after Ramadan. In a video posted by a local news site on YouTube (among other places) that has been viewed more than ten thousand times, representatives of the respective sides gave speeches thanking various branches of the government and the security apparatus like the *mukhābarāt* and signed an agreement promising to cease hostilities and surrender anyone who violated the truce to the police.[11] The video begins with a recitation of a Quranic verse warning of the dangers of dying in a state of spiritual impurity and entreating believers to "hold firmly to the rope of God" and "be not divided." The verse then continues that "you were enemies" "at the brink of the fiery pit," but that "by His grace" "He united your hearts . . . you became brothers" (3:103). In the ensuing speeches the respective "faces" representing the two sides played up their government connections, thanking everyone from the "Governor" to "the Minister of the Interior," "the Director of Public Security," "the director of the *mukhābarāt* in Irbid," and the "head of the Gendarmerie for the North." They spoke of Jordan and Sarih as a "big family" and averred that they were all "brothers." The implicit message here was that the community's leaders were now in lockstep with the state, and those who violated the terms of the truce would face a united front from the local authorities.

However, the reconciliation was also at pains to reestablish parity and acknowledge how the families had been moved by the "emotions" of the people of Irbid and the rest of Jordan. As a key stipulation of the government-organized truce, the two sides agreed to give up any personal or tribal rights to revenge or further civil penalties for the violence, including the burning of homes and businesses, injuries from the clashes, and the murders of both the original victim from the Shiyab and a young man from the 'Athamneh who had been killed later in retaliation. By relinquishing these personal and tribal rights and framing the feud as an exchange of a life for a life, the families at least in theory reestablished a balance with each other. Having done so, they placed themselves in the hands of God and the king and extolled the virtues of love, forgiveness, pardon, and mercy. The families of the two deceased then signed the truce agreement, which would be stored by the Public Security Directorate for future reference.

In what follows, I will explore how these concepts of envy, face, the deep state, and mercy might help make sense of not only Jordan's unique social media landscape but also the contemporary human condition more generally. Tribalism here evokes old-new forms of experimentation with personhood, political representation, and sociality that are by turn traditionalist and futurist, reactionary and radical. The fragmenting and reformation of the nation-state, the individual subject, and their supportive and enabling infrastructures entails the emergence of all manner of hybrids. This is a time of monsters. My aim, however, is not to simply lionize all Jordanian understandings of social media (or tribalism). Rather, I hope to offer an alternative to both the glib evocations of tribalism so common in pop social science and the strategy of avoidance so common in recent academic anthropology that has failed to offer a plausible account of the persistence of tribalism despite the widespread conviction that it represents an evolutionary "dead-end."

Conclusion

In this chapter I explained how I was forced by the conditions of my fieldwork in Jordan to take tribalism "seriously" (as anthropologists sometimes condescendingly put it). Instead of allowing the concept to be subsumed by quick-fix counterinsurgency strategies or teleological evolutionary "just-so" stories, I tried to engage with Jordanian tribalism as its proponents and critics understand it—contradictions and all. In doing so, tribalism emerges as an enticing vehicle for individual and collective self-knowledge, experimentation, and social transformation. Tribalism's implications may be by turns subversive, transformational, or tragic, but they are very real, and one ignores those implications at one's peril. This is all the more true in an era when digital infrastructures and transnational labor flows undermine the primacy of the nation-state by both surmounting and fragmenting national boundaries and state bureaucracies. If those "often mistakenly called tribes" have historically emerged from the "shatter zone" (Scott 2009, 13) left by retreating state projects, how might these older experiments anticipate new forms of nomadic deterritorialization and political fragmentation? And what if they insist on calling themselves tribal, following their forebearers in situating their own projects in opposition to common imperial cosmopolitical frameworks?

Islam's formation within an oscillation between tribal and more "civilized" modes of social organization (as opposed to a more simplistic narrative of progress from one to the other) here offers an interesting modality for thinking about social change distinct from both Christian apocalypticism and more modernist notions of historical progress. The highest flowering of this approach to history emerges in the work of the medieval historian ibn Khaldun's *Muqaddimah*: the introduction to his universal history. Merging earlier stories of Jewish prophets and the life of Muhammad with the political realities of medieval North Africa, ibn Khaldun posited a cyclical view of history. According to ibn Khaldun, prosperous city-states emerged in fertile river valleys yet remained forever vulnerable to the depredations of the Bedouin. Resembling an individual human's life cycle, they grew more powerful as they matured into their "adulthood," but inevitably a sort of senescence eventually set in. The group feeling or *'aṣabiyya* that served as a source of unity and dynamism inevitably fragmented as the temptations of urban life took hold. At this point, Bedouin tribes united by a greater measure of *'aṣabiyya* could seize their moment, riding out of the desert and installing themselves in power, allowing the cycle to begin anew as each tribe of invaders found itself succumbing to the same temptations that domesticated its predecessors. This is not to homogenize or romanticize tribalism, of course. As Talal Asad (1986) has noted, this would surely be a reductionist reading even of Islamic history. Yet given how "tribal and nomadic elements become no longer imaginable under colonial and national institutions" (Assi 2018, 12), I would argue they are worthy of reparative (as opposed to paranoid) reading (Sedgwick 2002). There will be plenty of time to linger on the human tendency toward motivated reasoning, hypocrisy, projection, and betrayal in the ensuing discussion of envy, face, the deep state, and mercy, but such is the essence of the discourse of tribalism itself.

CHAPTER 3

Envy

During interviews with a wide range of Jordanians about the uptake of social media in Jordan, I was often told that social media inflamed envy (*ḥasad*) among both individuals and groups—especially the tribes—even leading to spectacular tribal clashes like the one described in the last chapter in the village of Sarih. A common refrain went that "social media changed everything. Before these were family problems. Now they widen quickly." The following ethnographic vignette will further illustrate how talk of envy could inspire fascinating digressions about how new media incited invidious tribal logics that infected everything from mundane interpersonal rivalries to life-or-death geopolitical conflicts. Moreover, this was an understanding of envy that included a collective and at times even an occult dimension, challenging the limits of conventional understandings of emotion and affect in metropolitan theory. Far from being unique to the tribes, however, these sensibilities about the fundamentally tribal and collective nature of envy were shared by a broad cross-section of Jordanian society, including fierce critics of tribalism like the country's Islamic movement.

In June of 2017, my research brought me to the offices of Assabeel, a print and later online news source often associated with Jordan's officially proscribed but often-tolerated Muslim Brotherhood. It was founded in 1993 during a previous round of press liberalization (see chapter 1) and slowly moved online beginning in 2005 until by the time I interviewed them, most of their readership was online and they had a dedicated social media team. At the time, I was canvassing all of Jordan's major news sites to learn how they were responding to the changing media landscape amidst the Arab Spring, an upsurge in tribal clashes, the rapid adoption of social media, and increasingly stringent state censorship regimes. My host quickly noted that theirs was an "opposition" newspaper, but after the "Arab Spring," "now there is no opposition. But we're still here. The situation now is much worse than before the Arab Spring. Since 2013, you can go to jail for what you publish. Maybe you have heard of Zaki bani Arshid." Being familiar with the controversy around the deputy leader of Jordan's Muslim Brotherhood, who had been jailed for his criticism of the United Arab Emirates' decision to list the Brotherhood as a terrorist organization, I replied, "Yes, he was arrested just for sending a Tweet." The journalist replied, "Yes, just for criticizing the Emirates. Our editor has been to prison as have many other journalists." The editor in question looked up from the information sheet that I liked to hand ceremoniously to potential research participants and exclaimed, "You're studying envy! What do you mean by envy? Like sorcery (*dajal*)?"

I was a bit embarrassed and frustrated that the mere mention of *ḥasad* (envy) had once again derailed my attempt to understand how social media was transforming tribal politics in Jordan. The previous summer I had tried to make envy the cornerstone of my research, with mixed results: I collected all manner of fascinating stories about envy, but some people visibly recoiled at the mere mention of the word, while others were likewise confused by the term because it could have both psychological and supernatural connotations. More than one friend laughed and told me not to say the word aloud lest I attract its powers. Even though the word *ḥasad* was written in a normal font within a litany of subtopics that I listed as being of interest to my research, it was now at the center of the conversation. After all, this was why I had been drawn to the topic of envy in the first place: people kept pointing it out to me. While I am skeptical of the common conceit that envy (like its close relative the evil eye) is actually "a phenomenon familiar to all, but apparently as little described by ethnographers as it is discussed by those who fear it" (Spooner 1970, 311), envy does not always lend itself well to direct elicitation.[1] Worried that the editor would think I only meant envy's supernatural dimensions, I quickly replied: "I know that envy can mean sorcery in the Arabic language. But for the purposes of this project, I mean it as more of an emotion (*ʿāṭifa*) or a feeling (*shuʿūr*). People say the media causes a lot of envy. A lot of times when there is a tribal clash or some other sort of social conflict in Jordan, people in the comments will say that it is because of envy. So I reckon I'll need to understand envy if I want to write this book."

The editor laughed and said, "I will give you another example: The Emirates and Qatar." Here, the editor followed many of my interlocutors in framing the conflict between the two countries as a tribal rivalry between their ruling families: a scaled-up version of the neighborhood fights that often rocked Jordan, driven by the same sorts of passions. He continued: "This is a conflict caused by envy. The Emirates envies Qatar because it is more respected and powerful than its size, wealth and population [would imply]. For instance, I think it is Qatar that puts its name on the jerseys of [the] Barcelona [football club] and the Emirates that puts its name on the jerseys of [the] Real Madrid [football club]." I laughed at this because at the time they (or their national airlines to be more precise) had each bought the front chest panels of the jerseys of opposing sides of the most important football rivalry in the world. In doing so, Europe's "Premier League" had become a proxy battle in the ongoing struggle between two of the Arabian peninsula's most powerful lineages. He continued:

> . . . and the Emirates has convinced the king of Saudi Arabia to go along. And for what? First, they said because they were close to Iran. Then when this turned out to be false they said they were supporting *da'ish* [a derogatory term for the so-called Islamic State]. But this is not true either. Finally, they said it is because of support for the Muslim Brotherhood and Hamas. But this is weak. They have nothing. The Emirates envy Qatar because it is so popular even though [The Emirates] give more aid to the region. They envy *Al-Jazeera*'s popularity. They even want to start their own sports channels now to compete with Qatar.

I had caught the journalists at a moment of profound vulnerability: the dramatic opening salvos of a region-wide diplomatic crisis whose most significant manifestation would be a multi-year Saudi blockade of the Qatar peninsula, with demands to shut down various news channels like *Al-Jazeera* and isolate itself from Iran and Turkey in favor of the Gulf Cooperation Council. The long reach of Saudi Arabia and the Emirates' anti-Brotherhood and anti-Qatar campaign would be demonstrated most spectacularly and brutally, though, when *Al-Jazeera* contributor and Muslim Brotherhood proponent Jamaal Al-Khashoggi was assassinated and dismembered in the Saudi embassy in Turkey the next year. This was what made the editor's accusation that Saudi Arabia and the Emirates were acting out of envy so audacious: because it took the intriguing form of a claim of *envying down*, which has often been treated in studies of envy as a contradiction in terms. As George Foster (1972) and Helmut Schoeck (1969) both argued, one envies one's social betters, but in most cases it would be nonsensical for the wealthy to envy the poor or the powerful to envy the weak. In this case, however, while the editor happily granted that Saudi Arabia and the Emirates were wealthier and more powerful, he further asserted that their leaders could not help but despise how their poorer neighbors maintained their own support base nonetheless—which the journalists signaled in their own somewhat coy manner that they continued to support despite the mounting personal costs.

As was so often the case during my research, envy was a slippery and elusive emotion that emerged primarily in the form of accusations directed at critics and rivals. Admissions of envy were humiliating and vanishingly rare, which makes sense since, as I noted in the introduction drawing on the work of Sian Ngai, envy tends to be perceived as "unjustified and critically effete," as it is "reduced to signifying a static subjective trait: the 'lack' or 'deficiency' of the person who envies" (Ngai 2005, 21). Yet in this envy accusation and so many others I will describe in this chapter, envy (whether in more natural or supernatural guise) was not only a lack or deficiency, but a potent force in its own right, with far-reaching implications. After all, if the editor was correct, this was an envy that menaced entire countries and even threatened to send my interlocutors into the dungeons of Jordan's state security apparatus, or worse (hardly so "critically effete").

This sort of accusation of "envying down" is hard to understand so long as envy is conceptualized in the terms Ngai identifies as a sort of "lack" on the part of the envier (see also Schoeck 1969)—or even as the way the losers of a zero-sum game will understand their lot (Foster 1965; 1972). Envy could also be conceptualized, though (as my interlocutors did here) as a defensive impulse by those with positional advantages within a hierarchy who are determined to maintain that hierarchical advantage for its own sake. As Amitav Ghosh argued in his critique of earlier work on envy drawing upon his ethnographic fieldwork in an Egyptian village, "If envy arises whenever a household thinks it has a means of changing its position within the determinate set of relations . . . it is the well-to-do . . . who stand as the defenders of the determinacy of those relations and, so, as the most likely agents of envy" (1983, 221).[2] That being said, there is no reason why accusations of envy (in any direction) should necessarily be taken at face value as either reflections of what the accused believe or even as unimpeachable testimony about the internal mental state of the accuser.

In fact, the accusation that Qatar's opponents were motivated by envy threatened to implicate the accusers in the very invidious tribal sentiments that my interlocutors were trying to blame on Qatar's opponents, transforming them into partisans for Qatar's ruling family. Unsurprisingly, the journalists stressed their professional commitment to impartiality. As the editor said, "In all things we try to be balanced except for one thing and that is military occupation: we are against all occupations, in Palestine, Iraq, and Syria." Yet in much the same way that I have previously argued that the Islamic movement's mass weddings and other support for newlyweds could make them seem like just another tribe (Hughes 2021), so here the journalists struggled to defend the Muslim Brotherhood and its Qatari sponsors while maintaining critical distance. As the editor said, "We are committed to the law, to professionalism, to balance, and to objectivity," and he promised to send me a study from Jordan University showing that their election coverage was the least biased despite the fact that "some people say that we are behind [the Muslim Brotherhood's political party] the Islamic Action Front."

This will not be the last time in this chapter that I invite the reader to ask who is really envying whom here—or whether "emotions" in general might not be experienced through others (real or imagined) far more than is usually appreciated. Rather, I offer this as a particularly rich example of how claims about envy are deployed to various effects, potentially at vastly different scales and with vastly different degrees of plausibility. For the editor, beneath the apparent geopolitical conflict between Saudi Arabia and Iran lay a fractal, branching conflict between lineages reminiscent of the classic segmentary model described in the last chapter. Competition was refracted between the Emirati and Qatari ruling families, then down to the level of Jordan and its own internal politics—and then back in reverse from the newsroom floor to the geopolitical struggles of the day. Even Europe's Premier League was not safe. Yet this is still but a glimpse behind the curtain at a hypothesized world of dark psychic impulses to best and even dominate one's fellow human beings that many Jordanians believe exerts a powerful sway over human affairs.

In this chapter, I draw on similar discourses of envy that arose in the context of Jordan's increasingly technologically mediated tribal milieu to help dramatize not only how Jordanians understand social media as a tribal and invidious phenomenon, but also how Jordanian discourses of envy might inform contemporary theoretical fashions for emotion and affect more generally. I begin by sketching how scholarly interest in emotions and affects developed in the first place, emphasizing how commercial and political preoccupations about the nature of media have never been far from the surface, and how this implies the need for a certain critical skepticism about affect's facticity that has often been lacking. I then trace how envy or *ḥasad* emerged in mundane personal interactions and the broader context of tribal politics. I argue that Jordanian ideas about envy challenge the tendency of many media ideologies to attribute causal powers to the media's widely asserted emotionality. In doing so, Jordanian discourses offer a range of exciting avenues for further exploring the nature of inequality, subjectivity, and the self that suggest a detour back from the so-called "affective turn" to a more fine-grained understanding of the prevaricatory nature of "emotions" as they shift between social policing, routinized confession, and lived reality.

Envy, *Ḥasad*, and the Limits of the Affective Turn

Affect and emotion—two terms that seem to resist clear differentiation—have been invested with increasing power by contemporary social theorists in the last thirty years. While this work has helpfully captured how networks of human minds and bodies can create shared self-referential circuits of meaning among themselves and various nonhuman actors, the "affective turn" has also received its share of criticism. For instance, Claire Hemmings (2005) has asked about the wider implications of "invoking affect," arguing that the concept is often used to dismiss scholars who emphasize the determinacy of unequal social structures by urging them to be less pessimistic and paranoid about the liberatory potentials of affect. It is also worth historicizing affect as emerging from particular economic arrangements associated with a shift to postindustrial models of production that prioritize the sale of experiences over more traditional mass-produced commodities (Hardt 1999). In fact, while the affective turn has been increasingly embraced by the social sciences, it has historically emphasized individualistic engagements with media—especially reading (Deleuze 1997; Sedgwick and Frank 1995) and watching television (Massumi 1996). In this spirit, I attempt to engage with affect armed with the discourse of *ḥasad* that I encountered among Jordan's Bedouin tribespeople as they told me about their encounters with new media technologies.

Precisely because affects are said to resist discursivization, it remains an open question what we are even talking about (Beatty 2005). One might object that it is unfair to use something as occult and supernatural as *ḥasad* to test the limits of the affective turn, but I will suggest that this ambiguity around the existence of the phenomenon in question is actually the perfect means of interrogating what the also ephemeral and difficult-to-pin-down concept of "affect" is doing in contemporary metropolitan theory. After all, metropolitan theorists usually do not take accusations of sorcery and other uncanny phenomena at face value, so why the credulity for more culturally familiar accusations about various ugly emotions (Hughes et al. 2019; Hughes 2020)? Here, the tendency of the affective turn to ignore decades of ethnographic and anthropological research on emotions in a wide range of cultural contexts runs the risks of repeating many of its earlier mistakes by failing to interrogate the turn's own culture-laden assumptions.

As Ngai (2005) notes, the distinction between emotion and affect emerged early in psychoanalytic theory and practice, and the subsequent attempt to differentiate them highlights some of the key problems with this mode of explanation. The distinction was supposed to help differentiate between the more "subjective" aspect of feelings that were attached to the analysand's "I" in discourse (emotions) from the putatively more "objective" physical aspect that was outwardly observable to the analyst (affect). Thus one could imagine a patient who has an agitated disposition (speaking quickly, taking short breaths) yet claims when asked that they are just fine, even happy. Here, the affect-emotion distinction cleanly differentiates the physiological from the discursive, the scientific from the narrative, and the objective from the subjective. Unfortunately, few contexts allow for this sort of certainty in terms of role coherence and stable hierarchies of authoritative knowing. Subsequent work in critical psychology (Foucault 1961; Schraube and Osterkamp 2013) has also given plenty of reason to question whether even the most idealized practice of analysis can live up to this ideal.

If the concept of affect had maintained its original meaning from psychoanalysis, it probably would never have had this reincarnation in critical theory. Here, the work of two very different thinkers—Silvan Tomkins (1963) and Gilles Deleuze (1997)—proved instrumental. A psychologist, Tomkins would push back against what he felt was a tendency in the dominant behaviorist paradigm of his era to reduce affect to "drives." Instead, Tomkins emphasized how affects were *autotelic* (as in they had their own ends, like a laugh or yawn traveling around the room). For Tomkins and later proponents of affect, affects were profoundly *contagious*. Queer theorists like Eve Sedgwick and Adam Frank (1995) would build on this foundation, emphasizing how Tomkins's work on shame in particular could illuminate understudied aspects of the marginalization and stigmatization often inflicted upon those deemed to fall outside the boundaries of normality. Yet even in this early formulation there was tension between the fact that shame is clearly an *intersubjective* emotion (even if the other minds are often falsely imagined) and the attempt to emphasize the *autotelic* dimension of affect in order to create space for agency beyond discourse and its subjects.

Deleuze was particularly interested in the experience of reading about shame, affect, and sexuality. He devoted his widely cited discussion of affect in "The Shame and the Glory in T. E. Lawrence" (1997) to two specific episodes in the autobiographical account of the British colonial official who helped to set the stage for Britain's colonial administration of Jordan in the midst of the Ottoman defeat in World War I (see chapter 1): Lawrence's reports of contagious laughter amidst the slaughter of war and description of his "erection" "in the midst of his tortures" as he is raped by Ottoman soldiers (Deleuze 1997, 123).[3] This leads Deleuze to invoke Baruch Spinoza and William James on the ability of the body to assert its primacy over the mind. Deleuze argues that "the mind begins by coldly and curiously regarding what the body does, it is first of all a witness; then it becomes an impassioned witness, it experiences for itself affects that are not simply effects of the body but *veritable critical entities* that hover over the body and judge it" (Deleuze 1997, 123, emphasis in the original). Again, affect's relationship to the potentially alienating judgment of another (usually conceived as a projection of the self) is key to how affect is constructed as *autotelic* or (in Brian Massumi's phrasing) having an "autonomy" (1996).

Yet freeing affect from the constraints of discourse and its subjects always ran the risk of essentializing certain culturally specific emotional scripts and overplaying the universality of the unique preoccupations of critical theorists living in post-industrial societies, fond of employing metaphors of "networks" and "circuits" much as industrial-era theorists spoke of structures and mechanisms. Anthropologists working on both sides of the Atlantic had likewise been inspired from the early twentieth century by psychology and psychoanalysis to investigate the universality of family dynamics and emotions, and through cross-cultural studies often found important cultural differences. For instance, the early ethnographer Bronislaw Malinowski (1927) argued that in the Trobriand Islands, where strong matrilineal and matrilocal kinship patterns downplayed the importance of fatherhood, the Oedipus complex was largely absent (though men often had difficult relations with their mothers' brothers, who controlled important forms of property and made other important household decisions). American anthropology's culture and personality studies sought to apply psychological tests to people from different cultural backgrounds, often revealing significant cultural differences in responses (Wallace 1961).

Especially as anthropologists were pressed into the Allied war effort in World War II and "culture and personality" gave way to "national character studies" of wartime enemies conducted at a distance, anthropological approaches often veered into national stereotypes. Where Ruth Benedict once wrote of two Native American groups she had studied (the Pueblo and the Kwakiutl) as being respectively "Apollonian" and "Dionysian" (1935), she would go on to write *The Chrysanthemum and the Sword*, which helped popularize the distinction between "shame" and "guilt" cultures. Not speaking Japanese and unable to conduct fieldwork there, she relied primarily on mass media, literature, and interviews with Japanese-American citizens and Japanese prisoners of war. While the fact that the book was wildly influential in postwar Japan's discourse about itself and sold over 1.4 million copies in Japan surely indicates some validity, it is also a classic example of an orientalist text. As John Lie (2001) notes, Benedict grossly homogenizes Japanese society while failing to substantiate her claims about Japan's distinctiveness (for example, she puts much stock in the fact that Japan's national epic involves negotiating competing social obligations, but the same could be said of any epic almost by definition). This tendency to exaggerate intercultural differences and homogenize internal distinctions within culture also manifested in the other direction as well: for instance, Margaret Mead (1928) denied the existence of jealousy in her report on her fieldwork in Samoa—an idea taken up by anthropologists like Leslie White and George Murdock to argue that jealousy was not a universal emotion.[4]

At the same time, the attempt to epitomize cultures with single emotions (or their absence) was readily recognized to be highly reductive even within the culture and personality school. Benedict herself hedged profusely even as she generalized. As she wrote in the opening pages, "The Japanese are both aggressive and unaggressive, both militaristic and aesthetic, both insolent and polite, rigid and adaptable, submissive and resentful of being pushed around, loyal and treacherous, brave and timid" (1946, 2–3). As Lie notes, the piling up of contradictions here masks the determination to establish "The Japanese" as a legitimate object of generalization (2001, 252). Wallace, author of the influential textbook *Culture and Personality* (1961), argued that the propensity for "diagnostic labels" in national character studies "merely expresses the author's hostility towards the subjects of his description" (1961, 224). Yet clearly these labels did not "merely" express hostility. As others have noted, these anthropological studies legitimized wider discourses of national character that contributed to postwar nation-building projects in general. Ethnography was yet another media object alongside journalism, the novel, and advertising contributing to the construction of the nation as such (Neiburg et al. 1998).

The increasing realization that attributions of emotions to others often reveal more about those making the attributions has long been a characteristic of the social sciences' strangely fraught relationship with the study of envy. The fervently anticommunist sociologist Helmut Schoeck blamed a latent enthusiasm for leftist central planning in the social sciences for the fact that at the time when he was writing there were no subject entries in the major British and American social scientific journals for "envy," "resentment," or "jealousy" (1969, 13–14). As a result, the anthropologist George Foster (1965) could present his own studies of envy in the 1960s as novel due to how envy previously had been approached either via the occult (Evans-Pritchard 1937; Fortune 1932; Westermarck 1926) or largely in the negative and somewhat Rousseauian fashion in which Mead and White had treated it—as a disease of "civilization." Foster sought to establish envy as a sociological and anthropological phenomenon by grounding it in the economic realities of peasant society's "image of the limited good" (1965) in which finite resources ensure that others' advantages have to come at someone's expense—all while optimistically predicting that envy would become obsolete in an industrial capitalist economy where growth was potentially infinite. Thus it hardly seems coincidental that almost all of the anthropological work on envy in anthropology that I found when I began studying it in the mid-2010s had been written between the 1960s and 1980s and coincided with a period of unprecedented abundance in America and Europe—itself undergirded in no small part by seemingly limitless energy reserves in the Middle East (Mitchell 2013).

Work on that close relative of envy, the evil eye, during this period (like Clarence Maloney's 1976 edited volume) mirrored Foster's optimistic view of envy as a relic of preindustrial scarcity and developed a mixture of diffusionist, functionalist, and evolutionary explanations for the phenomenon. As John Roberts argued in his contribution to Maloney's volume drawing on a quantitative analysis of the 186 distinct human "cultures" in George Murdock's Human Relations Area Files with documented evil eye beliefs, there are high correlations between such beliefs and plough agriculture, the consumption of milk products, and premodern urbanization. This led Maloney and his collaborators to speculate that the belief arose somewhere in the Middle East before spreading outward, eventually reaching Latin America. Writing in the conclusion to that volume, Garrison and Arsenberg asserted that invidia—envy—and evil-eye beliefs "are emergents from behavioral processes involved in the more general categories of rivalry, cooperation, and competition in the context of dominance and submission mediated by patronage in stratified, but not yet bureaucratized societies." The authors went on to suggest that the evil eye's persistence in the "lower strata of the modern nation state" was a vestigial link to a bygone era, like witchcraft, which they saw as the evil eye's "equivalent in egalitarian and ranked societies" (Maloney 1976, 326). While the implicit evolutionary teleology and the smug sense that envy is somehow unique to the "lower strata" are clearly grossly simplistic, it is hard to deny the underlying point that social context has a profound influence on how even an emotion as seemingly specific as envy will manifest itself. If nothing else, Maloney's volume itself certainly represents a unique effort in human history to fix responsibility for envy on the correct culprits.

Especially as the politics of anthropological representation have grown more fraught, anthropologists have become increasingly uncomfortable with culturalist and sociological accounts of envy because of their propensity for essentialism. From the beginning, critical anthropologists remarked that Foster was offering a profoundly pathologizing way to understand peasants. Reviewing Foster's earlier work, Oscar Lewis (himself notoriously cynical about rural village life) felt compelled to title his own review "Some of My Best Friends Are Peasants" (1960). Chastened, perhaps, Foster would eventually aver that envy was a human universal and go so far as to argue that Americans systematically minimized its importance within their own society (1972). This more universalist bent would be the model for later ethnographic work on envy as well (Ghosh 1983; Pitt-Rivers [1992] 2017), "seeking out the underlying and universal emotions that make us all kin" (Lindholm 1982, xxxi). In some ways, however, a shift toward emphasizing envy's universality was an overcorrection and represented the exhaustion of anthropological interest until recent years.

As Lila Abu Lughod (1986) noted, however, in her ethnographic study of Bedouin women (a seemingly paradigmatic example of a shame culture), shame is experienced in radically different ways even within a single family, depending on where one sits in terms of age, gender, and parentage. In other words, social structures and cultural specificity matter for what we usually call emotions and affect, but one needs a good deal more social context to predict how individual people will experience these phenomena and react to them than some early anthropological studies implied. Most importantly, it is important to avoid treating particular regions like the Middle East as a "prestige zone" (Appadurai 1986; Abu Lughod 1989) for particular emotions like shame or (in my case) envy. The solution, however, is not to ignore difference, but rather to demand greater specificity from ethnographic descriptions, a theme I will return to in the next chapter.

In trying to carve out a space of independent action for affect as distinct from the social and the discursive, scholars of the affective turn risk reifying a more simplistic and individualistic model of the emotions than warranted. Worse, they risk repeating many of the worst reductive tendencies of behaviorism by failing to appreciate how culturally distinctive "affects" can be. This need not lead to an embrace of national stereotypes and crude cultural essentialism, however, and one must be especially aware of such pitfalls when discussing something as contentious as envy. Yet by focusing on *ḥasad*, it is possible to retain some of affect theory's original emphasis on intersubjectivity inherent in its treatment of shame while heightening the potential stakes of the other's judgments. After all, according to many of my interlocutors, envy is not merely an ugly feeling, but a potent and potentially destructive force in its own right. In what follows, I take affect theory and the anthropology of emotions back to its origins (of sorts) in jarring, para-ethnographic literary encounters with a potentially imaginary Orient. However, I will focus on discourses of envy or *ḥasad* and how they can further make us question (after Deleuze and Spinoza) "what a body can do."

In Search of Envy with Jordan's Bedouin Tribespeople

In retrospect, I was a terrible naïf when it came to the topic of envy, and I can only be thankful for the forbearance of the many Jordanian tribespeople who were kind enough to clue me into these dynamics over the years. As was often the case, my status as a foreigner encouraged a didacticism that made ethnography almost too easy—to the point where one might be almost seduced into ignoring what people did in favor of what they said. Fortunately, the discourses of envy that I recorded were themselves keenly fixated on this trap and constantly pointed to how envy itself played on the deceptiveness of surface appearances. Even amidst the otherwise mundane and rationalist context of a newsroom engaged in discussions of press censorship, envy's powers retained more than a hint of the occult and the metaphysical. Yet this should in no way detract from the fact that envy was also a very concrete and material feature of the social and physical landscape, with potentially far-reaching implications.

The aftermath of tribal clashes often brought talk of envy to the surface. There was a sort of conversational set piece that young Bedouin tribesmen who styled themselves as cynics would sometimes perform, mostly for their own amusement, but also for my benefit. One man would claim the recent clash—indeed all tribal clashes—were at base "because of girls," while another would claim they were all "because of money" and, if a third was available, all "because of land" (all embellished with the appropriate local gossip, naturally). After some back-and-forth about how the elders transformed women into land and money and back again through marriage exchanges, the men would eventually agree (hopefully to the delight of the audience) that money, land, and girls were basically the same thing to the tribes. According to this account, tribes were jealous (*ghayūr*) and covetous (*anānī*), seeing their neighbors' every advantage as a potential threat to their own position and hence something to be seized at the first opportunity, if possible. It was often argued, however, that it was precisely this ability of people to organize their envy collectively in the form of the tribes that could keep violent manifestations of such impulses to a minimum: the threat of tribal retribution could serve as an effective (if unequally available) check on the socially destructive tendencies of envy.

As I was repeatedly told, the advent of social media was a disaster on this front for such a "tribal" society, affording a vastly more public gaze for envy-inducing displays of feasting, expensive consumer goods, and vacations (a relatively new concept for most tribespeople I knew). I was often told without any prompting that especially because of the "tribal" nature of Jordanian society, the dissemination of photos (of women, but often just flamboyant displays of hospitality and consumption) threatened to inflame *ḥasad* in the community to the point of violence. A lot of older men (especially those who remembered going hungry as children) found the photographing of food particularly distasteful. Once at a barbecue by a scenic overlook, a boy of twelve pulled out his phone to take a picture of our chicken dinner (presumably to post online) and his father told him to stop: *fī nās mish lāgiyīn* (there are people going without). Thus, a considerable amount of energy online was devoted to denying and displacing envy and the implication of invidious intent. To this end, the international consortium responsible for emoji standards has created two anti-envy emojis at the time of this writing, both representing protective or *apotropaic* talismans that have been used to ward off envy's malign effects for millennia: the *naẓar* (a stylized—usually glass—eye, see figure 3.2) and the *khamsa* (a stylized—usually metal—hand, see figure 3.2). Social media users are endlessly creative in their own efforts to ward off envy as well. Certain Quranic phrases and verses are said to ward off envy (see figure 3.3), making them common utterances in online spaces as well as fodder for images and short clips alongside pre-Islamic eye and hand talismans.

Envy was not merely a negative trait, though, and here many Bedouin tribespeople I spoke with invoked Islamic philosophical and psychological precepts, even if they sometimes strayed into heterodoxy. One especially salient distinction here was between an envy that seeks to destroy others' good fortune versus an envy that seeks to exceed others in good deeds without taking anything away, known as *ghubṭa*. According to one popular prophetic saying, "[There should be] no envy except in two [cases]" (*la-ḥasad illa fī ithnayn*): a person who spends their God-given wealth appropriately and a person who uses their God-given wisdom to make righteous decisions and teach the people. The saying is a subtle critique of the invidious mentality as myopic and small-minded, arguing instead that it is such selfless acts of service to one's God and one's community that are truly enviable. In doing so, however, the saying further identifies an imitative but also competitive impulse as something valuable—indeed potentially indispensable—to a functioning society. Seeing someone blessed by God with the ability to do good deeds *should* feel bad—and it should stir people to do more good deeds so that they too can share in the blessing. While discussions about envy were at times paranoid and projective, my interlocutors were also fully capable of domesticating envy and incorporating it productively into their social worlds. Even envy's leveling powers were not seen as totally negative: if people were basically all the same before God, many tribespeople reckoned that maybe it was a good thing if the fear of envy drove hospitality, charity toward the poor, and a general attitude of self-abnegation on the part of the community's more privileged members.

Bedouin tribespeople (and indeed Jordanians more generally) were especially apt to tell me about the potential positive dimensions of envy and its close relative jealousy in the realm of gender and sexuality, something that arose frequently during my research on marriage. As an American, my presence almost certainly encouraged this because it furnished my interlocutors with a unique opportunity to process a lifetime's worth of jarring encounters with pornography and less intentionally explicit depictions of psycho-sexual dynamics that they often found profoundly alien. In particular, both men and women were often eager to discuss the perceived lack of concern on the part of the Western men they saw on television about the sexual and emotional lives of their wives, daughters, or sisters, even in seemingly "family-friendly" situation comedies and dramas. While some wanted to use this as a model of "modern," "open-minded" values that Arabs and Muslims should embrace, and to hear me back them up, more often than not my interlocutors brought this up to explain to me how wrong this sensibility was. An inability to appropriately express jealousy was interpreted as cold, uncaring, and dismissive in a way highly reminiscent of Suad Joseph's (1999) classic account of normative Arab family dynamics and their valorization of a more relational self. When comparing *Bollywood* to *Hollywood*, a few Jordanian women told me that this lack of jealousy in American and European male characters made them contemptible and hence led them to dislike Western films and television in general.

Sometimes I also suspected that my status as an agreeable (and potentially impressionable) foreigner led people to almost soliloquize about envy, giving themselves up to boasting in ways they would normally resist in front of a more sophisticated audience. As I asked after his family and showed an interest in his genealogy, many a taxi driver would confide about how his tribe was beset by problems because of the envy of their neighbors. It was not just that they had great lands or fabulous wealth or a surfeit of connections (*wasṭāt*) in government, but that their wives and daughters were the most beautiful and fair and their men were courageous—real "men the size of themselves" (*rijāl gid-ḥawalhum*). For instance, one driver told me proudly of how he was a member of one of the twelve tribes of the Circassians—a group of refugees from the northern Ottoman Empire who were resettled in Jordan in the nineteenth century in the aftermath of losses to Russia. As he was driving me out of Amman to a wedding in the steppe in his late-model hybrid Toyota Prius, he began to tell me how much his tribe was resented: "They envy us because we have the best lands, for instance. The Ottomans settled us near the water, around what is now Amman and this land has made us rich. Also, because we come from the north our women are blonde (*shaqra'*). And many of our sons have been ministers and officials in government. A lot of people envy us for our good relations with the king." If glamour is (as the art historian John Berger put it) "the happiness of being envied" (1972, 132) then this was the envy accusation as a fantasy in which one could luxuriate. I nodded along, lightly intoning "mashallah" to incite him to continue.

The Evil Eye: Affect in a Metaphysical Register

However, at least in Jordan, envy need not always be a "solitary reassurance" (Berger 1972, 133), and here my use of the phrase "mashallah" (literally *whatever God wills*) was itself a product of my increasing socialization into Jordanian discourses of envy. The phrase was a verbal talisman of sorts, said to ward off the malign effects of envy and the evil eye. As I was often reminded, it is only polite to reassure others of one's lack of invidious intent by deploying the phrase in response to any mention of good fortune, lest one ruin it. Drawing on a large sample of instances of the use of the phrase *mashallah* by Jordanian Arabic speakers, researchers at Jordan University of Science and Technology found that it was a highly ambiguous phrase deployed as "an invocation, a compliment, an expression of gladness, an expression of modesty, a marker of sarcasm, and as a conversational backchannel." They conclude, however, that "this formula serves as a membership marker whose use marks the speaker as a social insider who avoids acting in a way that would invite the 'evil eye'" (Migdadi et al. 2010, 480). The pragmatics of *mashallah* (specifically its ability to do all these things at once) offer a useful pathway into the ambiguities of envy in its more metaphysical guise of the "evil eye" and how it shapes the social worlds of those who fear its power. I hesitate to endorse the local stereotype that tribespeople are particularly fixated on envy, but the stereotype exists and tracks a very real cleavage between tribal and Islamic moral and cosmological frameworks.[5] Where Islam is more likely to challenge the legitimacy of envy's destructive side and to emphasize God's ultimate power, tribalism is far more open to both envy's moral logic and its supernatural powers.

As I kept realizing, to my horror, my attempts at flattery could not help but draw attention to inequalities and imbalances in the community, which implied that envy's leveling powers were not too far behind. When people did experience good fortune, they were keen to protect it. Sometimes this could be as simple as festooning a valuable object with the phrase "mashallah": indeed, it was commonly found not only online but also on cars, buildings, thresholds, and jewelry (see figures 3.1–3.3). However, people also sought to address these anxieties in more concrete ways. The fear of envy was often

Figure 3.1. A tow truck with *Mashallah*, "No strength but by God," and other apotropaic phrases.

proffered as an explanation for customs that were especially prevalent among tribespeople, like buying neighbors and colleagues sweets to celebrate an expensive purchase—or hosting an elaborate feast to celebrate the construction of a house. Complimenting Bedouin tribespeople's possessions often led to impassioned demands that I take them (after all, the compliment itself had already tarnished them). The more appropriate response was usually to skip the compliment and devote one's efforts to protecting the object of potential envy from its depredations: Your daughter is studying medicine at university? You redecorated your guest room? You have recently been promoted at work? *Mashallah. Maaashallah. Ma sha' Allah.*

When I asked about envy, a lot of people were not shy about blaming very specific problems on envy, often closely associated with either the failure to say *mashallah* or, worse, straightforward compliments. Giggling, a friend hissed the word *ḥasad* in a whisper to his friend before saying, "Don't talk about it, man!" Laughingly, he continued, "Envy has cost me 4,000!! [My friend here] lost 3,000! Gone! All from the eyes of the people! They envy, man, they envy! The other night my tent fell down! All envy. Don't talk about it, man!" Another friend's wife was initially perplexed by how I could possibly study something like envy but nonetheless launched into a litany of struggles with its malign effects: "When [my son] was a baby, certain people would see him, and they wouldn't say *mashallah*. He would be sick for weeks!" Pointing at her ceiling, she said, "Do you see that chandelier?" I noticed that there was a fine crystal-encrusted chandelier hanging from the intricately patterned plastered ceiling on one side of the room and a hole in the ceiling on the other with a wire sticking through. She continued, "Someone struck it with their eye and it fell down." Her husband responded: "You mean [so-and-so]? Damn their father's honor they never say *mashallah*."

Given envy's powers, it was no wonder, then, that *mashallah* was also a means of expressing modesty. To describe one's good fortune with a healthy dollop of *mashallahs* was to acknowledge not being so arrogant as to see oneself as the sole proprietor of one's good fortune. It first had to be acknowledged that (as a common phrase found on buildings that was purported to ward off envy put it) "this is from the pleasure of my lord [God]." Yet while some tribespeople insisted that those with true faith in God were immune from envy, it did not stop many of their kin from seeking to avoid stoking the envy of others, both practically, by addressing inequalities, and through more metaphysical means (including the use of specific Quranic verses believed to ward off envy).[6] In fact, the sheer ubiquity of the physical deployment of these phrases in the built environment was one of the more striking features of the whole envy complex. One evening, I decided to take photos in downtown Amman of apotropaic talismans in public places and managed to take more than forty photos in an hour or two, even with a moderate degree of selectivity about what I photographed as I quickly tired of the more mass-marketed fare that everyone seemed to have. There were keychains, decals for cars, gold-embroidered wall hangings, an endless supply of jewelry, limestone plaques for thresholds—and that was just a sampling of what was for sale in the market. There were also countless handmade charms of various sorts that incorporated Quranic verses, eyeballs, the outstretched hand, the color blue, and various permutations thereof (see figures 3.1–3.3). One driver told me a peacock feather hung from his rearview mirror was intended to ward off envy. Some people even attributed the practice of leaving exposed steel rebar sticking out of one's roof to a desire to ward off the envy of neighbors and the evil eye (alongside the more general practice of leaving the outside of houses unfinished, with a rough gray stucco finish).[7]

For a number of Bedouin tribespeople I spoke to, envy was quite literally at the root of all evil and offered a solution to the apparent contradiction between God's attributes of omnipotence and infinite justice in light of the existence of evil in the world (what theologians call the theodicy problem). Fashioning an interpretation of the account of Adam and Eve's fall contained in the *Qur'ān*, such interlocutors told me that the devil was originally motivated by envy. When God created Adam from mud and ordered all of creation to bow down before him, Satan refused, reasoning that because he had been created from fire, he was the superior being.[8] For this, Satan was banished from paradise, but as a sort of mercy he was given a reprieve and told he could try to take

Figure 3.2. Talismans to ward off envy.

Figure 3.3. Plaques featuring *Surat Al-Falaq* and *Surat Al-Nas* to ward off "envy" (as written in large letters at the bottom of the plaque on the right).

his revenge on Adam and his descendants by leading them astray until the day of judgment. As a non-Muslim, I was seen as particularly susceptible to the devil's snares, and so Bedouin—though also other Muslims—would often warn me to beware. The devil was an envier who loved to sow discord (*fitna*) among the people and degrade them to his own level. I would encourage them to elaborate and then thank them for their concern.

However, as with my attempts to make veiled compliments, to be agreeable to boasting acquaintances and to act humble and self-deprecating while being proselytized, the whole envy and evil eye complex could easily drift into sarcasm and self-parody. As one aphorism put it, "Nobody envies wealth except its owner" (*fīsh ḥada yaḥsud māl illa ṣāḥibuh*), implying that people had a tendency to be paranoid and get carried away when it came to envy—especially those who already had something to lose. Islamic authorities and those who followed them were more than happy to criticize the whole phenomenon of envy belief as fundamentally irrational and often strenuously objected to attempts to reframe Islam around envy. As the journalist in the opening vignette put it to me later in our conversation: "Envy in our society is a kind of sorcery. The uneducated people take a hand and put it on the wall to protect them. They think this idol will protect them from evil." He then proceeded to recommend a show on Egyptian television that I could find on YouTube which specialized in unmasking religious hucksters, including one who made money convincing people to buy camel urine from him. The journalist—himself clean-shaven and wearing smart business casual—complained that these days all one had to do to be taken for a man of religion by the masses was to grow a beard and wear robes.

When more observant Muslims sought to curb my enthusiasm about the role of envy in Islam, they often turned to the thirteenth- to fourteenth-century cleric ibn Taymiyyah, especially his *Diseases of the Hearts and Their Cures* (*amrāḍ al-qalūb wa-shifā'uha*), in which envy features prominently as one of two major "diseases of the heart" alongside passionate love. According to ibn Taymiyyah, Quranic verses that are often accorded apotropaic powers like "I take refuge in the lord of daybreak [God] . . . from the envier when he envies," (see figure 3.3) are clearly saying that it is God, not the words themselves and certainly not their physical manifestations, that protects believers from envy. For ibn Taymiyyah, the believer is often subject to the envy of others and must be patient (*ṣabūr*) and trust in God. Here the archetype is the biblical story of Yusuf (Joseph), who was forced to undergo a series of ordeals before receiving his ultimate reward after his brothers plotted to have him sold into slavery because they were jealous that he was his father's favorite.

What many of these different theories of envy have in common, though, is that they are highly redolent of what Weber (drawing on Nietzsche's theorization of *ressentiment*) termed the "theodicy of the disprivileged." Weber argued that Abrahamic monotheism lends itself well to an expectation that "the unequal distribution of mundane goods" will eventually be set right by "God's wrath" (1978, 494). Injustices were often rationalized as God giving an opportunity for the wicked and the good alike to show their true colors, and even those who despised ibn Taymiyyah often took Joseph as an exemplar here. After all, it is his brothers' initial betrayal that leads to him becoming a powerful Egyptian official in a position to save his brothers' lives before their treachery is revealed to their father (with Joseph's mercy further shaming them). It might seem counterintuitive that a traditionalist and iconoclast like ibn Taymiyyah often cited by militant groups to justify attacks on saints' graves and other alleged idols would have played such an important role in staking out something approaching a psychological theory of envy in Islam. Yet his position must be understood in the context of his commitment to a strong monotheism in which God's power is the main absolute.[9]

Lacking ibn Taymiyyah's commitment to monotheism, plenty of Jordanians were clearly sufficiently confident that the physicality of a Quranic verse as talisman could help somehow or other that they bought and installed such talismans with alacrity. Blue beads and eyes were more controversial yet, though. I once saw such beads become a particularly explosive flashpoint during a change of bus drivers when the new driver ripped down the eye-patterned beads, threw them on the ground outside of the bus, and screamed that the beads were a form of idolatry (*shirk*) and hence *ḥarām* or religiously forbidden. The critic of such talismans sported a long beard and short mustache (a sign of commitment to living as one imagines the prophet Muhammad and his companions lived in the seventh century), giving a sense again of how various Islamic revival movements from the more sartorially demure Muslim Brotherhood to the more flamboyant Salafis engage critically with ambient envy beliefs found in Jordanian society. As Engseng Ho notes, ibn Taymiyyah's rejection of idolatry and embrace of iconoclasm was not at all a rejection of superstition's efficacy (like the journalists at *Assabeel* and others of a modernist bent). To the contrary, the problem for ibn Taymiyyah with forms of idolatry ranging from talismans to the practice of grave visitation was that "they create powerful dynamics of signification with the potential to create communities based not on revelation but on something autochthonous and incipient" (Ho 2006, 25). In other words, the problem for ibn Taymiyyah (like contemporary traditionalists) was not that idolatry does not "work" but that it works all too well by leading people away from the structures of pious devotion they should cultivate.

The envy beliefs that I encountered in Jordan among self-styled tribespeople and their critics were certainly not uniform, but rather a source of lively debate that did not always map neatly onto simple binaries like Islamist-secularist, urban-rural, liberal-conservative, or tribal-nontribal. While the more orthodox Islamic interpretation of envy favors a psychological account of envy, others emphasized potentially occult dimensions. The dominant interpretation of Islam and its sacred text the *Qur'ān* as rejecting the whole notion of apotropaic powers constantly struggled with the proliferation of discordant interpretations. The phrase *mashallah* is clearly vulnerable to sarcasm. It's also ironic that the *Qur'ān* and its verses themselves are often pressed into service as tools of apotropaic magic. In the next section, I attempt to show how a general tendency across these distinctive approaches to envy to insist on the relational nature of the self and its full imbrication in broader circuits of sociality offers a useful corrective to the naïve psychologism so rife in current enthusiasms for emotions and affect. Instead of trying to separate affect from discourse and its subjects, I seek to reconnect affect and emotion with social institutions that are often predicated on profoundly violent and unequal distributions of power.

Envy, Balanced Opposition, and a Culture of Leveling

As I have argued, there was lively debate about the nature of envy among Jordan's Bedouin tribespeople and their critics—especially at its more occult fringes where tribal beliefs came into conflict with orthodox Islamic precepts. There was widespread agreement that at least one common manifestation of envy was in rivalries between individuals and groups in structurally similar positions in relation to each other. Archetypal relations of envy included brothers, neighbors, rival tribal leaders, and tribal segments of various sizes with similarly sized neighboring groupings. Moreover, social media was believed to incite envy—especially among the tribes. As one man said, "[Social media] involves a particular person from a particular tribe who is in front of the entire group and this encourages jealousy and envy. Facebook becomes a means of showing off . . . the Bedouin used to turn off the electricity before a feast so you could eat and take your rest (*raḥtak*). Now with social media it's the opposite. The goal is to show that you have a lot of guests and a lot of food. It's very shameful." While some Jordanians from both tribal and nontribal backgrounds were keen to follow ibn Taymiyyah in leaving any leveling of inequalities to God's wrath, others were more inclined to take matters into their own hands, or even to see their own actions as instruments of higher purposes. A subversive tribal culture of leveling manifested itself in the institution of the feud and in closely related practices of hospitality, raiding, and livestock theft, revealing how emotional phenomena like envy are shaped by their ambient social context.

While livestock theft was subject to much moralizing during my fieldwork as a sign of the fallen nature of our current times, there were also those who held the opposite view and told nostalgic tales of various capers. If ibn Taymiyyah argued that miserliness was at least slightly better than envy because the sinner only denied himself the good things in life and not others (1262, 115–117), more tribally oriented Jordanians tended to argue that it was the other way around and that the miser was the most contemptible figure in society (see also Ghosh 1983, 221). One tribesman tried to illustrate this sensibility using the following parable: "Once a sheikh had three guests: a rich man, a generous man and a thief. Why did he seat the generous man on his right, the thief on the left and the rich man further away on the left?" I responded that of course the most honored guests sit closest to the host and the most honored place is on the right, so the generous man was best and the thief was better than the rich man. The man said, "Exactly. Of course the generous man is best but the rich man is rich because he is a miser (*bakhīl*), whereas the thief is also generous.[10] You see in those days the thieves were not like the thieves now. They would steal livestock (*ḥalāl*) to share with the people. This made them much loved. Now people just spend the money on themselves."

The contention that today's thieves were merely acquisitive was not completely fair, however, and the invidious nature of their deeds continued to be viewed with a certain indulgence. I once attended a large Ramadan *ifṭār* or breakfast with perhaps a hundred other people where there was some muted discussion of how the host could afford such generosity as we photographed ourselves to post online later and ate our fill. All was revealed a few weeks later, though, when our host was arrested for livestock theft. Some attributed it to a sort of madness that had possessed him, which made him steal from his neighbor from another lineage for the sake of hospitality and the pride of having bested him. It was *ḥasad*, but while everyone assured me it was a sin and completely against the spirit of Ramadan, no one seemed particularly perturbed (though I never spoke to the man whose livestock had been stolen). To take a more extreme example of how livestock theft became a tool of economic leveling against suspected misers, there was another man to the south who was notorious for inviting his victims to feast on their own livestock. For his *coup de grace*, he would wait until his guest, having been consoled with a free dinner following his misfortune, told him *yākhlaf ʿalayk* (may God provide for you, as in, may your generosity be returned to you by God). At this point, the thief would proudly say, "No! God provide for *you*," removing any lingering doubt about where the meat had come from. In both cases, the tribal indulgence of invidious, leveling thefts (as in the tribal indulgence of revenge in the previous chapter) represents a break with Islamic ethics even as it is couched in Islamic practices, from Ramadan *ifṭār*s to formulaic blessings.

While there could be a subversive playfulness to this sort of theft and raiding, it was also a deadly serious business. One man I was close to, who I will call Abu Yassin, had his entire life's savings tied up in livestock to the tune of tens of thousands of dollars. The fear of thieves kept him up most nights with a loaded shotgun, so that he slept mostly during the day. It was not just the money, though. He told me, "Stealing someone's livestock is like stealing their wife. It's a great shame." A particularly good illustration of the segmentary logic that led to culturally specific manifestations of envy arose one day when Abu Yassin mentioned distinctive tribal brands used to identify livestock and prevent theft by rival groups. Fiddling with a piece of metal, he told me he was thinking of making his own brand: "We Huwaytat make a number seven (V in Arabic) like this—and those of us from [my section] add two horizontal lines. For sheep and goats we put it on the left ear. For horses and camels we put it on the rear left thigh. But now there are all of these Saba'awi (Palestinians from Bīr Saba') calling themselves Huwaytat and using our brand." His nephew immediately demurred: "No uncle, the Huwaytat brand is a number eight (an upside-down V in Arabic)." They went back and forth, both assuring me that if I looked on Google, I would see that they were right.

Nonetheless, both men agreed that some sort of "V" was the basis for the Huwaytat brand—although the images uploaded on the internet by various Bedouin with an enthusiasm for such folklore were far more diverse. Within this system (or so Abu Yassin and his nephew claimed), different "legs" or "fives" (as in five generations back) of the *'ashīra* (tribe or, literally, ten generations back) could add embellishments to differentiate their livestock. I asked if this regress continued, then what about individuals? Here, the nephew jumped in: "It's rare." Yet then he said, "My Grandmother (may God have mercy on her) used to put a personal mark under the ear. But that's not common. The most common is for the tribe as a whole." Again seemingly caught in a web of contradictions, he said (still speaking authoritatively), "Of course nowadays everyone just puts whatever they like. The tribes are not like before." I asked about the implications of these marks for livestock theft: "If someone was found with the livestock of another tribe, would the whole tribe rise up?" He smiled with a look of satisfaction and said, "Yes, before it was like this. Now, no. Maybe your close relatives and neighborhoods will help you look. Then you'll go to the police. Maybe they'll help you. Things aren't like before. Before, people lived on blessing alone." Again, contradictions between the ideal of segmentation and the realities of practice could be solved by appealing to imagined coherence elsewhere, if not online with the help of "Google," then in an idealized past.

If the theft of livestock represented a very particular way of relating to one's neighbors in social orders characterized by rivalry and inequality, the blood feud that would follow a homicide represented a more collective and extreme version of the phenomenon. It is easy to criticize the sterility of mathematical abstraction when considering envy in relationship to the feud. The feud would seem to take us beyond what economists and mathematicians call the "cake cutting problem" (Steinhaus 1948) in which the neutralization of "envy" is conceptualized as the even distribution of variegated goods between a set number of coherent individuals. As a model of envy, the feud and its reliance on the principle of balanced opposition is certainly more poetic: murder does, after all, raise the stakes. The principle of a life for a life might be the ideal solution to the problem of balanced opposition, but, as Emyrs Peters notes, it is rarely so simple. He documents a folk model of retribution for homicides wherein the progression from tertiary to secondary to primary segments maps onto an escalation from blood money and vengeance to feuding to raiding and total war on the model of Evans-Pritchard's (1940) Nuer findings—only to catalog all of the glaring inconsistencies with the model in practice, with different resolutions to different homicides seemingly deployed ad hoc. The idealized vengeance killing brings the series of killings to a close—whereas feud killings can theoretically continue indefinitely, since it is all too easy to view one's own tribespeople as more valuable than anyone else's. This applies all the more to blood money, which is sometimes rationalized in part by putting it toward payment of the bridewealth for another marriage, from which the first child can be named after the victim of the homicide: another take on a life for a life.

It is in the context of these sorts of social institutions that notions of honor and shame begin to make sense as analytical categories that take an obviously reductionist approach to the problem of envy reminiscent of economic and mathematical models, but do so while foregrounding problems of personhood and temporality. Instead of representing a single relation between two fixed entities at a single moment in time, the feud problematizes both the fixity of the two entities (person, group, or some emergent thereof) and the stability of their relationship in time. For instance, it might seem obvious that it is murders of individuals that cause the fracturing of tribal segments in the context of the feud, but as anthropologists studied such feuds more closely, they could not help but notice the disjuncture between the social model and the reality: not all homicides lead to feuds, and those feuds may not proceed along existing cleavages within lineages. Homicides often provoke realignments. To give an extreme example, the Bedouin of Cryrenaica reason that when a man kills his father, "the act itself proves that he cannot possibly be his son . . . relieving the males of the agnatic line of the responsibility and the odium" (Peters 1967, 275). In fact, the violence of feuds tends to reconfigure the social order as much as it follows the lines laid out by that social order. Jacob Black-Michaud (1985, 17), drawing on the implications of Peters's findings, emphasizes how homicides often come to be narrated as precipitating events when in fact they point to deeper fissional dynamics inherent in the struggle among descendants over a limited patrimony. Important killings are often inscribed with multiple meanings over time (Gilsenan 1996; Shryock 1997). This plays out at every scale, with homicides and blood money payments becoming the events that are later narrated as having precipitated various fissures and fusions. Groups openly change their lineage affiliations when necessary—through rituals, by participating in collective violence, and even through state fiat (Dresch 1988).

Normally, we would want to abandon a model that does not explain the empirical data. Yet as Dresch is quick to note, the persistence of a model that fails to account for "the course events take" *within* a social field we seek to study is at least as interesting as the persistence of a model that does. As with tribalism, there is a simplistic and projective understanding of envy that is easily elicited in interviews, which is both misleading but also produces enough self-validating structural effects to remain viable. Both concepts consequently point to structural dynamics that can unfold independently of the conscious (or unconscious) desires of the principals. Whether or not any of the individuals I have described here have ever actually felt envy begins to seem beside the point. In so many ways, one is expected to act like Abu Yassin and tribal mediators: *as if* envy were an ever-present threat, and *as if* the tribe were a stable and coherent entity. Anything else (as I often found) was simply socially illegible.

Conclusion

As I have argued previously (Hughes 2020), it is not the Middle East that is a privileged site for the study of envy so much as ethnography itself. With its preferred method of "participant observation," there is something inherently invidious about the whole project that affords a unique opportunity for studying envy's workings. After all, ethnographers are of necessity imitators who almost by definition can never be as good as the "natives" they hope to imitate. Yet as is typical of how envy is publicly signified, ethnographers are more prone to talk about their suspicions that their interlocutors envy them (Wolf 1979) than to confess their envy of their interlocutors. There has been much emphasis in recent years on the privileges of mobility and wealth that ethnographers often enjoy, but if my experience is any guide, ethnographers are also often vulnerable, at the mercy of their hosts, and in possession of an almost child-like understanding of what is unfolding around them. My hope here is not to revive tropes of the Orient as a prestige zone for the study of envy. To the contrary, my Bedouin interlocutors have encouraged me to wonder: who is really envying whom here? What is to be made of these fears that social media is making us envy each other?

I would argue that the discourses of envy I have encountered in Jordan have taught me to think much more critically about the possessive individualism (Macpherson 1962) that still exerts a powerful sway over social science's common sense and that has arguably prepared the ground for the current affective turn (despite its proponents' protestations to the contrary). I would even go so far as to say that my interlocutors have more often than not put me to shame with the sophistication of their approaches to various anthropological problems involving emotions and the problem of human intersubjectivity. While tribal and Islamic conceptions of envy that are popular among my Bedouin interlocutors may differ on the permissibility of spiteful, vengeful manifestations of envy, they converge on the compelling observation that envy remains an important dynamic in human affairs that cannot simply be ignored. My more devout tribal interlocutors are probably correct that envy cannot bring down chandeliers and tents (at least on its own), but the idea of the evil eye reminds us that people are often entangled with various others in ways they do not understand—and that the judgments of others can have far-reaching implications. Life in Jordan, with its relatively weak state and strong kinship structures, merely highlights what many of the societies in which theories of affect have been developed work so strenuously to efface and obviate. Emotions and affect can assist with this ideological work to a degree, but they can also help highlight the limits of possessive individualism. Like shame, envy in particular challenges attempts to extricate individuals and their bodies from the social order, and to imbue such bodily impulses with political agency by foregrounding what Deleuze might call "veritable critical entities that hover above the body and judge it." More than merely judge, however, envy carries within itself a powerful leveling impulse that threatens to take from those who have and give to those who do not. Whether or not social media itself is indeed inciting such passions, as so many seem to believe, the wider discourse about the invidiousness of social media suggests that the attempts of postindustrial societies to escape from these critical entities are meeting with mixed results.

CHAPTER 4

Face

Much of my fieldwork in Jordan involved being directed toward powerful senior men known as "faces" (*wujūh*), who were seen as the true experts on Jordan's tribes and their "customs and traditions." And as I have noted, one of the key leitmotifs of those conversations was a sort of elegiac monologue explaining wistfully how "these days, the youth don't sit and learn in the *dīwān* (the guest room) the way they used to. They're always on their phones! They're on Facebook, WhatsApp, and I don't know what else!" These men often counseled me that the time to conduct research on Jordan's tribes and their system of tribal justice had passed because these new technologies had so profoundly disrupted the traditional forms of face-to-face (*wajh-li-wajh*) sociality that undergirded them. Indeed, the adoption of the internet and ubiquitous mobile telephony in Jordan has been rapid and striking—and many Jordanians (young and old) cannot seem to put their phones down. However, as I have also noted, such criticism of young people's social media usage came at a time when social media teemed with reports of "tribal clashes" (*ishtibākāt 'ashā'iriyya*) across Jordan. Many of the younger men I knew in rural Jordan—in both their in-person and online personae—spoke enthusiastically on how social media allowed them to reconnect across distances and even borders with fellow tribesmen, learning more about their history and uncovering allegedly unresolved cases of "old blood" that became hot topics of debate. The subsequent breaking of truces that their elders had negotiated and then guaranteed years before, known as *taqṭiyya' al-wajh* (literally "cutting the face"), allowed younger men to abrogate the authority to act on behalf of the tribe to themselves. Suffice it to say that the concept of "face" had an important place in Bedouin understandings of the nature of human sociality, but it was highly contested and often easily unmoored from the literal body.

It was not simply the guarantors who vouch for their kin's compliance in truces who were "faces" here. The groups themselves (as well as their individual members) were also reckoned to have their own idiomatic "face," or discrete social reputation. It could be metaphorically "blackened" via various affronts, just as the coloring of one's face may literally darken in moments of interpersonal conflict as blood rushes to one's cheeks. In such a situation, unless one's metaphorical "face" was "cold" (incapable of experiencing shame), it became incumbent upon any self-respecting individual or kin grouping to "whiten" their face through remedial action. Such beliefs are long-standing, and, in many ways, "Face-book" is immediately recognizable as a tool for the extension of one's "face" (Miller 2011). While such continuities with older logics were widely accepted by interviewees, however, it was the disjunctures that fascinated them. This chapter uses the polysemy of the Arabic for "face" (both a term for a tribal leader and the organ most associated with shame) to show how shame and tribal authority become inextricably linked in Jordan's tribal communities. I emphasize how shame here is no longer merely an involuntary bodily reaction but something that becomes unmoored from the body and something that entire lineages may be subject to. In such a context, the authority of tribal "faces" is profoundly shaped by how shame is perceived to ripple through the body politic and impact the collective "face" of the group.

Beginning with my work as an English teacher and sometime after-school tutor, I saw how Bedouin children were frequently admonished when they misbehaved that their faces were cold. Asked what he meant by telling his younger brother that his face was cold, a friend once said, "It means that he's an animal—that he doesn't have shame (*ḥayāʾ*)." In other words, part of transforming children into fully fledged human beings required a steady stream of hissed or shouted exclamations of *ʿayb* (shame!) or *istaḥī* (be ashamed!) to cultivate the correct physiological response to social transgressions. Once I was standing with a neighbor in the nearby market town when a beggar in motley clothes called out, "Shilling? Shilling? Give me a shilling!" My neighbor mischievously tried pressing some coins into my hand as I instinctively resisted until he gave her the money himself. Once she was out of earshot he explained to me didactically, "She's begging [literally witnessing: *tashhad*]. This is charity (*ṣadaqa*) because of our Lord. If you give charity, our Lord will sustain you (*yarzugak*). . . . But lots of these people beg because they don't want to work. Like her." I replied in deadpan, "Really?" He continued, "But this is for our Lord. On judgment day, their faces will melt." I repeated the words quizzically back to him: "Their faces will melt?" "From the shame," he clarified. "On judgment day, when they stand before the fire, and are asked to account for their sins, their faces will melt from the shame." In other words, perhaps one might hold out hope that one day even the most incorrigible might finally learn to cultivate shame, but there was nothing natural or inevitable about it until the day of judgment.

However, the most telling manner in which it became clear that shame and "face" were at least as much social as physiological phenomena was in the practice of raising black or white flags. It is not uncommon in rural Jordan to see a white flag flying above a house from time to time. It is a widespread practice among many Bedouin groups, perhaps most memorably captured by Paul Dresch's work with the tribespeople of highland Yemen in "Placing the Blame" (1987). If asked about his white flag, a Jordanian homeowner might demur by saying something vague about heritage and tradition, but he might also give a very specific account of a duty he felt his family had to a neighboring family and how they believed themselves to have discharged it—thus "whitening" the family's face, as symbolized by the white flag. The reverse was less common in my experience, but also present: families would sometimes raise a black flag as a reminder that their collective "face" had been blackened and needed to be whitened. For instance, I once commented on the large black flags flying in front of a house as I was leaving a gathering and asked the man who had invited me about them. The self-styled "opposition" sheikh said, "It means they're at war with the Hashemites, those bastards and dogs. These people are Abu Mus'ab Al-Zarqawi's cousins (referring to the former Emir of Al Qaeda in Iraq). When the Hashemite house falls, they will have whitened their face and they will take the flags down." The ambition here, grandiose as it might seem, was to eventually avenge the death of their kinsman by upending the whole political order and driving the current ruling family from power.

What is notable here is that while the spread of social media has given new impetus to the question of how emotions and affects come to be mediated in human societies, it also offers an opportunity to reflect on how such emotions and affects long ago escaped from their embodied dimensions (if that was ever their true locus). With apologies to Marx, one could say that the weight of past mediations weighs like a nightmare on the brains of the living. In fact, as the ethnographer Andrew Shryock (1997) notes in his study of Jordanian historians, adapting discourses of (and *about*) a world of agonistic face-to-face encounters to new forms of mediation hardly began with the advent of social media. As Shryock chronicles in *Nationalism and the Genealogical Imagination*, the Jordanian tribesmen who were attempting to write history in the 1990s were already struggling with the challenge of relating scurrilous and defamatory narratives designed for the *dīwān*—"lies" (*kidhib*) in the local idiom—into texts that could circulate far beyond their originally intended publics. As Shryock seeks to collect oral histories and commit them

Figure 4.1. A typical *dīwān* or guest room. The *dīwān* is not reserved only for the wealthiest sheikhs, but rather is something that most Jordanians of all class backgrounds aspire to re-create in their homes—especially in rural areas. It is usually the nicest room of the house. This is a typical example of what a senior man of some stature (though by no means especially wealthy) might use for receiving guests and otherwise conducting business on behalf of his junior kin.

to tape, he quickly discovers his interlocutors fear that words transposed from one medium to another might betray their authors. Willingness to welcome the use of an analog tape recorder here is not so much diagnostic of veracity as it is of dominance: only the most powerful and well-insulated have the confidence to disseminate their narratives far beyond the *dīwān* (Shryock 1997, 179–182). The "digital" here appears yet again not as a qualitative shift so much as an intensification of older analog dynamics.

If such anxieties could be provoked so readily by older men's history-writing and a foreigner's tape recorder, then it is little wonder that the profusion of social networking and phones with recording capabilities greatly accentuates these fears. As I will show, amidst rapid technological change at the level of practice, tribal sociality remains ideologically committed to face-to-face encounters in the *dīwān* (see figure 4.1). Yet the materiality of new media challenges such commitments among the older generation, becoming part of a deeper history of technological transformation dating back to colonial sedentarization projects and the introduction of the automobile. This history underlines how there has long been a problematic disconnect between the ideology of face-to-face communication and the technical realities of actual tribal sociality. In fact, this was precisely why self-appointed guardians of the social order like these tribal "faces" were constantly counseling me not to confuse the violent goings-on of the moment with Jordan's venerable "customs and traditions"—an object lesson in how interview data is always revealing but is not necessarily the last word on a particular matter. In what follows, I try to emphasize both the plasticity of these traditions amidst rapid technological change while also emphasizing how certain core antagonisms (between generations, between tribe and state, and between dominant and subordinate lineages) perpetuate themselves through ever-changing media. I begin with a brief reflection on the troubled place of the face in modern social theory given its orientalist baggage before returning to Jordan, where face remains a powerful principle organizing social relations. I contrast the face-to-face sociality of the traditional tribal *dīwān* with the novel sorts of "face work" (Goffman 1967) that new media like Facebook and WhatsApp seem to enable, concluding that the contested notions of "face" that emerge here are not inherent in these technologies or some sort of psychological universalism, but are instead a product of historically situated struggles over their meaning between differently positioned social actors.

What's in a Face?

As with the other concepts that this book seeks to develop through its engagement with Bedouin discourses around social media, the idea of face has its fair share of orientalist baggage. As Matan Kaminer has noted (2022), the concept of face was already widely in use in transnational anglophone merchant circles in the nineteenth century long before it was taken up by the Chinese Boasian anthropologist Hsien-Chin Hu (1944) and then the sociologist Erving Goffman (1967). As Kaminer notes, however, for all of its propensity to be used to denigrate Asians as untrustworthy and overly concerned with appearances, the popularity of the term also implies something of a shared underlying logic that makes diverse groups of people receptive to it. After all, while the term "losing face" never completely shed its racializing connotations, it also offered a succinct way to characterize a key anxiety among the honor-obsessed Victorians. Crucially—as Hu noted—face is a quality not merely of individuals, but also of groups, and its salience may be especially heightened in moments of cross-cultural encounter. What is more, in many societies characterized by extreme inequality, "face" is likely to be unevenly distributed. As Hu notes, "The higher the social standing of a person the more dignity he has to maintain, and the more vulnerable this *lien* [face] becomes" (1944, 47). For all of social media's ability to heighten the anxieties of the notable and privileged about the risk of public humiliation, they also follow familiar and long-standing patterns of social behavior.

One could probably follow Maurice Bloch (2013) in drawing out how the face serves as a key conduit through which humans go *In and Out of Each Other's Bodies*, leveraging recent work in neuroscience on "mirror neurons" and the intriguing possibility that humans build little models of other minds in their brains that can be detected and mapped through physical sensors. However, as the anthropologist Emily Martin notes in expressing her dissatisfaction with a scientific study measuring her facial reactions that she participated in as an experimental subject, it is worth being skeptical of how such an appeal to affect relies on laboratory wizardry to produce an illusion of universality. As Martin notes, the notion of affect is ultimately tied to an ongoing and often fraught attempt to banish "subjectivity" from experimental psychology that at least in some regards is culturally specific precisely due to its very peculiar fixation on finding the universal and a particular sort of potentiality in the historically specific procedures of the laboratory itself (2013).

It is important to appreciate just how quickly ideas of "face" can detach from the literal face and become a powerful symbolic tool for the articulation of not just individual identities and intentions, but also those of groups and specific sorts of socially situated actors. As Webb Keane puts it, "face-work" is not only about "inner psychological states"—it "invokes the larger public world." To make any sort of moral claim in such a context ultimately "depends on being perceptible and being recognized as such to other people" (2016, 97). Such vulnerabilities to the judgments of others are widespread, of course, but require less recourse to such experimental paradigms and assertions of universality. Following Bourdieu, Keane notes the specific sorts of bodily dispositions that people develop around something like honor or shame are both distinctive depending on one's position but also subject to radical recontextualization, such as, for instance, if a Kabyle woman from Algeria brings her propensity to orient her body downward with her to France. All of a sudden, what was once read as an assertion of dignity is liable to be read as evidence of abjection (Keane 2016, 98).

As I noted in the last chapter, all of this implies that while attempts to use honor-shame discourses as a theoretical metonym for Arab, Middle Eastern, or Bedouin culture are bound to be distorting and stereotyping (Abu Lughod 1989), the universal is not the safe refuge it might at first appear to be. Such distortion is inevitable because, as Abu Lughod demonstrates so extensively in *Veiled Sentiments* (1986) and her pathbreaking work with Catherine Lutz in the anthropology of emotions (1990), the problem with such attempts to posit a sort of "national character" is not that they are too specific, but that they remain far too general. Because "face" as a key symbol for the articulation of honor and shame is fundamentally a social phenomenon, the phenomenon of "face" will manifest itself very differently depending on the social roles inhabited by the people in question. For that reason, in what follows I will discuss the avenues for disruption that the younger generation pursued through their adoption of social media before turning to the strategies elders aligned with the state have pursued to reassert their traditional prerogatives. Despite the rapid technopolitical transformation of Jordan and the wider world in the last century, the face continues to exert a sort of uncanny influence in patterns of sociality.

Feuding Goes Digital

Plenty of social media activity (and activity in general) in Jordan has nothing to do with feuding and tribalism—especially in urban areas. Jordanian social media users enjoy sharing jokes, poetry, inspirational images, and a lot of Islamic and nationalist content. They also take vast quantities of pictures of themselves, their friends, and their mundane activities. Yet the nature of preexisting rural Jordanian social networks tends to make kinship integral to the adoption of new media, which can mean exclusivity as well as inclusivity. To return to an earlier observation, because mobile phone companies used to offer discounts on calls within their networks, kin often pressured each other to switch carriers to save them money, leading to different carriers predominating among different lineages. Nowadays, Facebook groups specializing in tribal news like "The Sakhr News Network" and "The Huwaytat Tribe" boast followers in the tens and hundreds of thousands, and many tribal segments boast their own groups on WhatsApp, Signal, and other messaging applications. Likewise, when it comes time to "friend" or "follow" people on social media and share content, it is often to one's tribe that one turns: for connections as well as affirmative, noncontroversial material that can be unproblematically "liked" and "shared." The semiotics of such circulating images proclaiming tribal solidarity tend to revolve around connecting the name of one's tribe with other prestige symbols, including international brands, nationalistic symbols like flags, and traditional Bedouin regalia and paraphernalia. As a medium, Facebook seems to present vastly greater prospects for such strategies of extension. At the same time, though, "cutting the network"

(Strathern 1996) by precipitating the dissolution of preexisting social relationships offers another way to animate an inert kin network.

One of the most interesting and dynamic of these disjunctive "traditions" focused on cutting the network was a kinship category known as *khamsat al-dam* (the five of blood). The category is given its fullest expressive form in didactic commentaries that are imparted to children and visiting anthropologists alike in the *dīwān*. Holding an imaginary dagger with a clenched fist, the more senior man would explain to his juniors that all the relatives of the killer to "the fifth grandfather" are subject to a degree of collective responsibility for homicide. With each generation, a finger would be dramatically released until, after five generations, the imaginary dagger is relinquished. These are the people who, following a murder, are potentially subject to *jalwa* (banishment) or *tha'r* (revenge). It is a vivid and evocative image. It is also a very partial representation of the reality—as my patient teachers were always quick to note. It is assumed that some of the *khamsa* will try to wheedle their way out of responsibility, while more distant kin may seek to join the fray for various reasons: in the hopes of building new family coalitions, making off with some booty in subsequent raiding, or maybe just becoming a protagonist in a good story and earning some local renown.

There are also good reasons why, at various times, the principle of five generations of collective responsibility itself has been attacked as both overly broad and not broad enough. Perhaps the biggest threat to the concept of the *khamsat al-dam* related to me by my interlocutors was the introduction of the automobile to Jordan. All of a sudden, the potential for unintentional homicide skyrocketed, especially when compared to the sort of face-off implied by a knife fight or even a gunfight. While the impersonal nature of car-related deaths might mitigate claims of malicious intent, the victim was no less dead, and there remained a sense that families should be entitled to satisfaction following the loss of beloved kin. As a result, there is an ongoing effort to limit collective responsibility to three generations rather than five, thereby decreasing the number of people who would have to undergo the hardships of banishment and paying restitution (Shunnaq et al. 2025, 64–65). One respected local historian even told me that, since a man can hold a dagger with three fingers (and the ring and pinky fingers move together), only three generations should *ever* be banished, and that all of my interlocutors arguing to the contrary were ignorant. The government's tendency to encourage previously nomadic groups to sedentarize (and accept the state's authority in place of such stateless structures of dispute resolution) has further incentivized families to settle disputes quickly and with minimal violence while cutting off collective responsibility at three generations.

Although almost everyone I spoke to saw social media as creating conflict, my Jordanian interlocutors did not naively accept a dichotomy between dynamic modern technologies and a static, objectified tradition. Indeed, most of the Jordanians I encountered were intensely concerned with history and the historicity of their customs and traditions. Even the threats posed by technology to face-to-face sociality and sober attempts to prevent such conflicts from "widening" beyond a delimited group of responsible kinsmen were understood to predate the Jordanian state and the internet. From car crashes to ever-evolving systems of guarantorship and the institutionalized banishment of five (or three) generations of a killer's family, the technical mediation of such "face-to-face" relations among kin groups has long been a significant problem and part of the work that the *dīwān* is supposed to do. As I will demonstrate in the next section, the *dīwān* presents itself as an interactive space that can defuse conflicts involving sprawling networks of actors by focalizing them in the bodies of senior men and their assembled kin and then orchestrating their separation while tempers cool. Here, elders cut the network to avoid creating opportunities for kinsmen to "cut the face." Yet as the following examples will show, youths at least initially found plenty in social media that could aid them in frustrating the local gerontocracy's attempts to act as the faces of the tribes.

When I was close enough to a tribal clash to interview members of the tribes involved, it was *de rigeur* for the elders to complain that yet again this principle of the *khamsat al-dam* was being flouted. One particularly violent set of clashes that broke out between the Huwaytat and the Maʿani tribes in 2013 struck many of my interlocutors as epitomizing the schismogenic (Bateson 1935) potential of this combination of kinship and social media. Following a shooting at Hussein Bin Talal University that left four dead, there were reports of people being pulled off of buses, having their IDs checked, and being attacked on the basis of their last name. These sinister rumors, which turned out to be true, became far more concrete when a group of Sharia Court employees that I was working with (none of whom were from either family) began repeatedly watching a viral video on Facebook that claimed to show the corpses of two Maʿanis who had supposedly been killed by the Huwaytat.[1] Debate raged as the video was played and replayed: Was it real or fake (*kidhib*)? Were the corpses who they were purported to be? Most importantly: just what sort of agenda was pushing this video—and the conflict more broadly? Was this being disseminated by Huwaytat as a means to gloat, or by Maʿanis to rile up their kinsmen for another round of revenge? Might there be darker forces at work (Israel, the United States, the Ministry of the Interior) driving all of this to sow chaos in Jordan amidst the tumult of the "Arab Spring"?

Whatever grand machinations did or did not lie behind the clashes, as events progressed, they became less about the rival families and more about challenging all existing authority structures. A particularly striking post from a week after the four deaths at the university depicted four men with red *kūfiyyah*s covering their faces while holding a stolen "Ministry of the Interior" banner and rifles. The most popular comments were: "There's no correct solution but the correct one from long ago, which is for the Southern Desert to be independent from the rest of the governorate" and "the Huwaytat are an army that doesn't need training." The strategic covering of the face here recalls deeper histories of revolt. As Ted Swedenburg has written, the *kūfiyyah* that has now become almost synonymous with Palestinian national identity only gained that iconic status in the context of the revolt of 1936–1939. Though it was banned by the British as they restored order, militants succeeded amidst the ferment of the revolt in catalyzing the mass adoption of what had been a humble, rustic garment, transforming it into a tool of depersonalization allowing insurgents to operate undetected within the civilian population (Swedenburg 2003, 30–35). Tellingly, elder members of the Huwaytat complained that this was all ignoring the proper channels through which such conflicts were supposed to proceed, and that people were being attacked with little in the way of genealogical precision. They noted disapprovingly that most of the victims *and perpetrators* of these retaliatory attacks were not from the *khamsat al-dam* of those involved, and, in any event, the government had announced a truce and important men from both families had backed it. Here, elders demanded that culpability be carefully and exactingly parceled out with full genealogical due diligence. Meanwhile, masked youths—faces obscured—flouted the limits their elders and the state sought to impose, hijacking its own system of identification to enact their own version of justice even as they increasingly took up arms against the state apparatus itself.

Such generational divides were ubiquitous in my interview data and systematically informed how different actors construed the involvement of "face" in these clashes, betraying the often wildly divergent accounts that circulated about them. For instance, one morning while taking the bus to do some archival work, I looked over and saw another local bus blocking the road. Its windows had been smashed. As the passengers strained to look, my friend's son asked what had happened and another youth said, "It's between the Ajarmeh and the Showabkeh." When asked the cause, he simply replied, "girls" (*bināt*)—a refrain I would hear many times over the course of my much-more-eventful-than-usual commute that day as my fellow passengers and I tried to shame and cajole reticent drivers to take us through the areas where vehicles had been attacked. That evening, I asked my friend whose son had been on the bus with me that morning for his take on what had happened. The older man proudly declared, "I don't have any idea! It's just youths. I was over by the school when it happened too. It's up on top of the hill so I could look down on [the town in question] and I saw the youths and the gendarmerie fighting. I didn't even ask anyone who they were or why they were fighting." I asked why not, and he replied, "You know why I'm not worried? Because the sheikh of the Ajarmeh's daughter is married to the sheikh of the Showabkeh. When the faces (*wujūh*) of the Ajarmeh and Showabkeh want to solve it, it will be very simple. This is just between youths. It's not important and I don't want to make it important. It's like how Al-Jazeera will put any video of ten people protesting on television and turn it into something."

Just then, his son arrived, and—as I expected—he was eager to relate all of the twists and turns of the saga. He explained that the previous evening a girl from the Showabkeh was waiting for a bus when someone from the Ajarmeh (who lived farther down the road toward Amman) started harassing her. The Showabkeh attacked him and he fled, only to return with his relatives. This led to a pitched battle in Jurayna. The next morning, they switched to retaliatory attacks on buses. The Ajarmeh targeted the Madaba-Amman bus line since it was owned by the Showabkeh and passed through Ajarmeh territory. Meanwhile, the Showabkeh targeted the Madaba-Na'ur bus line since it was owned by the Ajarmeh and passed through Showabkeh territory. However, I received the most detailed and effusive account from a participant the next day when I ran into him working at his father's office just off the intersection where the bus had been smashed up the day before. Notably, his account included a very different reckoning of how "face" figured into things. He told me:

> This Ajrami was drunk and he came to Jurayna and started laying down rubber circles in our neighborhood [literally *mukhammis*—after the number five, which is represented as a circle in Arabic]. This is very disrespectful so some youths hit him and sent him away. He even had a gun. If we had had another five minutes we would have burnt his car! Then he came back with his relatives and we fought together until really late. We were all using [Facebook] Messenger and WhatsApp to bring all of our relatives. It was really fun. Then the next day, they shot the windows out of the Amman-Madaba bus [which was owned by a man from the Showabkeh] so we broke the Amman-Na'ur bus [which was owned by a man from the Ajarmeh] and used it to block the road. Then the gendarmerie came because you can't block the road. The road is for all the citizens. But we fought with them. They were shooting tear gas at us and we were cutting open onions just to help us breathe. But it's good to get into a fight every now and then.

Given how many people had attributed the conflict to "girls," I put that to him, and he responded with frustration: "People always say that fights start over girls if they don't know [the cause]! But this happened because the Ajrami was drunk and laying down rubber circles. . . . He was doing it in our face (*fī wajhna*). Do you understand? He was doing it in our face (*fī jakhimna*)!"

The nature of face was thus a site of struggle—especially between generations and between those more or less closely related to these conflicts (depending, for instance, on whether one was invested in a particular outcome or simply late to work). While young social media users tried to build tribal solidarity around their own highly distributed notion of face by fomenting conflicts with the government and sprawling rival kin groups, their elders tried to maintain order by cutting the network at the level of five generations and focalizing attention on certain "faces." This sort of fundamental need to cut the network (even as one extends it) was also central to much more mundane aspects of online sociality as well. When one administrator for one of the largest tribal Facebook pages in Jordan explained to me the constant need to ban people from the page, he said, "A lot of people just dislike the page in general. . . . Our tribe has maybe 22 or 23 families and one or two families are in the upper class. A lot of the members of parliament are from them . . . and they are not the biggest family either. . . . When we want something from the government and the people in the upper class don't give us this service, we put the problem on the page. It helps the average citizen, but they hate us for it." Again, the making and breaking of kin bonds emerge as two sides of the same coin; in this case, in the attempt to extend the network by nurturing a broad-based tribal political bloc to wrest more services from the government requires cutting the network by actively banning and excluding existing powerbrokers, or "faces." The next section will explore how Jordan's incumbents are increasingly taking an active role in shaping these conflicts online, before they reach the streets.

A Facebook Sheikh

If the emergence of social media had left those in their sixties or seventies confused and increasingly marginalized, a new generation of leaders in their forties and fifties began to blend many of the trappings of sheikhly authority with a bit of internet savvy to make their own claims to tribal authority. One of the most interesting examples of this new kind of leader is a man I will call Sheikh Abdullah. While I may seem to dwell on this encounter at length and highlight certain atypical aspects, much of it was completely typical of my interviews with other judges, from the rituals of hospitality to the depictions of tribal law and tribe-state relations, and will recall the profile I offered of Sheikh Salim in chapter 1 ("**The Many Faces of the State**"). In our discussion, he made clear that he saw tribal law much as tribesmen in many other parts of the former Ottoman Empire do: as "a self-conscious kind of social engineering, in which the older and more mature members of the community tried to manipulate a homicidal conflict in such a way that it first could be contained and then . . . be resolved" (Boehm 1984, 142). As the ensuing discussion will make clear, tribal conflict mediation in Jordan is likewise a moral project that places a high normative value on a kind of social harmony that seeks to accentuate and reify hierarchies of age, gender, and wealth. Yet despite his popular page with thousands of followers, including hundreds who would "like" everything he posted, the shiekh made clear through both his explicit answers to my questions and his tacit self-presentation how dependent he remained upon the interactive space of the *dīwān*.

I first met Sheikh Abdullah, appropriately enough, through Facebook. A tribal judge, he would frequently post pictures on his Facebook page of satisfied disputants reconciling in his *dīwān*, which was a goat-hair tent next to his posh, limestone-faced villa in the capital of Amman. Through a series of Facebook messages and some mutual friends, I arranged to meet the sheikh at his home one evening. When we arrived, he led us to his studied replica of a Bedouin tent with a ceiling fan, a flat screen television, and large, imposing pictures of his father and grandfather, Jordan's king, and its crown prince. He sat us down, and a young boy came out to pour us each a cup of coffee in a small, thimble-like cup before disappearing. The sheikh then took his leave, and three more boys emerged, each carrying a platter: dates, chocolates, and cookies. We demurred a bit. They insisted. After we had all taken some sweets, they filed out and left us to our own devices. My friends took pictures of themselves and remarked on the décor. When the sheikh presented himself again, we were interrupted by the arrival of another guest. Indeed, a couple of men would file through over the course of the meeting, although they barely registered in the conversation. A woman came out with tea and the sheikh remarked, "My Sudanese is off for the day." Presumably this was for my benefit, lest I naively think that he would ever have his daughter serve me—something other sheikhs simply noted outright when underlining that any women I saw were foreign servants.

The nature of this setup was highly typical. Framed around women and junior men providing tea, coffee, and food, the sheikh's hospitality in the *dīwān* required a host of invisible yet indispensable labor as its condition of possibility. The first question I asked him was, "What is the basis of the tribal system?" He replied, "The *dīwān*." He pointed to the tent we were in and said, "This is the *dīwān*. It is open to anyone. Anyone can come here. Now we have stone houses, but we still keep the *dīwān* for guests. This is where the sheikh is found. He's the big [man]. He fixes problems among the people. He judges. This is the basis of the tribal system." The *dīwān*'s modes of hospitality center certain senior men as the primary givers, subsuming and erasing women and junior men as mere extensions of these senior men in ways that in turn govern who can speak and when, with those who "give" hospitality encouraged to monopolize discourse in the *dīwān* while those who *enact* the hospitality are largely excluded. More than its physical space, it was this human component of the *dīwān* that most set it apart from the modes of online tribal sociality that people like Sheikh Abdullah are now turning to, where at least in theory anyone can have their own account and start their own pages.

I next asked the sheikh to explain the process of resolving disputes, and he said he would do so using the procedure for homicide as an example, strongly echoing the account offered by Sheikh Salim in "The Many Faces of the State" but usefully highlighting the roles of the tribal "faces." He told me that the first step after the governor and police deemed a homicide to be tribal (a determination heavily dependent on whether those involved responded as individuals or tribes) was for them to impose a "security truce" for three and a third days. At this point, the guilty party and those related to him through his family notebook (a government document listing one's patrilineal relatives) would be banished from the area, ostensibly for their own safety and reasons of public order. The two families would then be expected to agree upon a sheikh who would act as a tribal judge and organize the "truce of recognition." This second truce would involve a meeting of the guilty party and his banished kin and the victim's family under the protection of the tribal judge overseeing the truce in his own *dīwān*. There the two sides would agree to a blood money payment and choose guarantors from each side ("faces"), who would be held responsible if the truce was broken. The third truce or "tribal truce" would happen after some time had passed and some blood money had been collected, which would be paid following a delegation. When the last of the blood money had been paid (or before, with the sufferance of the victim's family), those banished from their homes could return. The reconciliation would be the fourth meeting of the disputants, marking the payment of the final sum and a return to normal social relations.

Proponents of tribal law like Sheikh Abdullah believed that the use of government courts and their jails brought nothing but "loss" because they did not lead to material compensation, reconciliation, or socially generative relations. The sheikh explained how the blood money is "lightened" by the people under tribal procedures. The delegation that is sent to the reconciliation asks for a particular sum, but it also asks for prayers for the prophet and his excellency the king (all of which is mirrored in the documents that participants sign at truces). Over time, the sum may be adjusted or the terms of the truce may be altered such that people can enter the other side's domain without violating the truce. In this way, demands for punitive damages are supposed to give way to mercy and then forgiveness on the part of the victim's family, the "owners of the blood." I will have more to say in chapter 6 ("**Mercy**") about this aphorism that "prison is loss" and how Bedouin see prison as denying them true closure.

The sheikh told me there were three types of cases: honor, cutting the face, and homicide. He estimated that he judged fifty cases a year, which would mean he had overseen about five hundred in his career. Of these cases, he estimated about 60 percent were homicide and 40 percent were honor. Of the homicides, many of these were car accidents in which the blood money payment had to be negotiated between the families, the police, and the insurance company. He said cases of "face" were exceedingly rare, yet also especially important, because without truces anarchy would reign, making such cases the key to stopping cycles of retaliatory violence. This was precisely why the notable failures in recent years of previously respected tribal "faces" to negotiate truces that would hold has led to such consternation. The "face" (or guarantor) is the "loser" if the truce is broken, having promised to pay a surety if someone on his side is found to have broken the truce, ranging from thousands to hundreds of thousands of dollars. Such "cutting the face" could range from an unauthorized revenge attack by a member of the *khamsat al-dam* to a family member simply wandering into the other side's territory during a truce.

Sheikh Abdullah was by far the most enthusiastic proponent of social media I encountered and surely represents an emerging pattern in which the gender and age hierarchies of the *dīwān* are increasingly projected into online spaces. After years of hearing almost nothing but complaints about Facebook, I was shocked when I asked him to compare it to the *dīwān* and he said, "The *dīwān* is face-to-face. You see the effects of words on the face of the other. . . . But now is better [because] everyone can see the reconciliation on the internet." Yet even he had to admit some ambivalence about the relationship between his online and offline personae and social media's violent potential. He complained that cases of "old revenge" would start on Facebook with youths relitigating old cases that had been settled by their elders decades ago until they spilled over into violent confrontations in the streets. He also related an example of a reconciliation he had overseen that had been "spoiled" when a young journalist published the blood money payment online in the midst of the proceedings in his *dīwān*. The two sides, angry over the publication of the monetary sum, had broken off the reconciliation, causing the gendarmerie to move in and prevent the return of forty families that had been previously banished. However, it is not only the new generation of sheikhs that is adapting to the new technological landscape—the state security apparatus is also learning to regulate social media, much as it used to regulate media before liberalization.

Bringing the State Back In

It is not just kin groups working to cut the network. Cutting the network has long been central to the work of the Jordanian state as well—and it is increasingly translating existing logics to social media. In the short term, Jordan's government has attempted to stop especially protracted clashes (following the basic logics of tribal law) by blockading the traditional domains of the respective families to keep them apart. Yet this itself has often led to more protests (media in tow, naturally) (Assabeel 2013). With the 2011 Arab Spring and its internet-mediated dimensions as backdrop, 2012 was the year that the Jordan government began applying its "Press and Publications Law" online, requiring websites to be registered with the government and to have a full-time editor with at least four years of membership in the Jordanian Press Association. In 2015, a new electronic crimes law came into effect, which now extends sanctions for libel and slander to online "speech" (El-Rayyes 2015). Through both of these laws, various sovereign prerogatives compete in an increasingly global system consisting of responsibilized guardians of social order. In fact, journalists themselves are increasingly under pressure to mediate conflict in ways redolent of tribal notables before them.

The dominant political debates in my conversations with journalists in 2016, 2017, 2019, and 2022 were about what people could legitimately articulate online. Chief among the controversies were a string of high-profile cases in which Islamists were arrested and accused of interfering with Jordan's foreign policy through social media by publicly criticizing its American and Gulf backers (Azzeh 2016; Sweis 2015): something I touch upon at the beginning of the last chapter ("**Envy**"). Then the Christian journalist Nahed Hattar was arrested for an allegedly blasphemous anti-Islamic State Facebook post that would soon lead to his assassination on the courthouse steps (Bulos 2016; Williams 2016). The cartoon featured the face of God peeking into a tent to tend to the needs of a figure associated with the so-called Islamic State named Abu Saleh. The man was depicted in bed, unclothed, smoking a cigarette, and flanked by two women, demanding wine and for the angel Gabriel to bring him some cashews (among other things). Hattar had captioned it "the God of Da'ish" (using a derogatory term for the so-called Islamic State). In a sense, Hattar had found himself the victim of context-collapse: his whole point was that this was no God at all, but rather a perverse travesty of religion, a judgment fully in line with the Jordanian government's official position as well as that of many Jordanians—especially after the release of a video of the group burning a downed Jordanian pilot alive.[2] Ironically, however, in trying to distance Islam from what he viewed as the extremist perversions of the "Islamic State" in Iraq and Syria, Hattar found himself appearing to be a Christian disseminating a blasphemous cartoon depicting the face of the Muslim God. Against the background of negative caricatures of Muhammad that were circulating at the time (Candea 2025), the subtleties of his intentions were easily lost against the wider backdrop of historical taboos among Jordan's Muslims around pictorial representations of faces.

Initially, the authorities claimed they had detained Hattar for his own safety, before later deciding to charge him with inciting sectarian hatred and racism. His kinspeople blocked roads in their historically Christian neighborhood in Amman as they demonstrated for his release. Hattar had positioned himself as something of a gadfly, becoming a public face of an emerging populist left movement that was critical of Jordan's relationship with Israel, but he also stridently rejected Islamist politics. Through his death, however, Hattar became something of a martyr himself, not only to ideals of press freedom and freedom of expression but also to Jordan itself. Authorities arrested people who had made threats against him, and the subsequent coverage was heavily controlled to emphasize that the preacher who had killed Hattar was to be viewed as a terrorist and an extremist. Hattar's killer himself would be executed the next year following a secretive trial in a state security court.

The journalists I interviewed were highly ambivalent about the increase in government regulation—especially as the state showed that it could not only attack journalists directly with criminal sanctions, but also indirectly by focusing public ire at them, or throttling their ability to reach readers or attract advertising. I met journalists who had served time in prison and been intimidated by politicians for video content that they had promoted to viral status. I met an editor who had resisted complying with the press law until he was left choosing between acquiescence and a government blockade on his website that left him unable to make payroll. He noted, though, that the authorities never tried to shut down his Facebook page—they just blocked his website and thus his source of advertising revenue. Even the frequent visits of the authorities to his office to encourage him to end the blockade by complying with the law had been (at least on the surface) cordial enough. At some point, virtually every journalist defensively told me, "We have freedom of expression like you do in the West." I certainly would not dismiss such claims—although I might question the degree to which "the West" actually lives up to the ideals they seemed to be envisioning—especially to the degree that it is in fact *Western* security concerns and specifically US security concerns that increasingly impinge on the exchange of ideas within Jordan's public culture.

I was particularly keen to understand how these journalists approached the tribal clashes at the center of this book, given their increasing centrality to the dissemination of information online as average citizens and opposition figures alike became more reticent in the face of such government crackdowns. I had noted that news of "tribal clashes" made up a significant portion of the content online news sites produced, on a par with drug busts and car pileups. Yet most journalists were relatively uninterested in these sorts of stories when I spoke to them, especially compared to issues of foreign policy and press freedom. I was repeatedly told that only someone who had spent a lot of time living in rural areas would care about such things. As I noted in chapter 1 ("**The Many Faces of the State**"), a number of journalists told me about how police press releases were often posted, unedited, without alerting the reader that they were verbatim government press releases.

In these press releases, the actions and claims of the "security apparatus" were discussed in the third person, pre-packaged for placement underneath the banner of a news site, at which point they came to read like ready-made short news items on local disturbances. The appeal here was obvious: competition was fierce, budgets were tight, and free content was not to be refused—even if such "*copy-paste*" was bemoaned as "unprofessional." When journalists did produce original content, they were mindful of the risks of getting the story wrong—and of providing the wrong kind of information and antagonizing the wrong people. Asked why journalists did not name the tribes involved in "tribal clashes" until they had grown protracted, I was told, "We don't want the fight to widen." As one journalist continued, "So for instance, if there is a clash in Ma'an, we don't want for people to read about it in Zarqa and then start a fight there." Again, for all the innovation necessary to make social media so ubiquitous, matters still seemed to boil down to a much older struggle over the way that names could circulate, focalize culpability, and attach to particular social actors with at least notionally discernible faces.

None of this has stopped these clashes or (as far as I can tell) necessarily lessened the amount of bloodshed and disruption caused by them—though the period around my early fieldwork from 2011 to 2013 does seem to have been the high-water mark in terms of the sheer number of such clashes. At the same time, whatever bad-faith motives might lie behind the attempt to use such examples of online incitement as a rationale for government regulation of the internet, there is little appetite in Jordan for romanticizing the violent clashes the authorities ostensibly want to put a stop to. More insidiously, though, the whole way in which people think about social conflict is influenced by the communicative restrictions that are slowly emerging. Ieva Jusionyte, drawing on fieldwork conducted among Argentinean journalists caught between shadowy informal networks and official corruption, has noted a trend in coverage toward what she terms "crimecraft" (2016). Like Jordanian journalists, these journalists find that the need to maintain good relations with the authorities encourages them to report the official narrative while allowing other truths and opinions to subtly emerge through the comments thread online, which can be moderated and subsequently disowned if need be. To become too prominent as the public face of narratives of conflict counter to those of the official state narrative was to risk meeting the same fate as Nahed Hattar—hardly a welcome prospect.

Yet the discourse of crime that is now challenging that of tribal conflict can be even more hostile to different sorts of claims-making by more or less marginalized voices than the highly regulated age and gender hierarchies of the *dīwān*. The concept of crime is very much consonant with the Weberian notion of the state as that entity that has a monopoly on the legitimate use of violence. It is almost tautological under modern states that citizen violence is "criminal" while state violence is not, although the persistence in Jordan of state-approved "tribal law" and its "tribal clashes" greatly complicates this. It would be deeply ironic if the internet, long believed to nurture and foster diverse viewpoints, was increasingly coming to homogenize a heterogeneous world of scurrilous face-to-face talk in cloistered *dīwān*s into a more neutral, state-endorsed hegemonic account of social conflict as "crime." Yet even this seems unlikely, as coverage of "tribal clashes" shows no sign of disappearing, despite a long history of attempts by both state and civil society actors to subsume it within a discourse of criminality. After all, just as the *kūfiyyah* has long mobilized faceless anonymity as a tool of resistance, so the internet affords new ways to efface one's identity without completely ceding the ability to act politically.

Conclusion

The Bedouin notion of "face" described here will no doubt seem highly culturally specific to most readers, shaped as it is by deeper histories of religious and political struggle in Jordan and the wider Levant. Bedouin themselves for the most part would surely agree given that they consciously ground their ideas of "face" as much in their "customs and traditions" as they do in the supposed biology of the human body or pop-technological determinism. My hope is that the discussion presented here helps to illuminate how the face as the visible seat of the emotions should not be essentialized through a vague appeal to affect. While materialism often presents itself as a form of demystification, it can easily serve as its own mode of mystification if the social is disarticulated into its material anchors without any appreciation for the ongoing need for coordinating action to maintain these relationships. Even as Jordan has been fundamentally transformed by technological changes in the past century, concepts like "face" and the "five of blood" that draw inspiration from the human body can also shed those attachments when needed to maintain specific social and political arrangements. Chief among these (as I have been arguing throughout this book) is a specific sort of relationship between state and society that has often been muddled by an appeal to the technological changes inherent in social media without appreciating how they depend on and facilitate changes to that state-society divide. In an era when states have experimented with more efficient modes of surveillance, subjectivation, and social control, the tribe and its various implements like "face" strike a retro-futurist pose, at once beguiling and terrifying. In the next chapter, I will try to draw out how Jordan and the broader Middle East have been at the forefront of the development of new imaginaries of the state that have become increasingly global, and how these imaginaries further illuminate some of the fundamentally *political* upheavals that have been too readily conflated with the widespread adoption of social media.

CHAPTER 5

The Deep State

Once upon a time, scholars diagnosed the "Arab Mind" as peculiarly susceptible to conspiracism and the belief that the political challenges of one's society were the result of nefarious foreign plots. In his spirited defense of the orientalist Rafael Patai's *The Arab Mind* in a 2006 foreword to the book, US Army Colonel Norvell DeAtkine, a self-described former "Psychological Operations" officer, wrote of an Arab "proclivity to praise themselves excessively and to attribute failures to some nefarious Western or Zionist plot." Drawing on the Egyptian intellectual Tareq Heggy, DeAtkine described this "very pronounced disinclination within the elite of the Arab world to admit any defect or failure" as "self-infatuation" (Patai 1973 [2007], xv). The performative contradiction of a psychological operations officer defending a failed military occupation by adducing Arab intellectuals who agreed with him about the disinclination of elite Arabs to admit any defect was always somewhat laughable. However, the whole conceit has become even more difficult to sustain as politics across the West have themselves taken a turn for the paranoid and self-exonerating. Amidst attempts to ban the popular Chinese-owned video-sharing platform TikTok and better regulate Facebook and other social media platforms, mainstream American politicians like Joseph Biden and Hillary Clinton blamed Russian and Chinese influence operations for their electoral woes. Not to be outdone, their upstart opponent, President Donald Trump, has turned a conspiratorial "deep state" into a powerful narrative foil and scapegoat. While much has been written about how social media has helped mainstream conspiracism by furnishing new channels for the dissemination of previously marginal ideas, I am more interested here in how they seem to have made elites more paranoid—and how this has helped move conspiracism and anxieties about the existence (or lack thereof) of a "deep state" to the heart of formal geopolitics.

Yet even the paranoid can have enemies. The idea of the deep state often represents a baseless conspiracy theory, but it emerged from a very concrete and well-documented set of events in Turkey—a country that witnessed several successive military coups, numerous counterinsurgencies, and widely publicized scandals unearthing corrupt ties between organized crime, the security services, and other facets of the state (Sooyler 2015). The most notorious of the latter began with a fatal car crash in 1996. While a member of parliament survived the crash, those killed included the deputy chief of the Istanbul police, a former leader of Turkey's shadowy nationalist group the "Gray Wolves" (who was on Interpol's "red list" for his involvement in multiple murders), and his mistress. The long-term defeat of Turkey's secularists and the rise of the Islamist Justice and Development Party have afforded a unique window into how the country's secular establishment cemented its power during the twentieth century through a wide-ranging prosecution that ensued from what is known as the Ergenekon case. For Turkish nationalists, Ergenekon is a mythical valley where the Turkish people were led to safety by a gray wolf. The myth articulates a paternalistic belief that the common people and even the formal political leadership cannot be fully trusted, and that the survival of the nation depends on the existence of "wolves" who are willing to step outside of normal ethics and morality (Kaya 2009; Unver 2009). Aside from the widespread coverage, the case and the wider Turkish debate around the "deep state" has found artistic expression in the wildly popular Turkish drama *Valley of Wolves*, which follows a police officer as he goes "under cover" to fight the nexus of organized crime and Western intelligence controlling his country.

Such modes of extra-parliamentary politics came home with a vengeance to the United States on the sixth of January in 2021, when Donald Trump attempted to prevent the certification of his opponent as the winner of the presidential election. Claiming the election was being stolen and often citing the communiqués of an anonymous, self-described member of the security services named "Q," crowds attempted to lay siege to the Capitol building and halt the proceedings. In the ensuing prosecutions, more than 890 people were found guilty of federal crimes for their involvement. The demographics of these prosecutions have become a subject of public interest, and one study suggested that more than a third were small-business owners and almost 20 percent were current or former law enforcement or military personnel (Denbeaux and Crawley 2023). The one person to die from gunfire—just outside the chambers as legislators were being evacuated in the face of the advancing crowd—had previously served fourteen years in the Air Force (Barry et al. 2021). Against the stereotype of the conspiracy theorist as the marginalized naïf who fails to grasp the nature of the state, those caught up here were often intimately familiar with the state and its workings.

That those convicted of wrongdoing in connection with the attack on Congress were all pardoned by Trump in 2025 in one of his first official acts might retrospectively validate at least some of their ideas about the nature of the "deep state," yet it mostly underlines how the deep state is both chimerical and politically useful.[1] Despite the frequent tendency to paint conspiracy theory as a primarily anti-systemic ideology, it is hard to ignore the fact that states are often enthusiastic producers and disseminators of conspiracy theories—and not just in the Middle East. What is striking about the Euro-American case is not so much that there is actually any less reliance on conspiracy theory as a tool of statecraft, but more the incessant insistence that it is primarily other people who do this. Perhaps the epitome of this, as Eve Sedgwick and others have noted, is the profound complacency of Richard Hofstadter's *The Paranoid Style in American Politics* (1963), which sought to banish paranoia to the "left" and "right" fringes of American politics with self-assured evenhandedness during the brief interregnum between McCarthyism and Nixonism (Sedgwick 2002, 142–143).

As Sedgwick notes, paranoia is not so much an affect as a theory about affects—and a strong one at that, which is not to say that it is always a correct one. Put briefly, Sedgwick frames paranoia around the imperative that there should be no unpleasant surprises (Sedgwick 2002, 130). Because there is simply no end to the unpleasant surprises one might encounter, anticipating them by modeling them conceptually may be endlessly productive as an epistemic project, but to what end? Is it even effective in lessening the unpleasantness of the surprise? What does placing so much faith in exposure (as Sedgwick puts it) really yield? Quite a bit, it turns out. While Sedgwick attempts to adopt the pose of the extreme cynic in asking what we would learn that we did not know already if the AIDS virus had been deliberately invented to wage biological warfare on gays and other marginalized groups, such details matter a lot—as many of my Jordanian interlocutors insisted amidst similar debates around the origins of the coronavirus. The relative admixture of malice and callous indifference can determine the shape and size of political coalitions—and therefore, ignoring how such determinations are mobilized in political claims-making risks its own complacencies. Perhaps nothing epitomizes the political efficacy of paranoia better than the coup d'état and its close relative, the "counter-coup," in which different constellations of power inside and outside of the state mobilize to assert the reality of their control while frustrating what they perceive to be the similar designs of their rivals.

In what follows, I am particularly interested in how the imaginative (if often paranoid) work around the concept of the "deep state" in contemporary, highly networked societies attempts to negotiate the increasing complexity and seeming autonomy of what moderns call "the state." In the 1990s, Jacques Derrida fretted that the emerging digital technologies of his day threatened to "[introduce] the police everywhere," potentially realizing a totalitarian, deontological ethic that he traced back to Kant's thought. He wrote that the "absolutely internalized police has its eyes and its ears everywhere, its detectors *a priori* in our internal telephones, our emails and the most secret faxes of our private lives" (2000, 69). Yet if the eyes and ears of the state are everywhere, this also opens up intriguing imaginative possibilities: perhaps anyone can play the role of the eyes and ears of the state. Maybe anyone can be the police. One guise in which this emerges is the popular phenomenon of so-called sous-veillance, where everyday citizens attempt to expose the crimes of the powerful by leveraging the virality of social media. However, I hope to argue that insurrectionary projects represent another contemporary manifestation of the new imaginative possibilities that new media can afford. Increasingly, everyone can indulge in the fantasy of playing the police. In this spirit, I define the deep state as an institutional phenomenon in which some elements within the state apparatus (or at least elements identifying strongly with that apparatus) attack other elements in the name of defending the state.

Here, I draw further inspiration from the recent revival of interest in anthropology in the work of A. M. Hocart, specifically his contention that the "machinery of government" was "blocked out" in the idiom of ritual and theological speculation, "not as a system of government, but of an organization to promote life, fertility [and] prosperity" ([1952] 1970, 3). Attempting to take this observation to its logical conclusion, David Graeber and Marshall Sahlins (2017) have noted that many of the societies that anthropologists have traditionally called "egalitarian" were—from their own perspective—nothing of the sort. Instead, as Sahlins puts it, such societies are usually governed by powerful "metapersons" (including the dead, divinities, and "species-masters") that give the impression to the outside observer that social hierarchy is not so much absent as displaced from human relations onto other sorts of relations that those of a more Cartesian bent might call natural or supernatural (Graeber and Sahlins 2017, 24). My interest here is not in the evolutionary just-so story or the ontological speculation about the merits of monism and dualism, but rather in the relationship between leveling practices and the concrete effects of the imaginative work of building a cosmic bureaucracy, the workings of which are always tantalizingly close to view.

My focus on this chapter will not be on instances in which paranoia and conspiracy theory turn out to be epistemologically valid—though plenty of such cases exist in the region's history, from the Sykes-Picot Agreement to the fabrication of evidence of weapons of mass destruction that justified the 2003 invasion of Iraq. Rather, I hope to highlight how even false intuitions about the lineaments of the deep state's machinations can be politically and socially productive. Here I follow a wider trend in anthropology toward theorizing conspiracy less in terms of its accurate or inaccurate representation of reality and more as a mode of social action that does things (Masco and Wedeen 2024). I begin at the margins, with accounts of marginalized people far from authority who sought unsuccessfully to mimic the machinations of the deep state, before moving to instances where increasingly powerful individuals were caught up in conspiracies that were—much to their detriment—all too real. I begin with the sad case of a murder in the town near where I was living during my dissertation fieldwork in which local youths allegedly attempted to copy what they had seen on the Turkish television show *Valley of Wolves*. I then shift to a murder trial that became a minor cause célèbre in which a Jordanian soldier opened fire on four US military trainers, successfully convincing many that he had been defending Jordan in doing so and problematizing Jordan's long-standing alliance with the West. I conclude with a case that struck the royal household itself, leading to the former Crown Prince Hamza being accused of sedition. The strong implication of the ensuing prosecutions was that the Trump administration had sought to replace Jordan's king with a more pliant alternative who would facilitate Trump's "Deal of the Century" by aligning Jordan even more closely with Israel, the United Arab Emirates, and Saudi Arabia within the unifying genealogical framework of the "Abraham Accords."[2] Conspiracy here emerges not as a deviation from the political norm, but rather as a manifestation of normal politics. Even so, however, I hope to emphasize that it is not always easy for even the most politically sophisticated to differentiate between efficacious manifestations of the deep state and their many impostors.

Valley of Wolves

One summer morning in 2012 as I was coming into the local market town of Madaba, I saw a column of armored personnel carriers and larger troop transporters lining the road to the offices of the municipality. The bus driver cursed the Hamideh tribe as we drove by, giving a pretty clear indication of who he blamed for what was about to happen. Having encountered several tribal clashes already by this point, I went and did my shopping quickly under the assumption that the fighting would not break out until the weather had cooled down more. Once in the shops, gossip about the impending tribal clashes was rife along with accompanying political commentary. One woman told the man at the till, "It needs to be a strong punishment so there will be fear." The shopkeeper tersely agreed, and, seeing that I was lingering, replied, "I gave you your change." Feeling shameless, I replied, "I know, but I want to hear what you're saying. I want to know why the town is full of gendarmerie." The shopkeeper replied that some youths from the Hamideh had killed someone from the Azideh. He continued, "Now there is a tribal clash (*mushājara 'ashā'iriyya*). If the state (*al-dawla*) solves this problem, it will be over tomorrow. If it's between the tribes, they won't solve it in seventy years. But the tribes are stronger than the state here (*al-'ashā'ir agwa min ad-dawla huna*)."

I would hear many iterations of this story in the coming days, albeit with a range of variations and embroiderings, depending on the sensibilities and loyalties of the speaker. Most agreed that (to quote a few common refrains): "It's something between the Hamideh and the Azideh." "They killed a taxi driver. Ḥarām! He had a wife and a child." "It was something about drugs." However, a far more bizarre story began to emerge soon after when online news sites and legacy, government-backed newspapers like *Al-Ra'i* alike began to attribute the crime to an adolescent attempt to imitate the Turkish serial drama *Valley of Wolves*. According to a confession the police extracted from the killers, the youths (ranging in age from seventeen to twenty) had sought to form an intelligence cell to fight corruption and crime, convincing themselves that the slain taxi driver was engaged in some sort of nefarious affair. They had lured him to his death and then taken his taxi and abandoned it (Al-Marayat 2012).

For some of my neighbors, the killing cemented a set of wider fears about the malign effects of the media. One man seemed particularly eager to discuss the case with me and asked what I had heard. I replied that I heard a bunch of things: Drugs, some secret society. . . . The man corrected me: "No. They were imitating a Turkish series called *Valley of Wolves*." I wanted to hear more about his reasoning, so I said that I had read that in the newspaper but was not convinced. He exclaimed, "You mean you don't see kids acting out what they see on television? I'll give you an example. *Tom and Jerry*. Everyone likes *Tom and Jerry*. It's the most popular show of all time maybe. Well, sometimes children imitate it. People in America see violent movies and then go shoot their classmates at school. Right or not?" He appealed here as well to his undergraduate studies in psychology. I replied, "I'm with you," but, wanting to hear his response, I asked: "Does art imitate life or does life imitate art?" His wife immediately said, "Art imitates life!" and offered that she thought children were drawn to media that reflected their interests, noting that her boys preferred romantic themes while her daughter preferred violence.

Suffice it to say that not everyone was convinced by the emerging official narrative—or even cared enough to learn the details. One man said, "Maybe drugs. Some people say honor. I don't know." Another speculated: "A fight over drugs. Someone owes someone money and so they kidnap him and take his car." I replied, "So wait. Was it theft or an argument over drugs?" He replied, "Well, when people are involved in drugs, they get greedy." Later that evening, I ran into some people who were related to the victim through matrilineal ties. By this time, it was dusk and the fighting had begun. A young man had just returned from Madaba with the latest news: "Madaba is burning. They're attacking the Hamideh market and the police. They set the police kiosk on fire. . . . The Azideh are demanding that the police give the criminals to them so they can hang them in front of the municipality building. This is their right in tribal law and Sharia [*qiṣāṣ*]. To kill a Muslim with no reason? The punishment is death." When I asked about the motive, I was told that the men from the Hamideh were selling drugs and feared that the driver's brother was going to inform on them, so they kidnapped the youth's older brother (the driver) and killed him. I responded that it didn't sound logical. If the driver was going to inform *before* they killed his brother, certainly he would inform *after* they killed his brother. The men shrugged. It was certainly a lot of crimes: "Drugs, kidnapping, theft, murder. . . . It's everything!"

Soon, we were joined by their cousin, an employee at the airport who used to be a police officer, who was excited to offer what he took to be his expert opinion and began talking at length: "Well, the Hamideh who have shops in the Hamideh market are eating wind right now. The criminals are from Dhiban (about forty-five minutes south of here) but the Azideh live right next to the Hamideh market. There are a lot of [Hamideh] too. . . . Maybe five or seven thousand. . . . And a lot of youths too. And the young and the old are of one mentality. They are together, and they are angry." One of the assembled men replied, "But how did they find the killers?" He said, "I used to be a police officer, and I can tell you. They used the phones." Asked what would happen to the killers, he said, "In this country? They'll get maybe twenty years. They'll leave prison before they're forty." His cousin replied: "You don't think they'll get the death penalty?" Again referring to his police experience, he said, "You see, these are a kind of youth (*shabāb*) called 'adolescents' (*murāhiqūn*). You see, an adolescent is like a youth, but they are under eighteen. They are not of sound mind yet. They can be violent and do crazy things. So it is difficult to hold them responsible. So to give you an example, the Azideh have many of these 'adolescents.' They are the ones making the problems now. It is difficult to punish such people."

I want to underline here that while the different factual claims were of great importance to those who asserted them, I am not in a particularly good position to judge and do not wish to privilege any one interpretation. Proximity to victimhood (or authority of various sorts) might confer some weight to certain theories, but these positionalities might also furnish motives for underlining (or for that matter downplaying) the wanton and criminal nature of the crime. Such special pleading is rife at the nexus of Jordan's tribal justice and official law. Over many years spent haunting the *dīwāns* of prominent men in Jordan, I have heard all sorts of sob stories about why people have landed in various legal predicaments, revealing a true wilderness of mirrors (Dresch 2000). To boil down a common tale, the relative who was caught with the large bag of contraband actually believed in good faith that they were participating in legitimate work in defense of the nation, something more plausible when the person in question at least has a job in the security services, of course. Yet as absurd as such claims may be, they can still mobilize important coalitions of actors—especially when wider structural factors encourage it and foreclose alternative courses of action. In this case, the mobilization was primarily negative: the Hamideh here "ate wind" and could not mobilize an effective response, while the Azideh united in collective outrage over a brazen murder. The story about imitating *Valley of Wolves* might have been useful in facilitating a confession, but the family of the victim was not exactly buying it. However, not every attempt to actualize various fantasies of the deep state ends in such sad abject failure—even if it does not ultimately succeed either.

The Abu Tayeh File

The "Abu Tayeh File," as it came to be known, was shrouded in controversy and secrecy from the beginning. The Jordanian at the center of it was a man named Ma'arek Abu Tayeh, a member of the Huwaytat tribe, which includes tens of thousands of tribesmen in Saudi Arabia, Egypt, and southern Jordan. What is more, he shared a name with 'Auda Abu Tayeh, the leader of the "Great Arab Revolt," the British-Arab assault on the crumbling Ottoman Empire at the end of World War I that brought the Hashemites to power and cemented the political accommodation between the monarchy and the tribes. Kinsmen described Ma'arek as a typical family man who had spent the better part of his adult life in the Jordanian Air Force. At the time of the incident, he was on guard duty in front of the base in his hometown of Jafr. While everyone agreed there was a firefight that left Abu Tayeh injured and three US military trainers dead, this was where accounts began to differ,[3] with supporters of Abu Tayeh offering a range of rationales defending him against accusations that he had murdered the trainers "in cold blood." When Abu Tayeh was convicted of their murder by a state security court that had largely operated under the radar of mainstream Jordanian news since the incident, the south of Jordan erupted in protests fueled in large part by social media and tribal Facebook pages. The genealogical link between the Abu Tayeh name and the current political accommodation between his kinsmen, the West, and the Hashemite family seemed to open up an irresistible imaginative space for reconceptualizing relationships between kin groups, the nation, and the great powers.

Ma'arek's defense in court sought to counteract the government's claims that (for reasons that had purportedly nothing to do with terrorism but that were never entirely clear) he had intentionally and without justification opened fire on four US military trainers who had been operating out of the base for some time. His public defense, mirroring the initial official account offered by the Jordanian authorities themselves, was that the Americans had failed to identify themselves, and that his response had followed the rules of engagement under which he was supposed to operate given the heightened threat of terrorism. In numerous discussions with his kinsmen at weddings and other gatherings (including interviews with some of his most prominent public defenders), there seemed to be genuine shock when he was convicted. The Huwaytat had been under the impression that this would all be hushed up, and that if they cooperated with the security apparatus, their kinsman would not be punished for what were clearly the Americans' missteps. They believed that his prosecution after the initial, exculpatory claims by the Jordanian authorities had been little more than an attempt to pander to the Americans. Even after the conviction, some of the more cautious argued that the family should take a docile stance and wait for the families of the Americans to relax their pressure on the US embassy so that the king could pardon Abu Tayeh.

In the absence of coverage on most of the major news sites and with most of the protests happening in isolated, rural areas, tribal Facebook groups that spread like wildfire in the aftermath of the verdict seemed to be the real center of the action, with the largest nearing one hundred thousand followers. What had previously been sleepy clearinghouses for the electoral slates of various sections of the tribe morphed into the aspiring voices of a tribe—indeed the aspiring voices of a nation. The content highlighted youths in Bedouin regalia engaged in hit-and-run acts of vandalism and sabotage across the southern desert, especially burning tires and waving guns in the streets. These scenes were accompanied by threats to cut the power and water supplies to the capital and begin a wider insurrection—all expressed as a defense of Jordan's sovereignty. Amidst the photographs and the communiqués, a large conference was organized that drew support from thousands of tribesmen from all over the country, gaining widespread press coverage, whereas hit-and-run attacks on isolated and unguarded stretches of infrastructure dramatized through viral pictures and video had not.

Among the family and, increasingly, among a wide cross-section of Jordanians, a more sinister account of what was going on began to spread. In a lighter version of the pro-Ma'arek narrative, a group of violent, corrupt, drunk, and out-of-control mercenaries had come back after a bad night out and attacked the base wantonly. Especially for those closer to the family and to the base where this had happened, an even more sinister version percolated. This version focused on the covert US aid to the Syrian opposition that seemed to be at the heart of the case: conflicts over the sizable amounts of money, weapons, and training opportunities that were at stake. Here, Ma'arek became the fall guy for war profiteers. In this version of the story, the soldiers were not even necessarily killed by Ma'arek. Many believed that they were "liquidated" after the fact in a cover-up,[4] along with a number of Syrians who were purportedly buried somewhere in the desert.[5] Kinsmen appealed to their intensive local knowledge of the isolated desert terrain, claiming (to me, among others) that they had stayed quiet about what was happening at the base for a decade. A common refrain was, "People wouldn't have believed us anyway. . . . But we live there. We know everything."

In a wide-ranging interview at a villa in the capital with of one of Ma'arek's defenders with ties to the royal court and the security services, family members were eager to name names and counsel me that US intelligence assets were out of control and needed to be reined in. In a moment of anger, the patriarch became especially agitated: "Fox News understands a little and Al-Jazeera English understands a little. . . . [But] For nine months there has been a campaign against us. All they say is 'killed in cold blood, killed in cold blood, killed in cold blood.' It's all documented but they only publish his name, Abu Tayeh, Abu Tayeh, Abu Tayeh, cold blood, cold blood." The phrase seemed to drip off his tongue like black bile. Despite my best efforts to assure everyone I spoke to that I was neither a spy nor a back channel to the US embassy, family members pleaded their case with alacrity. At times, they seemed genuinely convinced of their kinsman's innocence and determined to find an American who would hear them out. They even told me that, in light of the hundred-year, mutually beneficial relationship between the family and the West, they had made extensive efforts to reach out to the families of the dead to explain what a terrible misunderstanding this all had been. At other times, though, they complained bitterly of sky-high unemployment in the community, a lack of development, low pay in the security services, and exclusion from emerging paths to upward social mobility, implying none too subtly that these issues might have also factored into the case somehow.

The attempt to turn the Abu Tayeh File into a cause célèbre quickly ran into a range of problems, though. Members of the Abu Tayeh section of the Huwaytat resented how a rival faction known as the bin Jazi had come to control the Facebook group with the most followers. In an ironic recapitulation of history, this was the same tribal section that had best capitalized on the Hashemite ascendency and left the Abu Tayeh section of the family working government jobs in the desert while the bin Jazi moved into elite positions in the capital and became the paramount sheikhs. At the same time, the killing of a Jordanian handyman in Amman by an Israeli embassy guard over a screwdriver (purportedly one which could have been used as a weapon) put pressure on supporters of the two cases to combine causes. Yet both eyed the other with suspicion, not wanting to fully dilute a family issue with a broader national issue. Members of the Huwaytat were keen to distinguish their "genuine" case from the "true crime" that had occurred in Amman, and to remind me that they were not like those city folk. As a number of Ma'arek's tribesmen insisted to me, "There are only ten real Jordanians in Amman." Ultimately, combining forces proved impossible. The specter of deep state conspiracies and foreign interference could be the basis of powerful political alliances, but only within limits. One of Ma'arek's more tireless defenders reasoned, "If I put [out] 'the great Satan' and 'Death to America,' they will all stand with us, all of Amman . . . Al-Manar (Hezbollah's TV station), Al-Mayadin (a Lebanese station), Russia Today, leftist parties, rightist parties, the *ḥirāk* [social movements] . . . one word issued from the Bedouin and they will all stand with us." Yet in the end, he could not seem to do it.

The final blow to the Abu Tayeh cause seemed to come when, after weeks of protests and angry demands for surveillance footage of the clash to be released, the Jordanian government released a video that was then widely disseminated via the online media (Philips and Hubbard 2017). The video showed in painstaking detail a group of soldiers arriving at a base—all meticulously following proper procedures—being shot at for about four minutes while trying to deescalate the situation as the Jordanian soldiers in the base looked on. Many of Abu Tayeh's kinsmen found the video comical at first, joking that "he's not Rambo" and that the movements of the soldiers looked stilted, like bad acting. What I always wondered was why none of Abu Tayeh's Jordanian comrades did anything to stop him. Yet while his kinsmen were adamant that the video was fake, most interest in the case—including the protests—died out soon afterward. At the time of writing, the family is still waiting for the king to come to their aid. Most tellingly, the case never seemed to be able to produce a leader with his own name and face. Instead, it was as if the eponymous Abu Tayeh himself was the only person suitably positioned to lead the revolt—from beyond the grave. Others shrank from the task, either afraid to risk their villas and titles or not of sufficient account to matter.

Ultimately, the actual course of events here is somewhat beside the point. What is more important is how particular narratives about Abu Tayeh's fateful encounter with the four US military trainers created an imaginative space in which different political coalitions could think about their relationship to the state and also experiment with alternative configurations. In particular, of course, what made this so irresistible was the fact that the younger Abu Tayeh's killings allowed his kin to reimagine his eponymous ancestor's own fateful decision to ally with the West differently: what if the elder Abu Tayeh had turned on Lawrence of Arabia and the British instead of inviting them in? What then? The Huwaytat of course live far from the capital and are vastly overrepresented in the military and security services, which provides a financial lifeline to their often-isolated villages. Yet this does not mean that they can simply be bought—or that they do not wonder if there might be better offers out there. The brief moment of political unity forged around the younger Abu Tayeh was an intimation of significant dissent to Jordan's foreign policy within the security services. Yet it was never able to deal with the contradictions between Jordanian nationalism's skepticism of alliances with Western powers and its concerns about the political implications of Jordan's large Palestinian population should the pro-Western monarchy ever be replaced with something more representative. Thus, the family could not bring themselves to ally with a Palestinian family whose kinsman had been killed at the Israeli embassy. The abortive nature of the cause célèbre around the Abu Tayeh case (especially as the courts unified against him and new evidence was released) merely underlines that the deep state is an often-chimerical phenomenon, but one that can take in even politically savvy operators in self-valorizing ways. This is because the idea of the deep state keys into important features of everyday work of security provision in modern states (including the interplay between publicity and secrecy, official and unofficial channels, and the letter and spirit of the law itself).

A Very Jordanian Coup

It is one thing for an impressionable youth to find himself too deep in a conspiratorial world of murderous deep state intrigue, but it is obviously somewhat different when the murderer is a longtime veteran of the security services. It at least implies that any delusions involved are not primarily due to a lack of familiarity with the workings of power. Perhaps Abu Tayeh too was driven by a kind of madness (I was struck by how the specter of a highly specific personal sleight lingered behind many of the accusations despite resisting clear articulation). Yet one can hardly blame the impetuousness of youth. As I have been arguing, though, it is even harder to dismiss claims about the deep state when prominent tribal personalities and veterans of the security apparatus take those claims seriously and begin to act as if they were true. A decade on from the Arab Spring in 2021, even Jordan's royal household itself found that it was no longer immune from such intrigues when Jordan's former Crown Prince Hamza was accused of plotting to overthrow Jordan's king—possibly even with the assistance of the Trump administration. Again, paranoid conspiracy theorizing is best understood not in epistemological terms, but rather for how it mobilizes coalitions and enables political claims-making.

When I first heard that Jordan's former Crown Prince Hamza had been formally implicated in a suspected coup, I immediately thought back to numerous conversations over the years that I had been party to in which Jordanian nationalists from tribal backgrounds with anti-monarchist views had pinned their hopes on Hamza. These were people who were dissatisfied with Jordan's neoliberal turn under Abdullah, which, although it had started with the hollowing out of Jordan's public sector under his father, had really accelerated under Abdullah's reign. Hailing from families who had historically been rewarded with the very jobs that were now less and less desirable as structural adjustment forced greater austerity on the public sector, such erstwhile regime loyalists sought to reconcile their historic loyalty to Jordan and the Hashemites. A common move here was to blame the king's marriage to the Palestinian-Jordanian Queen Rania as a sort of national betrayal, despite the fact that the Hashemites themselves hailed from the Arabian peninsula. Given this background, the whole scenario sounded like something plucked from the midst of a rant one might hear in a café or an informal gathering at someone's house, perhaps after a series of scurrilous accusations about drug dealing, sex trafficking, and sorcery. Yet here it was being taken extremely seriously, not just by the Jordanian authorities, but by the global media.

The details were—as in the other two cases I have described here—rather murky and contradictory, and again it was never totally clear who was really setting up whom. After all, it can be lonely at the top. As the "Crown Prince" from the time of his half-brother's ascent to the throne in 1999 until 2004, Hamza was always going to be a lightning rod of sorts, focalizing the aspirations of disenchanted loyalists and the anxieties of the incumbent leadership (BBC 2021). Yet over time, Hamza also began to style himself as an anti-corruption crusader of sorts—always a dangerous proposition for a man in his position—and even criticized his half-brother the king. The precipitating event according to numerous news sources was a widely publicized case of medical negligence at the height of the COVID-19 pandemic when six patients at a new hospital facility in the town of Salt died due to an oxygen shortage. When Hamza visited the bereaved families amidst protests over their deaths before the king could pay his respects, it was seen as a major breach of protocol. Suleiman Al-Khalidi (2021) of Reuters quoted a "senior official" who called the visit "the straw that broke the camel's back."

When the palace tried to place Prince Hamza under house arrest, he responded by releasing a video in English in which he complained of the lack of tolerance for dissent in the country while denying that he was part of any conspiracy.[6] The video went viral. His mother, the American-born Queen Noor, took to Twitter, where she wrote obliquely that "truth and justice will prevail for all the innocent victims of this wicked slander" (Sweis et al. 2021). In a since-deleted response, Princess Firyal more directly criticized the "blind ambition" of "Queen Noor and her sons" (Sweis et al. 2021). However, the palace moved quickly to repair the breach. Within forty-eight hours, a typed letter signed by Hamza was released in which he affirmed his loyalty to the king (Ward 2021). The next year, the palace released another letter from Hamza in which he apologized and asked the king for forgiveness (BBC 2022).

The swirling rumors in Jordan were virtually indistinguishable from what I read in the English-language press. In the prosecutions of the two central conspirators, Bassem Awadallah and Sharif Hassan bin Zaid, prosecutors relied heavily on intercepted communications in which Hamza had sought to induce tribal leaders to swear allegiance to him. *The Guardian* reported on the basis of "regional sources" that the episode might have been an "epilogue" to Trump's Abraham Accords and attempts to advance his elusive "Deal of the Century" between Israel and neighboring Arab states (Chulov and Safi 2021). Here, the journalists Martin Chulov and Michael Safi argued it was significant that Awadallah had been a key figure in the Abraham Accords negotiations, which had threatened to marginalize Jordan and its king, especially his status as the official custodian of the Al-Aqsa mosque. Yet speculation simultaneously ran rife that the whole plot was overblown (if not outright fabricated) to discourage dissent at a time when the king was subject to a wide range of criticisms (Ward 2021).

Again, the issue is not so much whether a particular account matches the paranoid structure of a conspiracy theory—because almost any plausible account must admit the existence of plotting somewhere—but rather how particular accounts can plausibly mobilize useful political coalitions. In this regard, the fact that this happened after a change in leadership in the United States is almost certainly significant—and not only because important evidence was purportedly handed over to Jordanian officials by US intelligence in March of 2021 (Chulov and Safi 2021). Rather, the replacement of Trump with a more sympathetic administration increased the king's room for maneuver and ability to settle scores. To the degree that the coup attempt was ever real rather than pretextual on the part of Jordan's king and security services, such reports suggest an act of desperation as a group of increasingly marginalized retainers sought to maintain their relevance and privileges even as powerful patrons fell away and the walls began to close in around them.

Conclusion

While the state (*polis*) is the *locus classicus* of politics, recent decades have seen an increasing focus on the role of the media in politics in both scholarship (Calhoun 1992; Habermas 1989; Lynch 1999; 2005; Warner 2002) and in the popular imagination. However, the increasing prominence of the act of mediation itself has had strange effects on how people conceptualize the state, and here Jordan and the wider Middle East might (if anything) merely be early adopters. In this chapter, I have tried to argue that the widespread fascination with the figure of the "deep state" that has emerged of late in scholarly and lay explanatory frameworks reflects—but also advances—a marked renegotiation of the state-society divide (Mitchell 1991) that has often been embodied in the shifting technopolitical configuration of the so-called "media." With its odd mix of unpredictably anarchic social dynamics and grindingly panoptic surveillance, social media seems to simultaneously promote the notion that real power must lie elsewhere, just out of view. In this sense, folk theories of the "deep state" represent one way of "bringing the state back in" (Skocpol 1985) at a time when reports of its death might be premature. Yet—crucially—the deep state is not simply a description of reality, but rather an attempt to bring new realities into being through acts of collective imagination.

As I noted in the introduction and first chapter, Middle Eastern countries like Jordan merely accentuate the more general transformation in regulatory frameworks that have diffused globally in recent decades. If the twentieth century saw what the historian of Russia Peter Kenez has called "the birth of the propaganda state" (1985), then the twenty-first century at least initially seemed to see that propaganda state in full retreat. It is easy to forget that there was a time when even proponents of liberal democracy saw state propaganda (Lipmann 1922) or at least state-backed progressive education (Dewey 1927) not as impediments to the liberal state but indeed as some of their most important tools. Yet times have changed—and not just in the heartlands of liberal democracy. Even self-styled authoritarian regimes like those in Russia (Price et al. 2002; Sparks 2008; Skillen 2016) and China (Brady 2008; 2012; He 2000; Lynch 1999; Zhao 1998; Zhu 2012) have largely outsourced their media operations since the 1980s, a trend reflected in countries like Jordan as well. At the same time, however, the need to shape media coverage never went away—the modes of action have simply become more oblique and indeed conspiratorial. A period of hybridization in which public and private became more entwined than ever has ensued.

Authority itself consequently comes to seem both more diffuse and more totalizing. Perhaps the most notable manifestation of this is a shift away from the authoritative, monologic voice of official media toward the increasing authority—even within official discourse—accorded to found evidence in the form of security recordings, intercepted conversations, and other "leaks" (El-Ariss 2019). If the figures of the state and the media no longer seem like plausible loci of authority, it must reside somewhere else that is both submerged within the obvious institutions of authority but also boasts unknowable depths. Based on the Jordanian case, I would argue that the associated changes are both global and local in nature, combining broader shifts in technology and elite governance paradigms with deep local histories of contestation and accommodation involving global powers, local government institutions, and their citizenries. At least in Jordan, far from being a purely disruptive phenomenon, the emerging accommodation between old authority structures and new media is breathing new life into tribal modes of social organization whose decline has been predicted for well over a century (Layne 1994, 14). The resulting dynamic offers new ways to act on behalf of lineages of various sizes and, indeed, the nation itself—but without necessarily needing either sheikhs or formal state backing. At the same time, however, astute observers know well that the deep state is a chimerical and elusive entity, and that it is not always easy to differentiate between efficacious manifestations of the deep state and their many imitators.

CHAPTER 6

Mercy

In recent years social media has been widely credited with catalyzing a number of movements from below concerned with questions of punishment, repair, and justice. Anti-police and anti-carceral movements have spread themselves by exploiting the viral appeal of shocking images of everyday state violence, leading to protests against police brutality and extrajudicial murders. While this phenomenon is often associated in the anglophone world with #BlackLivesMatter and the protests that followed the police killings of Michael Brown and George Floyd, it has also manifested in related movements in Latin America (Scott 2019) and Africa (Táíwò 2022). In fact, the Arab Spring itself was initially catalyzed by protests against police violence, from Mohamed Bouazizi's self-immolation in protest of police harassment and his subsequent transformation into the symbol of the Tunisian revolution to the role of the Kulna Khaled Said Facebook page in sparking the Egyptian revolution as it transitioned from disseminating videos of police brutality to calling people into the streets (Amar 2013). At the heart of this global upsurge of criticism directed at the increasing role of the state in dispensing justice has been a critique of how logics of disposability have rendered certain populations disposable and unworthy or incapable of rehabilitation, especially the poor, the marginalized, and the minoritized.

At the same time, marginalized people and especially women have used the public and highly distributed nature of social media to draw attention to abuses of the powerful that were once deemed private, often associated with #MeToo. Both of these trends have manifested in particular Jordanian form in the ethnography so far, from the protests against Jordanian, US, and Israeli security personnel detailed in chapter 5 ("**The Deep State**") to the pervasive fears of public humiliation and "cutting the face" that I described in chapter 4 ("**Face**"). It is notable that these globally networked movements from below have in turn catalyzed equally global elite moral panics that have developed into networked social movements in their own right. Between the demands from below and the elite backlash against them, the issue of carcerality looms large as often marginalized people who lack confidence in the state and its carceral systems seek to evade and frustrate those systems but also to build something more responsive to their needs in its place. At the heart of all these debates has been the fundamental question of when and how to forgive and forget. That brings me to the topic of mercy, which I will argue might help cast some of these debates in a more illuminating light.

In this chapter, I will take a by now familiar tack of beginning with an account of how the Bedouin tribespeople I came to know in Jordan taught me to think differently about social media, here with a focus on the nature of justice and especially the instrumental role that *raḥma* (mercy) played in their thinking. I begin with the common aphorism that "prison is loss," laying out why the idea of prison offended the sensibilities of so many of my Bedouin interlocutors. I will then focus on a particular case I was especially close to (a car accident) and how it impressed upon me just how intimately Jordan's older systems of tribal justice have become interwoven with the modern administrative state, in ways that allow perpetrators to be nonviolently diverted from the carceral system, often to the mutual satisfaction of victims and victimizers alike. However, not wanting to leave the impression that this is utopian or egalitarian, I will then shift to focus on those who are still excluded by these forms of justice, especially women, the poor, and the poorly connected, emphasizing how media itself becomes politicized as a key strategic terrain in the struggle for justice. I will conclude with a wider consideration of the conservative and revolutionary potentials latent within the act of mercy, and specifically how the idea of mercy might help to move beyond a simplistic punitive-reparative binary in the pursuit of justice. At a time when carcerality seems almost inescapable as the centerpiece of any modern "justice system," I argue that the idea of mercy might offer a possible escape hatch.

"Prison Is Loss"

From my earliest days living in Jordan's southern desert, one thing that many of the self-styled Bedouin tribespeople I met were keen to discuss with me was the oddness—even perversity—of the prisons that they associated with European colonization.[1] It was something of a cliché for these Bedouin that "prison is loss," which could mean a number of things. Most obviously, as a replacement for the practice of paying blood money or *diyya*, incarceration struck many as grievously inadequate for the victim—who now received no restitution. Some even questioned whether prison was a punishment at all, and a number exclaimed incredulously that they even *feed* prisoners. What sort of punishment was this—and to whose benefit? In contrast—the reasoning went—taking away money was taking away something that people really wanted. Even better, that money could be reapportioned to people who had been wronged. While money (historically in the form of precious metals or livestock) could never fully make up for the loss of a life in the most extreme cases of harm, it was still a form of reified potentiality that could be generative in various ways. One could even use it to support new marriages and new families—even naming the first child after the deceased. Yet from a more distanced and benevolent perspective, there was also the loss of the opportunity to ask for and to grant mercy (*raḥma*)—with all its socially productive potentials. In fact, the more heinous the crime, the more inadequate monetary compensation could ever be. What I hope to argue in what follows is that Bedouin notions of mercy could not be reduced to a simplistic binary between forgiveness and revenge. Instead, my interlocutors generally preferred to reconcile these two impulses processually, as punitive impulses were meant to give way to reparative ones.

This emphasis on mercy among Bedouin tribespeople might initially seem incongruous given the many violent and punitive facets of Bedouin justice that I have already described at length, yet, as I will argue, that might be an effect of precisely this increasingly reified distinction between punishment and repair. In what follows, I will not shy away from the violence of burning people's houses, banishment (*jalwa*), and the right of *lex talionis*, from a claw for a claw to a life for a life (the latter known in Arabic by the Quranic term of art of *qiṣāṣ*). Nor will I neglect the forms of violent corporal punishment that Muslim jurists and Bedouin alike refer to as the *ḥudūd* or "boundaries" that include amputation, stoning, crucifixion, and lashing. Yet while there are certainly Bedouin—and Muslims more generally—that revel in the idea of violent retribution, this coexists with a widely held belief that the "boundaries" are precisely that: extreme solutions to extreme problems that need only be implemented in the most egregious cases. In fact, as my Bedouin interlocutors were often keen to emphasize when trying to convert me to Islam, the *ḥadīth* literature chronicling the prophet Muhammad's approach to justice is replete with examples of him finding creative reasons not to apply such sanctions. This is not merely a preoccupation of my Bedouin interlocutors either. This emphasis on the prophet's mercy is a long-standing facet of the tradition transcending traditional and modern or urban and rural binaries (see, for instance Qutb 1970, 145–147). Moreover, the contention I often heard that the *ḥudūd* were never intended to be implemented systematically on any sort of scale also finds support among modern scholars (Brown 2005, 180–181; Hallaq 2009, 311).

Without discounting how the *ḥudūd* have become entangled in confessional apologetics and polemics, it is worth considering how such punishments constitute merely a starting point for negotiations between victims, victimizers, and the wider community. Some men told me that Bedouin loved to commit adultery, and that this was why Islam was so appropriate for them: while the punishment was death, its implementation required four eyewitnesses to the act of penetration itself, making it virtually unenforceable. There were similar apologetic claims about theft, noting that extreme punishments were reserved for those who stole especially valuable things and did not steal out of need. I was often told that the Islamic golden age had no need for such punishments because their welfare policies solved poverty and the positive influence of living in a just society also led individuals to be more just. While such imaginaries predicated on past and/or future worlds of abundance might point to the more utopian and aspirational dimensions of Bedouin justice, they should not detract from the existence of a more hard-headed set of logics at work in the act of mercy.

As I have intimated, the idea of justice (*ʿadl*) in play here has a strong connotation of balancing, and indeed there was an obsession with reestablishing a respectable parity between the two "sides" in the conflict that manifested itself in many guises. Perhaps the most scandalous to modern sensibilities in Jordan was the practice of *ghirra*, in which a woman from the tribe of a murderer would be married to someone from the tribe of the victim until she bore them a child—at which point she could be divorced and returned to her family. I heard about this practice several times during my research on marriage, usually intended by my interlocutors as an example of how godless and wild Jordan had been in the past so that I would not romanticize it. However, some traditionalists told me about it with a sort of pride to poke at what they assumed to be my more modern sensibilities. One man even told me about how his own family had resolved a blood feud with such a marriage in the 1950s, noting with satisfaction that the woman bore the other tribe a daughter, releasing his tribe from their obligations without delivering a like-for-like replacement for the son they had lost.

Yet while Bedouin justice affords no shortage of avenues for human cruelty, it seeks to channel them toward a resolution, and here the idea of mercy comes into play. Early treatments of such patterns of feuding like Evans-Pritchard's *The Nuer* (1940) tended in high-functionalist fashion to privilege the rebalancing of relations between segments as the social structure's telos, which is not unreasonable given that ethnographic interlocutors emphasize how important this is. At the same time, the conflict itself can have generative effects too. Influenced by the Manchester School's focus on conflict, Emyrs Peters (1967) and Jacob Black-Michaud (1975) explored how social groupings themselves might emerge from these cycles of infraction, negotiation over restitution, and eventual reconciliation. For Peters, the temporal dimension is key: the process of atoning for a homicide must take at least four or five years, because "a single payment of the full amount would only terminate relationships. . . . Where there is no debt, there are no relationships. Debt must be allowed to run between groups, for it is this which creates obligations and perpetuates social relationships" (Peters 1967, 267). Peters here is extending a more general observation that the negotiation is in many ways more visible (if not also more important) than the blood money itself. With each round, the give-and-take of claim and counterclaim helps constitute not only the relationships between the sides but also their internal structures as groups in their own right. It is this work of mutual *recognition* (Sangren 2022) that my Bedouin interlocutors seemed to find most compelling, allowing them to move from enmity to, if not friendship, at least a sense of resolution. It seemed that this was what was ultimately at the heart of the common complaint that prison is "loss": that whatever one thought of the punishment being meted out, it could not complete the balancing operation that justice demanded.

Yet somewhat paradoxically, acts of mercy—the more flamboyant the better—can also become a means to frustrate that very desire for closure and resolution, cudgels that instantiate new kinds of relationship. Here, mercy emerges as a kind of sport, perhaps even what George Bataille (1949) might call a sort of "pure expenditure" that has the potential to channel society's excesses in new and generative directions. I have been told that in the old days, when the family of a victim was especially resistant to reconciling, the family of the murderer might strip the perpetrator naked and tie him to a horse bearing his own dagger and drive the animal into the victim's village. To kill someone so helpless would of course itself violate deeply ingrained expectations of graciousness, making it a safer gambit than it might appear at first blush. At the same time, as a move within a larger attempt to rebalance relations between the two "sides," the gracious refusal of the offer of a life for a life would still represent a power play in its own right. In this way, everyone involved could hope to maintain their own account of how they had ultimately gotten one over on the other side, evading a truly equal accounting.

The use of flamboyant acts of mercy as a cudgel persists in a fashion even within Jordan's criminal justice system. In a particularly memorable episode while I was calling on a friend, a man who had lost his son to a violent altercation brandished a pistol in front of us amidst a torrent of vitriol against his killer, boasting that he had fought for the lightest possible sentence for the murderer—so that he could kill him as soon as he was freed from prison (something he said he made clear in the trial, emphasizing that he wanted his son's killer to spend every day dreading his eventual release). Disturbed by this outburst, I asked my friend later if we should do something. He said no, that this was simply his way of regaining some semblance of control over the situation and coming to terms with the death of his son.

If most Muslims see mercy as a quintessentially Islamic value, it is worth noting that the system of justice being described here predates the advent of Islam and extends to Christian, Druze, Jewish, and polytheistic communities throughout North Africa, the Middle East, and Southern Europe (Black-Michaud 1975; Boehm 1984; Pely 2016). Like the Torah, the *Qur'ān* explicitly endorses the principle of a life for a life. Yet to relinquish this right in a case of murder by forgiving the murderer and sparing a life is a Godly act. This is something the speeches in truces and reconciliations and the texts of the agreements themselves were always at pains to make clear. Reflecting this sensibility, much of the action around truces and reconciliations is aimed toward extolling the virtues of mercy for the individual souls of victims as well as the wider community. Islam does, however, foreground the concept of mercy with alacrity—and it repeatedly encourages believers to reflect on it as a key virtue. In fact, the opening verse of the *Qur'ān* (which is itself typically used as a preamble to tribal truces) reads, "In the name of God the gracious (*al-raḥmān*) and the merciful (*al-raḥīm*)." Like its Hebrew cognate *racham*, *raḥma* is derived from the same root as the word for womb (*raḥim* or *rechem* in Hebrew) and connotes a refusal by a stronger party to exercise their rights over a weaker party—especially the right to revenge. Instead, believers are encouraged to forgive and extend mercy in the face of wrongdoing. Helping unrelated people with the payment of blood money to victims can even be a means of earning religious merit for oneself.

However, mercy takes on a very specific meaning in the context of Jordan's contemporary regime of overlapping legal codes, in which tribal law continues to play a very specific role. Moreover, because my Bedouin interlocutors are often so intimately tied to the security services, they are often extremely well placed to convert more familiar facets of the administrative state and its underlying technical infrastructures into fodder for their projects of withholding and ultimately conferring mercy. In what follows, I have tried to select two cases (a fatal crash and a case of domestic violence) that show the potential transformative power of mercy, but also its limitations and tendency to benefit those who benefit from patriarchy, personal wealth, proximity to state power, and—increasingly—the ability to plead one's case through the skillful manipulation of media. The aim here is very much to show a system that is anything but utopian, but hence far more plausible, and also to suggest that prison might not be as intrinsic to modern social order as is often assumed.

A Crash

For years I never really pursued these issues around justice and dispute resolution, but then a family I was close to was struck by a sadly familiar sort of tragedy: their kinsman was involved in a fatal car crash. It was all made more complex by the fact that he was a bus driver in the security services—and that he was clearly speeding along the winding rural roads when he collided with a tractor trailer, suffering life-changing injuries in the process, killing one man, and injuring tribesmen from across the kingdom who were returning home from the base where they had been stationed. Aside from the frequent hospital visits, the family was suddenly plunged into a complicated social, legal, and financial predicament. Since the police investigators had deemed their kinsman's driving to be reckless, he was potentially looking at serious criminal charges—possibly even something on the order of manslaughter. Moreover, the family of the deceased and the families of those injured were angry and demanded satisfaction in the form of blood money. In the coming months, my friends would have to walk a tightrope: mollify the victims through the institutions of tribal law and the payment of blood money, and, through securing their cooperation, dissuade the authorities from pursuing formal charges against their kinsman and imprisoning him.

What I remember the most are the phone calls, which were almost daily, for weeks on end at times. Being closest to the brother who had taken primary responsibility for the negotiations, I saw firsthand how his whole relationship to his phone was transformed by the constant demands. He would often sheepishly draw the phone from his pocket, check the number, furrow his brow, and decline to answer. This, in turn, would lead to calls rebuking him for not returning calls, and calls threatening his family with retaliation should they fail to make things right. There was also of course the need to raise money, which my friends made clear was deeply wounding to their pride. This necessarily involved expensive hospitality—itself often interrupted by more unpleasant phone calls—but while eager to maintain their dignity, they also knew they had to seem at least somewhat pitiful, so they were simultaneously forced to lean into their straightened conditions.

Sitting in the hospital with the man at the center of the tragedy, I listened for hours as he began to look back on his life while questions swirled about whether he would ever walk again, whether he would go to jail, and whether his family could ever recover from the financial burden of keeping him out of jail. If I was the respected *duktūr* of anthropology, the perpetrator here (who I'll call Rashid) was a "doctor in lying," his brothers and sisters and nieces and nephews teased. He introspected a lot about his misspent youth: skipping school, smoking, even drinking alcohol and smoking hashish. He spoke of how he had gained a reputation among the officers for how fast he could make the trip. Everyone knew him for being fearless as he took those winding turns at high speed. He said that this was why he had crashed the bus. Now he had to live with the fact that he had killed a man and injured a lot of his best comrades. Some of them might never return to the service. Rashid talked a lot about how he needed to turn his life around now, that he had been consulting with a local Imam about how he might purify himself through fasting and prayer, and perhaps even redeem himself despite being a "murderer" (*qātil*). "He's spoiled the world," the children would sometimes say to sum up, making sure I was getting the point.

In some very concrete ways, Rashid had certainly spoiled those children's world: for years to come, the family's activities and finances would revolve almost completely around this single careless act. His family would ultimately be forced to organize several delegations to various tribes to arrange truces, pay blood money, and, eventually, reconcile with those who had suffered as the result of the crash. These too would follow a very specific pattern. As with other delegations, we would begin by assembling before heading off. Yet instead of directly approaching the family of the victim, we would first need to be received by the mediator. There, in a tent or even a large purpose-built hall, we would assemble in our plastic or metal chairs to be served coffee before heading off to be received by the victims while under the protection of our intermediaries. The truces and reconciliations themselves could drag on for hours—though many only lasted an hour. Especially in the early phases, there were threats, lurid accusations, and raised voices. One of the things that made things so complicated was that the insurance money involved could potentially go some way toward mollifying the victims—especially the relatives of the deceased, who represented by far the gravest threat in terms of criminal charges. Yet that final payment was contingent on everyone who had been involved in the crash signing off on the final report of events for the insurance company, and many of the survivors did not want to sign until they had been paid. Realizing the power their signatures represented within the wider negotiations afoot, victims argued vehemently for the severity of their individual plights.

Over time, my friends unwound the various disputes, truce by truce, reconciliation by reconciliation. The final reconciliation with the family of the deceased happened well over a year after the crash, on a cold winter day. It was a rather joyless affair and somewhat perfunctory in the end. The family of the deceased accepted the money and the sincere apologies of Rashid's family. Speakers took turns averring that they knew that there was no ill intent, that Rashid had indeed been a comrade of the victim, and that ultimately it was God's will. Especially given what everyone now agreed was the inherent lack of malice in such an accident, speakers reasoned that there was no need to add to the world's suffering with further thoughts of vengeance. Instead, the family of the deceased spoke of how God would want them to show mercy given the perpetrator's sincere regrets, and the family of the perpetrator averred that it was brave and godly of the victims to extend them such mercy. It was repeatedly suggested that, perhaps, this might have brought them all together for some greater purpose. They prayed together for God's forgiveness, and after about an hour everyone went back to their cars and left.

In the end, Rashid managed to avoid prison. No one wanted to pursue charges against him, and he eventually recovered enough to work again and support his family. For their part, the rest of the family slowly clawed their way out of debt and—after a few years—even found the money to again host weddings and engagement parties and build new houses for their children. Such cases are frequent in Jordan, and, as I have noted, the introduction of the automobile has led to a shift in notions of collective responsibility such that, where five generations were once held liable in cases of homicide, a growing chorus insists that three generations should suffice.[2] The move to limit responsibility to three generations—especially in cases of car crashes—reflects not only the presumed lack of malice, but also the sheer increase in the number of homicides. It also of course reflects the continued demand on the part of many Jordanian victims' families that even unintentional homicides should be followed by some sort of reckoning between victims and perpetrators.

A Case of Domestic Violence

While Rashid and his family may have been able to reach an amicable resolution through a mixture of Bedouin justice and the bureaucracy of the modern administrative state, this was in no small part because of his substantial privileges. A member of the state security apparatus himself, he also had a family willing and able to support him by raising substantial sums of money and engaging all the aggrieved parties in extensive negotiations. It is hard not to recall here Angela Davis's warning that "alternatives [to prison] that fail to address racism, male dominance, homophobia, class bias, and other structures of domination will not, in the final analysis, lead to decarceration and will not advance the goal of abolition" (2003, 108). The state is only one source of inequality among many, and such an example should highlight how noncarceral systems of justice can be just as biased as the carceral state. Nonetheless, Jordan continues to illustrate how the whole emphasis in modern approaches to justice on solving problems through the state criminal justice system can obscure how other logics often continue to operate alongside it, exerting their own effects (for better or worse).

As I have noted a number of times already, my ethnography was greatly facilitated by the fact that self-styled sheikhs often took an interest in me, usually because they liked the idea of a foreigner following them around and recording their important deeds. For my part, while I sometimes found myself somewhat horrified by what they were doing—usually all the more so because I was mindful of the local mores they were flouting—I also found the access they afforded me to be irresistible. So when an acquaintance I will call Dr. Saqr invited me to come with him to the home of a prominent sheikh in West Amman, I said yes without checking what the purpose of our visit would be. It would slowly emerge that he and our host were in the process of insinuating themselves into a domestic dispute involving a woman who had been beaten by her husband, who was threatening to report him to the police. Dr. Saqr would attempt to represent her in the dispute by leveraging his status as a well-known personality in her tribe, while our host Mithqal sought to take on the role of tribal judge in reconciling them with the powerful tribe from which the husband hailed.

It is hard to overstate the luxuriousness of the villa—or the elaborateness of the hospitality to which we would be treated: copious tea and coffee, fruit, and a lunch featuring platters piled high with meat that would cost a week's salary for many. After some awkward greetings and a reminder that I should write down everything that happened, Dr. Saqr launched into the heart of the matter: what he began by referring to as "the case of honor." He spoke about how he "knew the family." He said of his kinspeople, "These people are cold. They have no shame. They sell their women. Unfortunately, these days, we have many families like this among us. All they care about is money. They don't understand honor at all. I know that all the father wants is money. This can be solved easily."

The conversation continued, somewhat one-sidedly, in this vein for a while. But Dr. Saqr had a problem: "They won't answer me when I call them. These people are cowards. I have a policy where I call someone three times at different times of day and if they don't return my call, I delete them from my phone. Can you imagine? They are afraid to talk to me." Our host slouched on the couch, dragging on his cigarette, and waited for a pause before he muttered, "You have to tell them not to go to the police." Dr. Saqr snapped back into action: "I told them they didn't want to go to the police. If they go to the police, they won't help them. . . . If [the perpetrator] goes [home to his village] they won't be able to bring him, not even the king himself. The police here are nothing to be afraid of." This was somewhat beside the point, though, as Mithqal made clear: the real problem was that the husband was a soldier, and if he was charged with assaulting his wife, he would be subject to military justice: courts martial, the possibility of a dishonorable discharge, and consequently his family's loss of not only his salary but also his pension and benefits, including health care for life and the possibility of a free university education for his children.

It was because the husband's job was potentially in jeopardy that our host counseled a light touch so as not to upset the negotiations. After more criticism of the family of the "girl," and more effusive boasting about his own ability to solve the matter, Dr. Saqr placed a phone call. He first contacted a relative of his and began berating his "cousin" (*bin 'ām*) for not returning his phone calls. Taking a more conciliatory tack, he then began complaining about how the father of the "girl" would not answer his calls. It transpired that Dr. Saqr had the wrong number—though it was unclear to me whether this was due to an honest transposition error or an artful attempt by the principals in the case to dodge a powerful and domineering man trying to make them accept a settlement they were not ready to accept. I soon began to suspect the latter explanation. Dr. Saqr then called the father of the woman. This time, Dr. Saqr took a much more solicitous tack. He asked after the man's health and then said, "I've been trying to call you but the number was wrong. The eight was in the place of the five and the five was in the place of the eight." As he said this, he laughed in an awkward, contrived way as his audience looked on. He then set up a meeting for 5:30 that evening and wished the man well. When he had hung up the phone, he assured everyone that it was all settled now: he would go talk to the man and then he would accede to arbitration.

From there, the conversation drifted to other matters. The men talked politics, history, and genealogy. Dr. Saqr's musings went in a characteristically apocalyptic direction: "We'll be riding on camels like our grandfathers," he exclaimed. They spoke of the decline of the great sheikhly lineages, and Dr. Saqr was keen for me to write down his thoughts on each. This allowed him to return to one of his favorite topics: the weakness of the Hashemites and their negative impact on Jordan. Rising to take the bait, Mithqal complained about how he had been ordered by the palace to ensure that one thousand tribesmen were in attendance at a recent visit of the king and the US embassy staff to the area. But why would these people want to attend, the sheikh asked rhetorically: "They've never met the king, they've only seen him on TV!"

One of the younger men in attendance interrupted and introduced himself by way of his tribe (which was unrelated to any of the parties to the dispute) before asking me about my background, noting that he had spent significant time in America himself. I gave him some relevant details from my CV and then returned the favor by asking after his background. He said he had been in San Diego in February for work, and that he was a lawyer for one of the leading telecom providers in Jordan. As Dr. Saqr continued to lay out his vision of a tribal republic that could replace the current monarchy, the young man then said, standing up, "We [referring to his tribe] don't want tribalism anymore. It's over." When asked what the alternative was, he said, "an Islamic State," to chuckles and smiles. The young man addressed Dr. Saqr now, telling him, "The new generation is not like the old. We don't want tribes. We don't listen to our parents or the state or any authority. We're not afraid of anything. In the old days you would go to bed at seven o'clock and your parents would tell you, 'Don't go outside or the *ghūla* (ghoul) will catch you.' But today we have the internet. You can't scare us with these stories. We criticize everything, even the king. There are no more red lines. They're all gone."

Instead of answering any of this directly, Dr. Saqr began a long description of how the foreign powers methodically destroyed the original sheikhs of Jordan. He was eager that I take notes and frequently asked Mithqal to assent to his characterization of events. Dr. Saqr said, "Now there are none of the original sheikhs left in Jordan. The British and the Zionists and the Americans got rid of them all. They like to pick people who are weak, people they can control." Eventually, the other men grew impatient, though: "And [your tribe]?" Dr. Saqr waffled a bit and threw out some names with the qualification, "I hate them, but this is known and documented. They were the last traditional leaders . . . I brought an alternative. I didn't bring my power from my father. I made it myself. They tried to put seven leaders in my place, but they never solved people's problems. The current leader is quiet. Instead, the people come to me. Now no one can solve problems but me." The assembled men called out, "To your strength!"

At this point Dr. Saqr asked to be excused to do his ablutions so he could pray before going to his meeting at 5:30. Before leaving, they rehearsed the important points for organizing the coming reconciliation between the two families. Mithqal said, "Tell them that even if you have one hundred witnesses and the best connections that if you go to the state they will waste you and it will take years." Then: "The important thing is that they don't go to the police." We said our goodbyes as we were escorted out to the car. They rehearsed the rationale for not going to the police one last time, and we got in the car. Finally alone, I asked Dr. Saqr what the case was about, and he said, "Cold people [meaning without shame]. Hitting and insulting. The girl insulted the man! Can you imagine! Shame! A woman shouldn't insult her husband. And then he hit the girl! Shame! We have to solve this before it goes further." Yet as 5:30 approached, there was no further answer to Dr. Saqr's phone calls. He seemed absolutely furious when I parted ways, and when I asked him about it later on, it became clear that this was the last that I was ever going to hear about this case from him.

I admit that for all I know this was all quietly hushed up, much as men I had met seemed to hope it would be, and no one outside of the families would ever be the wiser. Yet whether these men failed to engineer this specific "reconciliation," these were powerful people thanks to the fact that similar gambits often do work out for them. The claim that the tribal system was over and represented little more than a ghost story in the face of social media expressed a widespread sentiment, but it also seems premature. New communications technologies gave these men new ways to demonstrate their power and reach as they tried to force their kin into particular concessions—even as their kinsmen dodged their phone calls. Crucially, however, while no one involved in the negotiations I witnessed took the victim's grievances seriously, the synergy between tribal logics and the criminal justice system and its largely administrative tools for compelling compliance forced the perpetrator and his kin to try—however crudely—to anticipate and meet the victim's needs. Moreover, no matter how much Dr. Saqr might protest to the contrary, the process of forgiveness could never be divorced from the social work wrapped up in the concept of "honor" that he constantly invoked (if only to negate it). To capture this dynamic, I now shift away from the minutiae of tribal dispute resolution to try and place it within a wider global context of colonialism and postcolonial state-building. Again, however, retributive and restorative dimensions need not be contradictory, and in fact they often work in tandem where they become fused processually in acts of mercy.

Mercy Beyond Retributive and Restorative Justice

As I have written elsewhere (Hughes 2024), the colonial encounter seems to have done a lot to reify the distinction between systems of retributive and restorative justice and state and stateless justice. The early sociologist Emile

Durkheim ([1893] 1984) optimistically predicted that modernization would lead to a shift from an emphasis on punishment to one on providing restitution through administrative remedies like fines as societies became less conformist and increasingly defined by a complex division of labor. While the punitive/restitutive distinction was taken up enthusiastically by later anthropologists like Radcliffe-Brown and his student Isaac Schapera, the polarity came to be reversed: in the face of the brutal violence meted out by colonial states, it was difficult to argue that law was becoming less punitive (Niehaus 2021, 142–143). Instead, anthropologists like Radcliffe-Brown increasingly held up the "native" systems of justice that they encountered as a more enlightened alternative, with an emphasis on their consensual and noncoercive elements (themselves accentuated by the settler state's claim to a monopoly on the legitimate use of violence) (Niehaus 2021, 135–137). It is little wonder, then, that the movement for restorative justice that emerged in the latter half of the twentieth century has often taken so-called "indigenous" systems of justice as a model—though proponents like Howard Zehr are quick to frame this as a "debt" and not a "myth of origin" (1990, 140). Even so, it is worth questioning whether such a sharp dichotomy is accurate—or even politically useful—and how the Bedouin concept of mercy might offer a more nuanced understanding of the subtle interplay of revenge and repair in the pursuit of justice.

Even as anthropologists were rushing to study indigenous systems of justice, though, those very systems were being profoundly transformed by the expansion of settler states and their highly developed repressive apparatuses. At a very basic level, the pursuit of personal vendettas without recourse to settler courts—against settlers, of course, but even other indigenes—was inevitably taken as challenging state legitimacy and often punished, much to the understandable outrage of erstwhile victims in search of justice. In such a context, the division between retribution and restitution was inevitably reified: stripped of their sovereignty and terrorized by the violence of settlers, indigenous peoples had to make do with forms of justice that did not rely on violence or coercion. If anything, decolonization has only further reified the distinction, perhaps nowhere more than in South Africa, with its widely discussed Truth and Reconciliation Commission. While some scholars have pushed back on the idea of restorative justice as a quintessential element of indigenous African justice, it came to be a key aspect of the post-Apartheid state's claims to legitimacy. It sought to placate skeptical white publics at home and abroad while also asserting a very specific sort of indigenous sovereignty (Wilson 2000).

At the same time—and often responding to firsthand experiences with the violence inherent within settler systems of "justice"—Black and Indigenous scholars have developed their own trenchant critiques of the carceral state that range from reformist to abolitionist. Especially in the wake of the uprisings that have followed widely publicized state murders of unarmed Black and Indigenous citizens in the United States, there is a growing interest in the work of abolitionist scholars like Angela Davis (2003), Ruth Wilson Gilmore (2022), and Miriame Kaba (2021). When asked about alternatives to the status quo, they are often unapologetically radical. To return to Davis, this abolitionist vision can only succeed to the degree that it also confronts "racism, male dominance, homophobia, class bias, and other structures of domination" (2003, 108). Here, systems of justice that reject the carceral state can be *good to think with*, but it would be a mistake to assume they are necessarily egalitarian. As I discussed in chapter 2 ("**Tribalism**"), especially to the degree that they lionize and reify a gender binary and map it onto a strict domestic-public division, Jordan's self-styled tribespeople embrace some hierarchies (around age, gender, and birth in particular) even as they reject others.

Indigenous systems of justice predicated on reconciliation, restoration, and restitution have not been without their critics, of course—nor has the tendency to romanticize them gone unchallenged. For instance, while the implementation of "traditional" justice in South Africa might involve touching scenes of forgiveness like those sometimes observed in the country's Truth and Reconciliation Commission (cf. Davis 2003, 114–115), Richard Wilson notes that it could also be quite violent—like a publicly administered beating with whips or golf clubs (2000, 85). Even the emphasis on reconciliation itself has not been without its principled critics. The anthropologist Laura Nader has long critiqued what she sees as a "harmony ideology" found in many indigenous communities, like the Zapotec communities of southern Mexico where she has conducted extensive fieldwork. While useful in maintaining group solidarity in the face of the encroaching Mexican state, she argues that it also leaves the socially marginal at the mercy of the resulting "controlling processes" (1990). Moreover, Nader has pointedly extended her critique of "harmony ideology" to the explosion of interest in Alternative Dispute Resolution (which often involves an emphasis on restorative justice) (1988)—arguing that ADR can mystify power relations and constitute an insidious form of social control against the socially marginal. In a similar vein, Nayanika Mookherjee (2022) has recently advocated for the value of *irreconciliation* and the refusal of forgiveness in the face of real harm that has been perpetrated against vulnerable people.

None of this is news to abolitionist activists, of course—many of whom have personal experience of being revictimized by the refusal of authorities and even their own communities to take their victimization seriously. Miriame Kaba, for instance, has written, "accountability is not punishment" (2021) and sought to emphasize the importance of demanding the former even as she is critical of the latter. As Mia Mingus (2022) has written, accountability is challenging and involves four things: reflecting on the harm to survivors, apologizing, repairing the damage, and "most importantly" working to change one's behavior. While I have tried to emphasize the darker side of Bedouin conceptions of mercy here, I would also emphasize that much of the work of reconciliation is concerned with forcing perpetrators into a similar sort of accountability process with their victims. Against a glib, utopian conception of mercy and restorative justice, Jordan's Bedouin have taught me to see just how challenging this can be for all involved.

Conclusion

As I have argued, one of the main things this form of justice holds out to all involved (and simultaneously demands) is *mercy* and its close relative *grace*, both of which can be rendered in Arabic as *raḥma*. As in matters of gift-giving with grace, so in matters of crime and punishment with mercy: it is very much "the thought that counts." In "The Place of Grace in Anthropology," Julian Pitt-Rivers argues that "the moral obligation is only to return grace and what is resented if it is not returned is not the material loss but the rejection of the victim's self" ([1992] 2017; 97). So while money may certainly help (as Dr. Saqr insisted), it is often about much more than that. Even the money itself is often better understood as a proxy for other sorts of social effects ranging from throttling the consumption of the perpetrator's family to acknowledgment of the victims' suffering and standing in the wider community. Acts of mercy and grace, while they can become deeply entangled with the workings of law and contract, must in some ways remain unbound by them. In this way, mercy can serve over time as a bridge from retribution to restitution and eventually restoration, precisely to the degree that it actively resists the application of standardized sanctions. This means that the guilty party must take responsibility not knowing where the process will lead, and the victims likewise must take a leap of faith in extending first temporary truces and eventually full reconciliation.

The forms of carcerality that emerged in the modern era in the West were designed to be more humane (Davis 2003; Foucault 1977), which at least in part meant relieving individuals and society as a whole of the burdensome uncertainty inherent in the act of mercy. At the same time, the attempt to replace the act of mercy with a more carefully delineated schedule of acceptable forms of retribution and restitution has led to its own problems. There is a marked tendency here to render certain populations, usually indigenous and minoritized, as irredeemable—and hence suitable for punishment, all while extending endless grace to others (Wacquant 2009). This need not lead to a romanticization of alternatives, though. If modern criminal justice systems often tear families apart, leaving deep scars in the process, Bedouin justice makes no apologies for doing the same in its own way. As I was often told, if you *really* want to hurt someone, hurt the ones they love. There is also the question of who gets to demand and receive mercy, which is highly contested and—absent strong countervailing forces—tends to privilege the already privileged: men, the wealthy, and the well-connected.

Echoing Davis's (2003) warning, both of these cases demonstrate that simply shifting conflicts away from the carceral system will not necessarily solve deeply entrenched inequalities grounded in gender, class, race, and ethnicity. Nonetheless, in an imperfect world full of flawed institutions and people, mercy does hold within itself a transformative potential: it can certainly serve deeply conservative ends, pressuring the vulnerable to go along to get along. At the same time, mercy can truly remake social relations, especially in the face of moral outrage, where the threat of sanctions can force people into uncomfortable reckonings they might otherwise avoid. In this spirit, I would like to close by suggesting that, at a time when elite impunity often seems to coexist with the hyper-policing of the most disenfranchised, such a rebalancing between retributive and restorative dimensions of justice might do everyone some good.

EPILOGUE

Locking Down

I am wrapping up this story in the wake of the marked infrastructural realignment that accompanied the COVID-19 pandemic and further normalized social media and its newfound ubiquity in an increasingly regulated and policed form. However, the acutely stringent controls limiting the freedom of movement and other rights that were felt not only in Jordan but also globally through 2020 and 2021 punctuated a more general shift toward increasingly direct state control of the media and many other facets of life, with liberalization initiatives seemingly in full retreat. Practices of *ḥiṣār* (blockade, siege, or embargo) have proliferated in recent years, from the open siege warfare of Gaza and Saudi Arabia's attempts to blockade Qatar during the Gulf Crisis to more mundane practices of embargoing websites that violate certain red lines in their coverage and limiting people's movements to prevent the spread of disease. This is a moment of generalized retro-futurism, where practices that an increasingly shaky liberal order had consigned to the past are making a comeback—from state censorship to the use of starvation as an increasingly legitimized weapon of war and the return of stringent public health measures like quarantine. Perhaps tribalism is making a comeback as well—though not in the way it has often been glibly invoked. As I have argued throughout, the idea of tribalism as an evolved but "primitive" module in the brain that primarily makes *other people* unreasonably groupish is a bit too convenient. What is another matter entirely is when specific kin-based identities come to be reified and policed in the social environment as *matters of state* through increasingly physical, public, and irrevocable media of representation.

When I returned to Jordan following a three-year absence in 2022 as restrictions on movement eased, I made a point early on of stopping by to see one of my closer friends in the Jordanian press: an opposition figure and owner of a prominent news site who I will call Bassim. When I arrived at the new office, Bassim immediately ushered me into a cool, dimly lit, and immaculately clean set of rooms. He was the only one there, and I saw scented candles burning in every room, with the air conditioner humming quietly in the background. He asked me to take off my shoes before I stepped in any farther, and I quickly complied. He said that since the lockdown (*ḥiṣār*), the employees all work from their houses: "We realized that we could do everything online, so I sent them all home." As he was saying this, I reckoned that the new office was also much smaller and in a less-prominent part of town than the old office, which would undoubtedly save him a substantial sum of money on rent. He insisted I drink something and asked what I wanted. Seeing that there were no employees left to make tea or coffee, I initially demurred. After some back-and-forth, we settled on an iced coffee he pulled out of the fridge before ushering me into his office.

"Journalism Is Like Farming Now"

I had returned to Jordan to see firsthand how COVID-19 and Jordan's response to it had impacted the lives of those I had come to know there over the past sixteen years. I was especially interested in how restrictions on movement might have further transformed people's relationship to technologies like social media. In many ways, the lockdown or *ḥiṣār* that was implemented by the Jordanian government in response to the global COVID-19 pandemic offers a fitting coda for this book: Jordanians found themselves subject to stringent restrictions on their movement, which in turn encouraged even more movement onto an increasingly regulated internet. At first, Jordanians were largely restricted to their homes, and the government even tried to reverse the normal flow of transit infrastructure, using it to deliver bread and other staples across the kingdom (rather than bringing workers into urban areas). However, this led to crowding as anxious citizens afraid they would be overlooked congregated along major thoroughfares, which of course defeated the whole point of the initiative (Hughes 2021). Having failed to enact an older patriarchal statist imaginary in which the king and his government serves as breadwinner for the people (Martinez 2022), authorities fell back on repression: curfews were imposed in the evenings and on weekends to discourage gatherings where the virus might spread, and those who attempted to drive had their cars impounded. As a result, it has become increasingly common even following the lifting of these restrictions for people to avoid weddings, engagement parties, and funerals by sending online congratulations or condolences instead—a development that a number of interviewees underlined they were actually quite happy about.

In most of the interviews I conducted in 2022, people remembered the restrictions more than the disease itself—perhaps not surprising for a country where the median age is about twenty-four. People certainly died of COVID, but as elsewhere they tended to be older, and—due to Jordan's rapid population growth—there were proportionately fewer of them than in many other countries. Jordan ended up with approximately 130 excess deaths per 100,000 people between the beginning of the pandemic and 2024 (Our World in Data 2024)—on par with Australia, China, and other countries that pursued what many of my interlocutors referred to at the time as the "Chinese Model." Whether because of population structure, the success of the mitigation restrictions, or a combination of these mixed with other local idiosyncrasies, Jordan emerged healthy—though not necessarily happy. While there are often good reasons to justify decisions in terms of lives not lost, crises, and even civil wars and revolutions averted, there is no guarantee that people will accept those justifications.

When I interviewed Jordanians about their experiences with the pandemic and the resulting changes in their relationship to technology, people's recollections of that time period ranged from vitriolic to indifferent. Some were even nostalgic. Many observations might seem banal and familiar: some people reported putting on weight from being at home all day; many people reported spending more of their money on data packages to access the internet. I heard a lot and—as is customary—I asked a lot about *ḥaraka* (movement, turnover, business): "How's the movement?" (basically, "How's business?"). As a common saying goes, *ḥaraka baraka* (movement is blessing). Work, movement, turnover: these are inherent goods—a blessing. Almost everyone I spoke with was keen to move on, but certain shifts were readily apparent: there was a massive increase in the amount of personal protective equipment like gloves and face masks worn by those working as cleaners, cooks, and other unpleasant, low-waged jobs. By far the most common complaint I heard in my interviews was about the restrictions on *movement* and the resulting economic impact—especially on the small businesses that make up an increasingly important segment of Jordan's overall economy.

I asked Bassim how things were going, and he started out by giving a rather optimistic account of things: he said the website was more popular than ever, and that it had cemented its reputation in the Jordanian press for its high standards. However, it did not take long before the problems and struggles he was facing came to the fore. I focus here on his interview because—despite the bravado that I reproduce in the interests of accuracy and transparency—he was more forthright than most due to his already somewhat tenuous status. He began his lament by saying that "journalism is like farming now" before launching into a description of the shifting industry to unpack this somewhat cryptic statement. He scribbled on a notepad as he talked: "You have the American social media sites like Facebook, Twitter, and such. You have the Jordanian security services and now they all have agreements with each other. They can block your IP [address], they can arrest you and put you in jail. . . . Some other sites have had articles disappear." "Really?" I asked. "Oh yes," he said. "Not us but those who don't understand security. They are hacked. But what happens is that you post your article now and very few people come to your site. They are lazy and they wait for the news to come to them on WhatsApp groups, Facebook, or Twitter. Sometimes, depending on the algorithm, you might have ten thousand people, but other days maybe only one hundred." I responded by bringing it back to his initial observation: "So like the farmer who plants his fields and prays for rain, you write your articles and hope for the algorithm to bring the audience?" He nodded in assent.

Bassim said that this was most difficult for him as the owner, repeating the lament of many small-business owners that "the employees all receive their salary but as the owner, I only receive what is left over and it is difficult because the big sites like Google, Facebook, and Twitter steal our work. They receive the benefit for our efforts." To make matters worse, he said that the big American technology companies increasingly outsource moderation and censorship to national governments in countries like Jordan: "They work with the security services so certain topics will not show up, like the Palestinian file and certain subjects connected to public security. If you violate certain red lines, they will ban your IP for fourteen days [or] a month. And I was arrested for something I wrote about corruption." I asked him how long he was in jail, and he said, "Nine hours, but people protested so they released me," underlining how capricious the government's grip can be.

He continued, "You have to be very careful if you are in the opposition. You need to have documents, and you need to be absolutely sure of everything. Most journalists are journalists in name only. They take their information from the government. They develop relationships with decision makers, and the decision makers feed particular stories to people they like as exclusives. They compete to flatter the government and decision makers so they can receive exclusives, so the government controls them. Since we are in the opposition we cannot compete against them like this." I replied, "Of course—so how do you compete?" He said, "So I wait until they post one of their exclusives and then I write a big article. I really focus on the issue and bring together lots of information from all angles of the issue. I dive in depth."

He said, "The problem is that a lot of the stories in the media are stupid and meant to distract. They have no real significance. Like [a recent case of sexual harassment that was trending on Facebook and Twitter]. We saw that and immediately knew it was a manufactured controversy. We looked at the accounts and saw all of their electronic flies promoting the story." He codeswitched into English and asked, "Do you know what electronic flies are?" He then explained that these were networks of accounts controlled by organized state and nonstate actors to shape opinion, concluding, "Remember this word." I asked skeptically whether he thought the story about harassment was fabricated, and he said, "No, it's probably true, but it's stupid. It doesn't matter. Besides, when you have been in journalism for twenty-three years like me you can just smell a manufactured story. They are using it to distract from price increases and the economic crisis. No one writes about these anymore."

I asked whether libel law was a problem as well: "And what about defamation? Like where a citizen attacks a news site?" He said, "It's not citizens who sue for defamation—it's the decision makers! The citizen cannot use the courts. But we have a very good lawyer, and we check everything with him before we publish, so if someone complains he already knows everything about the case." I said, "So the courts are somewhat independent?" He replied, "No, there is no somewhat independent or not. You either are or you aren't. The same with lying. Can someone be a bit of a liar or not? Obviously, you either are a liar or you aren't a liar."

I tried to push back. I said, "I understand how you say that as a journalist, but there is a difference over time from a sociological perspective. In the seventies and eighties, the government really controlled everything. Then there was an opening with the internet around the time of the Arab Spring, and now they are controlling things more carefully again. So these differences are important." He replied, "Okay. So yes, when the internet first came to Jordan, you know I started [another news site that he was later pressured to sell] and the government didn't understand it. They didn't know how to control us. But now they control almost all of the journalists in Jordan. It is only a few like me who are independent. But I write anything I want. No one can control me."

I decided not to push the point. He then began telling me about how much money he had saved by switching to working from home: the employees preferred it, and he found it unnecessary for them to be in the office. They could meet on Zoom or communicate via text. He said, "I saved so much money. Now I only come to the office when I have a meeting like this. I saved two hundred a month for electricity. They would use the air conditioning all of the time in the summer. And in the winter, they would use it for heat, plus gas for the space heater and making tea and coffee. I let the secretary go. I can make my own coffee and clean up the dishes. I have a woman who cleans my house twice per week, and now I have her come here to clean once a week for ten JD [dinar]. I also let the cameraman go too. There's no need." What had begun originally in the post–Arab Spring era as a twenty-four-hour breaking news site had now been reimagined as a long-form commentary site relying primarily on the owner's own analysis. Despite the attempts to put on a brave face, it felt like a real shrinking of horizons, and there was a barely sublimated resignation to the whole conversation.

He then turned things around and asked what I was working on and what differences I had noticed in Jordan. I explained to him that I was doing exploratory research on the impact of COVID, hoping to also finish up my book on social media and make sure I understood the current situation. However, I said I thought that COVID was a bad topic, and that people were tired of hearing about it. He said, "Oh yeah, if you try to talk to people about COVID they will fight you! Everyone is fed up with it. They want to forget about it! And the way everyone stopped talking about it when the war in Ukraine started made people believe it was a conspiracy and fake. But imagine: For one, two years it was all anyone wanted to read about. It was very stupid. And then everyone stopped. So you can see why people started to believe the conspiracy theories."

I said one thing that I had noticed other people disagreed with was my sense that there had been a decrease in *ḥaraka* or movement and especially in traffic. He said "No, man! You just need to go out during rush hour! In the mornings and from 3:30 to 5:30. Just the other day I spent forty-five minutes going one-third of a kilometer. Usually it takes three minutes, but it took forty-five minutes." I said, "Yes, this is what people say, but I took the bus back from Irbid at 4:00 yesterday and was home by 6:30." He was amazed: "You mean from the Northern bus station to Sweileh? Impossible!" I said, "Maybe it was luck. I was surprised!" I continued, "Another thing is that people tell me everyone has gone back to the office, but then the same people will tell me that 'I am working consulting now internationally' or 'I am tutoring students online now for money.'" He said, "That is very true. The internet has become a part of business in a way it never was before." I replied, "Don't you think that has an effect on traffic, though? Even students tell me that they meet to study on Zoom now instead of meeting face to face." He replied, "Yes, my son used to go to a center to take extra classes after school, and it would take him an hour each way. Now he takes the classes online, so he saves time and also of course the fares."

In the midst of this little digression about congestion, he received word that the head of the teachers' syndicate had been arrested and posted a report. This was public information from the Public Security Directorate, but he asked, "Is this news when the head of the teachers' syndicate is arrested?" I replied, "Of course." He also mentioned that more teachers had been arrested with him, first sixteen, then nineteen, and later twenty-one. He then invited me "to take a tour" of his competitors to see what they were reporting on: he highlighted stories like, "Economic Conference at the Dead Sea," "A Minister Drinks Water," "What Makes the King Laugh?" and "What Did the Mosque Lecturer Say in Morocco?" As we checked the different sites and noted the overlap in the trivial stories, the same full-page ad from Jordan's now-privatized Housing Bank kept popping up. Practically spitting out his words, Bassim said, "I hate these! I refuse them! Sure, I have banners at the top, but I respect my readers! This is too much!" He continued, "They really control everything now. There was a time when people would go to the streets if prices rose five *gurūsh* (about ten cents). Now there are five price increases at once and nothing."

My conversation with Bassim crystalized for me something of the increasingly anxious and isolating experience of life in Jordan that I observed during that visit. Alone in his hermetically sealed and carefully curated bubble filled with air-conditioning and aromatherapy, Bassim continued to resist the powerful forces increasingly arrayed against press freedom in Jordan. He refused to give up on the transformative potential of the media—or on his independence. As he had challenged me earlier, one cannot be *a bit of* a liar: one either was or was not a liar as far as he was concerned. Yet to what end? He felt like he was completely at the mercy of technology firms, most of them American, that had opaque agreements with Jordan's security services, which determined whether his voice could be heard or even what counted as an important news story. Like a peasant, the best he could do was to sow his fields (or speak his mind) and hope that powers beyond his control might enable him to reap his reward. Others I spoke with had been more successful, but no one was claiming Bassim's style of outsider strategy was working that well. In 2020, Freedom House even went so far as to downgrade Jordan to "not free" following the lead of many international NGOs that have been critical of the resurgence of authoritarian rule in many parts of the world. Perhaps the Jordanian journalists that I have come to know had always lived in a velvet prison, but in that moment, it felt perhaps as claustrophobic and hopeless as it ever had.

Cracks in the Screen?

Of course, much as the level of social control witnessed globally at the height of the pandemic could not last forever, neither will the current regime of restrictions that constrain journalists like Bassim and everyday citizens alike. If the backlash to the Arab Spring has helped dispense with any illusions about the liberatory potential that was supposed to be inherent in social media, social media nevertheless continues to cause no end of headaches for those in positions of authority. Despite increasing recourse to libel litigation, vague "cybercrime" legislation, and long-standing but previously unenforced regulations on journalism, Jordan's security apparatus remains unable to completely stamp out dissent. Tribal clashes continue—though not at the rate I experienced during my dissertation fieldwork in 2011–2012. Price increases still provoke Jordanians to take to the streets, as they did in late 2022 in clashes that ended in a government-imposed ban on TikTok after a police officer was killed in the violence. The recourse to the blunt instrument of a blanket ban showed the limits of the sort of state-private partnership that has blossomed since Jordan began liberalizing in the nineties, but also that the state has a lot of room for maneuver when it comes to modulating its oversight of the public sphere. While the ban has made an important statement about a small country's willingness to attack the business interests of large multinational companies that fail to prioritize its security concerns, it has also driven an increasing number of Jordanians to rely on Virtual Private Networks to disguise their online identity. Such tradeoffs highlight how the technological advances of the past 150 years have done little to alter some of the basic dynamics around the state control of media: regulate too much and people disengage and find meaning elsewhere, but the commercial nature of modern media simultaneously ensures that the state will always have ample levers to pressure important media figures over the longue durée.

I would argue that it is in the context of this sort of renegotiation of the state-society divide that the appeal of tribalism as foil, analytical concept, and even as an aspirational political identity starts to make sense. Unfortunately, the pop sociology of social media–induced "tribalism" has tended to discard this line of analysis in favor of depoliticized explanations that rely on various forms of determinism (at least for other people) that gloss over the crucial role of political choices in shaping the contemporary media landscape. The decision, simultaneously individual and collective, to route so many of our relationships (commercial, political—even intimate) through these particular networks could not but entail a dramatic reworking of the infrastructure of everyday life and, in turn, the institutional relationships that those infrastructures both depend upon and legitimize. Of course, humans have not made this history purely by choice. They have been constrained in innumerable ways, not least by the state-centric political order that has become the hallmark of modernity. However, the idea that states could completely monopolize the realm of the political was always ambitious, and tribalism in part has clearly come to stand in for the idea of emergent gaps and even escape hatches within the state's matrix of control.

In retrospect, the emergence of cyberspace itself as a new, more virtual frontier just as older, more physical frontiers were giving way to a hermetic matrix of international borders does not seem merely fortuitous. Built on repurposed military technologies that were originally intended to maintain command and control functions amidst threats of infiltration and nuclear war (Edwards 1995; Harris 2023), the internet's liberatory aspects were always overstated. Much like the tribal frontiers of old, social media can resemble a peripheral zone of freedom and escape, but it is also a key site where new forms of social control are developed, perfected, and deployed. Like earlier, more physical frontiers, the internet actually represents a more nuanced set of social and political possibilities than the fantasies of escape that so often dominate in the popular imagination. These possibilities are neither liberatory nor totalitarian per se, but they do turn on specific practices of encompassment and evasion that were earlier pioneered in more physical forms.

Here, some recent reflections on the deep history of tribal frontier zones can be highly illustrative. In a brief but pointed survey of the discourse of tribalism in Asia, Sumit Guha masterfully illustrates how the idea of the tribe was not merely a Western colonial imposition, but something that long preceded the arrival of Europeans in Asia and in turn shaped the course of colonization (2021, 11–30). As Guha notes, most extant discourses of statecraft that were developed across Asia in the past few millennia involved something akin to the notion of a tribal frontier that the state would seek to manage by exploiting family loyalties, complete with its own colorful folk sociology of tribalism's environmental determinants. If "tribals" have been tied to the desert in the commonplace environmental account of tribalism in the Middle East that I have described in this book, similar political formations are associated with the forest in India, the steppe in China, and the mountains in Southeast Asia. As Guha notes, these environments represent zones that are vast, difficult for states to traverse, and lacking in easily extractable resources that would make them economically sustainable to control and police. However, these are also environments that are actively produced by those who flee to them in the service of their varying political projects, including both forms of marronage based on the radical egalitarian rejection of centralizing state hierarchies *and* rearguard actions aiming to capture and further perfect the rapacious efficiency of centralizing state hierarchies (Guha 2021, 45–66). The shifting digital architecture of social media here resembles the advances and setbacks of rivals bringing with them vast herds against tilled fields—or dense thickets against forest-clearing parties.

Social media itself can be seen here as resembling the classic tendency of states to farm out the regulation of peripheral but potentially restive or unexpectedly profitable peripheral zones to ambitious aspiring magnates, some of whom in turn begin to resemble states in scale, human labor power, and assets (if not a capacity for direct violence—yet). The urge here for routinization and registration has not merely come from without. Social media have certainly emerged in their current form in no small part due to governance agendas focusing on preventing their use for a familiar set of crimes ranging from money laundering to fraud, incitement, and sedition. However, social media have also made online worlds more hospitable both to those who inhabit them and to newcomers, leading in turn to all sorts of opportunities to engage in precisely the sorts of activities that states have been so concerned to stamp out.

Nowhere is this more apparent than in neighboring Palestine, which has emerged as a new sort of hybrid frontier in the aftermath of Palestinian militants' Al Aqsa Flood Operation and the ensuing invasion of Gaza in 2023. For a Jordanian state that has struggled for decades to extricate itself from the question of Palestine, it again presents both a virtual front in a media war and also an all-too-real site of violence threatening to spill over. Despite repeatedly rejecting any sort of involvement in the absence of progress on a Palestinian state, there have been repeated overtures for cooperation from Israel and its allies along with familiar talk of exploiting Palestinian clan structures to bypass existing political groups like the Palestinian Authority and Gaza's Islamic Resistance Movement (known colloquially by its Arabic acronym Hamas).[1] At the same time, Palestinians have mobilized social media throughout the diaspora (including in Jordan) to lend their stories unprecedented reach. While protests in solidarity with Palestine have been suppressed in Jordan and around the globe, the theory that Palestine could simply be ignored and set aside in favor of normalization between states (Kaminer 2024) has been largely abandoned. The growing sense in the immediate aftermath of the pandemic that there could be no outside to the regional nation-state system has been roundly reversed.

All the same, just because political projects are organized in these borderlands does not necessarily imply any liberatory potential, or even any contradiction with processes of centralization and state formation. As in more physical frontier zones, the virtual worlds that social media have spawned allow for rapid self-reinvention. Writing about the fortunes of the state in contemporary frontier zones along the north and south of the Sahara, the anthropologist Judith Scheele observes, "People, meanwhile, move in and out of state and non-state categories with vertiginous speed: from rebel to soldier to minister to rebel again—or internationally, from blue helmet to road-cutter to mercenary to Islamic terrorist—mostly mediated through large payments of cash, obtained through international loans" (Scheele 2021, 920). The recent trajectory of Syria's new leader Ahmed Al-Sharaa, who went from being a wanted terrorist with a $10 million bounty on his head to shaking hands with the US president in a matter of months, is a particularly striking example (Doucet 2025). Similarly, a proliferation of different platforms allows contemporary Jordanians to compliment each other on their recent promotions through the ranks of the state security apparatus on Facebook while sharing insurgent combat footage and rumors on WhatsApp and Telegram. Scrutiny is greater than ever, but so is the sophistication of the techniques of indirect speech and plausible deniability.

While social media garnered much of their initial sheen of novelty and potentiality from their ability to disavow a relationship to the state, even the countries with the most robust free speech protections increasingly take for granted the need to regulate social media. In such a context, there is a real need for more analysis of social media as a sort of "public-private partnership" that tries to negotiate the state-society divide in a way that creates engaged and economically sustainable publics that are suitably politically quiescent. Here, soft authoritarian regimes like Jordan are helpful because they readily dispense with the incorrect (if sometimes reassuring) idea that social media simply cannot be regulated. At the same time, countries like Jordan also offer countless examples of how media regulation often leads to perverse incentives and unintended consequences. There is also a need here for more research on how "social media" is itself somewhat chimerical and varies in significant ways from place to place depending on wider political dynamics and cultural beliefs. Formal regulatory structures matter here, but so do much more diffuse cultural sensibilities around the nature of subjectivity, the social scripts appropriate to managing conflict, and folk theories of human emotions and wider motivations. In this regard, there is also a need for more work on how the widely held belief in social media's emotionality can be mobilized in different ways depending on local media ideologies about the ability of media to mobilize certain kinds of emotions for political ends. At the same time, other elements of social media may reflect more abstract, structural political dynamics that lend themselves well to cross-cultural generalizations. This is why I have suggested throughout that research on social media might benefit from engaging with research on tribalism that treats it as a political phenomenon and examines its entanglements with states and their attempts to manage their frontiers. Since most traditions of statecraft must contend with a frontier of some sort, the frontier might serve in many contexts as a model for managing the internet along locally meaningful yet still more widely legible—and comparable—lines.

Precisely because my Jordanian Bedouin interlocutors bring such a different set of traditions and personal experiences to their analysis of the state than much of contemporary metropolitan social theory, I believe they are worth thinking with, even when they are clearly mistaken about their own social reality. After all, people might tend to be eloquent and impassioned narrators of their own conditions, but they are not always accurate. However, a deep familiarity with state attempts to corral them into tribal structures, set them against one another, carefully register their identities, and subordinate them to the state has sensitized my interlocutors to dynamics that the denizens of more avowedly "modern" political formations have too often ignored. All the same, the Bedouin concepts of tribalism, face, envy, the deep state, and mercy that I have emphasized are not only interesting for what they say about a specific political moment in a specific part of the world. These are ultimately anthropological concepts, and, while they bear the hallmarks of their community of origin, they also extend outward and offer a means (however flawed) for reaching across vast cultural divides.

Acknowledgments

I have accrued many debts in the course of researching and writing this book, too many of which must remain unpaid—at least for now. First and foremost, I am forever indebted to the Jordanians who offered me their warm hospitality and taught me so much about both themselves and the world in which we all live. This includes those who hosted me as a Peace Corps volunteer from 2006 to 2008 and initially taught me about the Bedouin and their tribes. It also includes those who hosted me during my dissertation research in 2010, 2011–2012, and 2013, and those more directly involved in this project, especially the journalists and tribal leaders who were so generous with their time. Given the current political climate of intensifying repression both in Jordan and around the world, I am reticent about naming names here. I hope that someday we will all be in a position where I can honor them properly in writing.

I also owe a debt of gratitude to a number of mentors and academic interlocutors who have encouraged me, read drafts, and otherwise helped me craft this book. Andrew Shryock was an extremely generous dissertation mentor and has remained a constant source of advice and inspiration ever since. Gillian Feeley-Harnik and Thomas Trautmann also played a formative role in my thinking on these topics through their graduate seminar on kinship at the University of Michigan. Since my move to the UK, Harry West, Matthew Engelke, and the late David Graeber have played important mentoring roles and shaped my thinking in both subtle and profound ways. Among those who read drafts for me and otherwise helped me clarify my thinking at various points, I would like to thank Matan Kaminer, Blaire Andres, Stuart Strange, James Meador, Kristen Kao, Christine Sargent, Kawa

Morad, Susannah Crockford, Arsalan Khan, Fuad Musallam, Megnaa Mehtta, Chiara Bresciani, Lucy Osler, Amy Penfield, Ellen Lust, Sam Shuman, Wael Al-Khatib, Nick Long, Tyler Brunet, Giovanna Colombetti, Narmala Halstead, Doug Farrer, Tom Roberts, Adrian Currie, Kirsten Walsh, and Joel Kruger. I would also like to thank audiences at Cambridge University, the University of Exeter, Oslo University, the American Anthropological Association, the London School of Economics, Bristol University, Brunel University, and the American Center of Research in Amman for their excellent questions and provocations. Finally, I would like to thank my students, first at the London School of Economics and more recently at Exeter, who consistently inspire me through their sharp questions and their own contributions to ongoing debates in the discipline.

I also received significant institutional support at every step of the way that I must acknowledge. As I noted, my initial exposure to the social dynamics I describe in this book were somewhat fortuitous and grew out of my time as a Peace Corps volunteer in a rural Bedouin community. As an academic researcher, I received substantial support from the University of Michigan and then the National Science Foundation (award number 1154785) that formed the foundation for this project. Fieldwork in the summer of 2016 was funded by the London School of Economics and Political Science, while fieldwork in the summer of 2017 was funded by the National Endowment for the Humanities and supported by the American Center of Research in Amman. In the summer of 2019, I received funding from the British Academy for fieldwork that was supported by the Council for British Research in the Levant. My most recent field trip in the summer of 2022 was funded by the University of Exeter. Jim Burr and the University of Texas Press have been extremely helpful throughout the publication process.

Finally, I would like to thank my family, including my parents, Michael and Gloria (my first teachers), my brother Sean, my partner, Blaire Andres, and our son Isaac, all of whom continue to inspire me every day.

Any errors of course are mine alone.

Notes

Introduction. Tribalism and the Politics of an Accusation

1. National Public Radio made the veiled reference to Trump explicit in its coverage (Horsley 2016).
2. The next year, Obama would build upon this analysis in warning of the threat of political "balkanization." Comparing social media to television, he said, "One of the dangers of the Internet is that people can have entirely different realities. They can just be cocooned in information that reinforces their current biases" (Wamsley 2017). However, such concerns around social media are very much a cross-ideological fixation, given that Trump's vice president, J. D. Vance, has voiced similar reservations about how social media leads to invidious comparisons and social division, even crediting the realization for his conversion to Catholicism in 2019: "Mired in the swamp of social media, we identified a scapegoat and digitally pounced. We were keyboard warriors, unloading on people via Facebook and Twitter, blind to our own problems. We fought over jobs we didn't actually want while pretending we didn't fight for them at all" (Ward 2024).
3. Scott Morrison made his remarks in front of the Australia-Israel Chamber of Commerce in the wake of the Christchurch massacre, during which an Australian citizen killed forty Muslim worshippers at a mosque in New Zealand (Department of the Prime Minister and Cabinet 2019).
4. See also M. Aouragh, "Framing the Internet in the Arab Revolutions: Myth Meets Modernity," *Cinema Journal* 52 (1): 148–156.
5. In fact, given Obama's enthusiasm for Friedman's analysis of the region (Fernández 2011, 30), Friedman's column may even have been the inspiration for Obama's subsequent comments before the United Nations.
6. For Habermas, this idea of an intimacy between author and reader (which simultaneously effaces its own institutional and infrastructural conditions of possibility) is central to the emergence of the public sphere as such. He writes that "the relations between author, work, and public changed. They became intimate mutual relationships between privatized individuals who were psychologically interested in what was 'human,' in self-knowledge, and in empathy" (Habermas, quoted in

Calhoun 1992, 12). This sense that one is engaging directly with the words of a person who might be *just like you* is further developed in the emergence of the various oppositional, minoritarian, and queer "counterpublics" that followed (Warner 2002). By the twentieth century, a whole range of more or less authentic forms of self-publishing had swept the globe, from cassette tape cultures (Hirschkind 2006; Simon 2022) to zines and samizdat.

7. Though see Carmody (2012) for a critical evaluation of the literature on mobile phones and technological "leapfrogging."
8. Internet cafés were usually small, independently run establishments where customers could pay around a dollar per hour to use one of several computers provided by the proprietor, all hooked up to the internet via a Local Area Network.
9. This approach to tribalism does not deny that people organized themselves along family lines before the emergence of the first states, but it recognizes that historical accounts of tribes are almost exclusively the product of states, and that such an "idiom of administration" should not be taken naively as "evidence of autochthonous kin organization" (Sneath 2009, 106).
10. See *Vexed* by James Mumford (2020), Amy Chua's *Political Tribes* (2019), and the Policy Commons paper "Europe's Political Tribes" (Raines, Goodwin, and Cutts 2017).
11. Talal Asad also advances a version of this argument about the intimate relationship between colonial administration, anthropological knowledge production, and the idea of the tribe in the opening pages of *Anthropology and the Colonial Encounter*. He suggests that the "shift in political power from 'tribal' leaders to nationalistic bourgeoisie" along with "rural development projects" and a growing academic critique of functionalism were "concrete developments in the world outside" that "pushed functional anthropology until it collapsed into micro-sociology" (1973, 13). In "The Idea of an Anthropology of Islam" (1986), Asad further develops these arguments in an extended critique of Ernst Gellner's use of the idea of tribe in his structural-functional model of "Muslim Society." Seraje Assi continues in this vein in *The History and Politics of the Bedouin*, linking the production of anthropological knowledge about tribes with tactics of colonial domination (2018, 7–10 *et passim*).
12. At the same time, opinions on tribalism among Arab intellectuals have never been uniform—or static. Arab intellectuals, especially those who write in English, are certainly more inclined than others to see tribalism as a source of social problems, including corruption and nepotism (Al-Saleh 2016), antidemocratic divide-and-rule politics (Al-'oudat and Alshboul 2010; Massad 2001), and violence against women (Faqir 2001). However, there are Jordanian academics who write quite positively about tribalism, like Dr. Ahmad Owaidi Abbadi (2006) and the other tribal historians profiled in Andrew Shryock's *Nationalism and the Genealogical Imagination* (1997). Yazan Doughan (2019) has suggested that there has been a revival of interest among Jordan's activists in recent years in fashioning the country's legacy of tribal resistance to state authority into a usable history. Other Jordanian intellectuals express more nuanced normative perspectives, noting that tribal justice can offer mutually agreeable solutions to hard problems but also that it can disadvantage women in particular—most starkly in cases of "honor" where women's sexual purity is demanded on pain of death (Emad 2021; Shunnaq et al. 2025). Others, like

Muhammad Badarneh (2023), write about it more matter-of-factly because it is an important part of local society that cannot be easily ignored.

13. The term "Arab world" that Abu Lughod employs in the title of her landmark review of the literature is itself a controversial one. While it has been critiqued as essentializing, homogenizing, and totalizing (Deeb and Winegar 2012, 538–539), it remains a powerful aspiration and reference point for many. I will use it from time to time to show my involvement in (and complicity with) certain worldmaking projects. In one memorable (though by no means unique) experience during an interview, a man paused after I asked him a question about the "Arab world" (*al-umma al-ʿarabiyya*) to thank me and tell me how much he liked the phrase, adding, "This is why we like having you around."
14. The modern genealogical preoccupation here is not merely archival. It also draws force from folk enthusiasm for genetics (El-Haj 2012; Strathern 1992).
15. Elizabeth Chin, *My Life with Things: The Consumer Diaries* (Durham, NC: Duke University Press, 2016), 26–27.
16. For more on this long-running debate in science and technology studies, see Jacques Ellul's *The Technological Society* (1964) for a strong argument in favor of the power of technology to shape social life. For a more nuanced view, see Langdon Winner's "Do Artifacts Have Politics?" (1980).
17. One of the memes that circulated online in the wake of this incident can be found in Hughes and Walter (2021, 93).

Chapter 1. The Many Faces of the State—the Sheikh, the Policeman, and the Journalist

1. The nation has come to be a staple example of a social construct, an "imagined community" as Benedict Anderson (1983) puts it (see also Chatterjee 1993).
2. The Marxist tradition of course has always been skeptical of the liberal belief in the autonomy of "civil society" and the "private sphere," something developed by Gramsci (1971) and his latter-day critics and interpreters (Althusser 1971, 141; Poulantzas 1973, 124–140).
3. Jordan's first official gazette was initially called the *Arab East* before it was later renamed as simply the *Official Gazette*. According to Avi Ayalon, four newspapers were then started in 1927, including *Al-urdun*, which started in Haifa in 1923 and lasted into the second half of the century (1995, 101). Ayalon draws strong parallels between these developments and earlier precedents set by Muhammad Ali in Cairo and then the Ottoman Sultan Mahmud in Istanbul in the early nineteenth century (Ayalon 1995, 11–21).
4. Like most of the judges, the sheikh attributed the special status of these three crimes to an agreement that emerged from a meeting between Jordan's King Hussein and the tribes in response to an attempt by the parliament in 1985 to abolish tribal law. For a discussion of this controversy, see Layne (1989) and Antoun (2000).
5. The government's gesture of distributing water and juice to protesters early on was widely covered in the Western media (Baker 2011; Amos 2013).
6. While most street-level police (like most of the general public) were adamant that crime was increasing, the people at the courthouse with access to the statistics were

equally adamant that the increase was completely in line with population growth and thus overblown. Journalists sometimes wondered if their coverage encouraged crime, but they also tended to defend themselves by saying, "The difference is that now we hear about it."

7. Abu Tayeh had no particular loyalty to the Hashemites, but the weapons and money he gained from the British and his raids on the Ottomans allowed him to fulfill his obligations as a sheikh to his people many times over.
8. The most overt challenge to Hashemite authority came in 1923 in the form of the 'Adwan Revolt, which was quickly crushed by forces led by Frederick Peake (Alon 2007, 54–56).
9. As one might expect, Lynch also makes much of this in his argument for the importance of the Arab public sphere as something King Hussein and the security services could not simply turn off with the flick of a switch in spite of the ensuing international isolation (1999, 151–165).
10. As Ebithal Mahadeen notes, the Jordan Press Association is a state-dominated syndicate for journalists established in 1953, and nonmembers who practice journalism (including online since 2014) are violating the law in doing so. This is but one of the "dizzying array of laws" for journalists that change frequently, creating a climate of fear, uncertainty, and self-censorship (2020, 21–22).
11. To illustrate how common it was to plagiarize official sources in the industry without attribution, the journalists in one of the more professional newsrooms where I did fieldwork once forwarded me the day's press releases from the public security directorate so I could see how pervasively they were incorporated verbatim into online news articles.
12. For a press account of the controversy and subsequent murder, see Bulos (2016).
13. As Quintan Wiktorowicz notes, much of what looks like regime support for the Muslim Brotherhood might better be seen as merely the absence of the sort of active criminalization competing organizations encounter, allowing for the creation of a uniquely sprawling network of NGOs providing various services by circulating money and jobs in the community (1999, 7).
14. For a press account of the national soul-searching around "university violence," see Sweis (2013).

Chapter 2. Tribalism

1. Many examples from the genre can be found on YouTube by searching with Arabic script for variations of "*fariq walid al-biduwi al-ḥaḍari*"—though the example that I encountered most frequently in the course of my fieldwork and describe here was shared over Bluetooth and is not readily available there.
2. By self-orientalizing, I mean that my interlocutors framed Jordanian politics as underdeveloped and "backward" (*mutakhallif*), sometimes in sorrow and sometimes with outright glee. The tendency of some in the Middle East to embrace orientalist stereotypes has been primarily explored in the context of tourism (Feighery 2012; Henderson 2008; Morgan & Pritchard 1998), but it is much more widespread. This was also an example of what I call in this book and elsewhere a "refusal of coevalness" (Hughes 2023), which had the interesting effect of

undermining my ethnographic authority by asserting my interlocutor's participation in temporalities and worlds that I was subtly excluded from. Whether or not I agree, I want to mark the disjuncture they were asserting—and my inability to ignore the assertion.

3. The concept of "honor killing" has come in for sustained criticism for othering and culturalizing more widespread dynamics of domestic violence, violence against women, and femicide under a vague and often misleading umbrella (Abu Lughod 2013; Ewing 2008). After all, could not most violence against women in Europe and the Americas be explained in terms of honor too? As Fadia Faqir notes, the Jordanian law that most perpetrators appeal to in order to mitigate their culpability in these cases is descended from the French legal code's stipulation of reduced sentences for husbands in "crimes of passion" (2001, 73). Such critiques highlight how the category of honor crime is itself a product of modern state bureaucracy and transnational feminist advocacy that has yielded a whole infrastructure of investigation and reporting, which reframes attempts to uphold certain sexual mores as crimes themselves. Yet as Faqir notes, if patriarchy tends to figure the domestic sphere as a refuge for women while in fact rendering it "one of the most dangerous places for women" (Schechter 1982, 5), it is worth understanding how the specific dynamics of that violence may differ: prerogatives that in Europe were conferred on husbands are reinterpreted in Jordan as more appropriate to a woman's own natal family.
4. Yazan Doughan's (2024) treatment of *wāsṭa* and "corruption" more generally as a "problem" space offers a number of rich ethnographic descriptions of this lively trade in allegations of *wāsṭa*, as does Susan Macdougall's (2019) treatment of Jordanian discourses of *maṣlaḥa* or [self]-interest.
5. Evans-Pritchard's *Nuer* has been extensively critiqued since its publication. It is, as Audrey Richards put it, "an irritating book" "in the best sense of the word" (1941, quoted in McKinnon 2000, 35). In fact, as Paul Dresch notes, Evans-Pritchard's treatment of his own Nuer material shifts markedly over the course of his engagement with it: in his earliest articles, his treatment is like that of a historian in search of facts about the past that can explain the present, seeking to understand how the genealogies of various Nuer clans and tribes explain contemporary political dynamics. In his second attempt marked by the publication of the monograph, however, Dresch argues that Evans-Pritchard "began to perceive a history that was the product of present concerns." Dresch goes on to note that Evans-Pritchard would continue to revise his ideas in the ensuing decades, producing a third attempt that would be less a history of the Nuer than a "view of Nuer history" (1988, 59).
6. In fact, it would be a mistake to overemphasize the degree to which his classic work among the Nuer was the genesis of later anthropological work on tribalism or what would come to be known as *segmentation*. As the literary theorist Mary Louise Pratt argues in "Fieldwork in Common Places," Evans-Pritchard followed standard generic conventions of ethnography by introducing his work with an "arrival scene" drawing on the tropology of travel writing. Pratt identifies Evans-Pritchard with the "gruff Victorian explorer-adventurer" (1986, 39) and shows how the ensuing self-deprecating story about being abandoned by his "servants" and having to figure out how to convince the Nuer to sympathize with his

plight was a close reprisal of earlier travel accounts like that of Sir Richard Burton (1868).

7. Dresch notes the irony that "the genealogies formed a framework in which the tribes (whatever they had been to begin with) became regiments in the garrisons of empire. The first segmentary, total genealogy, whose form was later to be taken as typical of certain 'stateless' societies, was thus the product of a growing state" (Dresch 1988, 53).
8. Leach suggested that "the ethnographer has often only managed to discern the existence of '*a* tribe' because he took it as axiomatic that this kind of cultural entity must in fact exist" (1954, 291). See also Leach's "Tribal Ethnography: Past, Present and Future" (1986).
9. Take, for example, how Amy Chua begins her 2019 book *Political Tribes* by arguing that an "ideological" investment in "democracy" and an inability to appreciate the importance of "primal group identities" has been responsible for major US foreign policy failures in Vietnam and Iraq. By this logic, the United States is figured as a political naïf whose cardinal sin is overestimating the goodness of those subjected to its ministrations, whether by underestimating the extent of Vietnamese animosity toward the disproportionately successful ethnic Chinese minority in the case of the former or the Sunni-Shi'i divide in the case of the latter (2019, 9–10). Of course, this conveniently overlooks how sectarian and tribal identification in Iraq was not a given: it waxed and waned over the course of the twentieth century in response to Ba'th Party policies, initially antithetical to its Arab nationalism but increasingly central to regime stability under Saddam Hussein's personalistic rule (Baram 1997). Such an account also overlooks how sectarian divisions were actively institutionalized by the US-led Coalition Provisional Authority in the immediate aftermath of the invasion of the country in 2003 through both de-ba'thification and the sectarian distribution of seats on the Iraqi Governing Council (Haddad 2011). Unsurprisingly, Chua's analysis has nothing to say about the extensive push to mobilize anthropological knowledge of the country's tribal and sectarian divides via the so-called Human Terrain System following the invasion. While there is much evidence these attempts to manipulate tribal and sectarian divides backfired as an insurgency against a foreign occupation fragmented into a civil war, it is difficult to argue US occupation authorities failed to appreciate the importance of tribalism. In fact, the US military has long been an enthusiastic purveyor of tribalism, something it recognizes itself when it deploys "Old West" metaphors like "Indian country" to describe parts of the Middle East it views as hostile (Silliman 2008).
10. Ahmed develops this argument through his depiction of Osama bin Laden's attempt to negotiate his identities as a Muslim tribesman, connecting his trajectory to a wider tribal struggle within Saudi Arabia stretching back to the dramatic assault on Mecca by his fellow tribesman and Islamist Juhayman Al-Otaibi in 1979. Like bin Laden's later assault on the United States, Al-Otaibi "achieved what he set out to do" by "drawing negative attention to the Saudis" (Ahmed 2013, 116), a dynamic reminiscent of the Bedouin practice of "cutting the face," which I describe in the chapter "**Face**," where those nominally included within a tribal formation humiliate would-be leaders through spectacular acts of unauthorized violence.

11. A video of this reconciliation titled *ṣulha ʿashāʾirī bayn āl al-shiyāb wa āl al-ʿathāmneh* can be found on the "rumonline" channel on YouTube, where it was published on July 1, 2017. It was still available in June of 2025: https://www.youtube.com/watch?v=mHd3K2rSFQ8&t=3s.

Chapter 3. Envy

1. The most recent interdisciplinary volume about envy continues the venerable tradition of claiming that it is somehow understudied, bemoaning how little anthropologists have written on the topic (Smith 2008, 11–12).
2. In a similar vein, Fredric Jameson has argued that theories of resentment and *ressentiment* have an inherently auto-referential character to the degree that they seem to cathect upon the elite's own discomfort at "seemingly gratuitous lower-class agitation" (1981, 202).
3. This episode was added to the account of his capture by soldiers of the Ottoman *Bey* in Deraa in later editions, and most of his biographers, including Andrew Greaves (2007, 146), Desmond Stewart (1977, 240–244), and James Barr (2008, 203–206) have dismissed the account as a sexual fantasy rather than a real event.
4. In his excoriating book-length treatment of Mead's work on Samoa, the later anthropologist Derek Freeman adduced a number of lurid examples and more general reports of the Samoan propensity for jealousy, and suggested White and Murdock were wrong to question the universality of jealousy (1983, 242–244).
5. Attempts to separate tribal and Islamic beliefs about envy are difficult, for a few reasons. As Aref Abu-Rabia argues, from the standpoint of the Bedouin, there is generally "no inconsistency" between their "folk beliefs (including the evil eye)" and Islam (2005, 242), so many tribespeople will deny that there is anything un-Islamic about these beliefs and practices. Yet tribespeople can also be intensely monotheistic in attributing all agency to God (and thus radically limiting the scope of envy's powers), and since tribal membership is rarely—if ever—a matter of one's metaphysical commitments (unlike Islam's *umma*), such generalizing can only lead to oversimplification.
6. Among the Quranic verses that are widely believed to have strong apotropaic powers, there is the so-called throne verse and the last three *sūra*s or chapters of the *Qur'ān*.
7. Or as Andrew Shryock (1997, 46) reports, people might paint their houses pale blue or green, colors purported to deflect envy.
8. The fall is depicted several times in the *Qur'ān*, first in the second book ("The Cow") and then the seventh ("The Heights"). In verse 7:11, God responds to Satan's invidious reasoning about how fire is superior to clay by banishing Satan from paradise, reproaching him that "it is not for you to be arrogant here" (*famā yakūnu lak ann tatakabbar fīha*). Some interpretations like ibn Kathir's *Tafsīr* explicitly interpret Satan's motivation as envy as well as "disbelief, stubbornness, arrogance and false pride" ([1372] 2000, 393). Yet despite sometimes validating the role of envy in the fall from paradise that some of my Bedouin interlocutors emphasized, the written tradition is markedly less effusive about its centrality.

9. Ibn Taymiyyah's psychologism here also anticipates the contemporary Salafi movement's tendency to psychologize spirit possession (Vinea 2018).
10. For more on the relationship between envy and miserliness, see Ghosh (1983) and Al-Jahiz's *The Book of Misers*.

Chapter 4. Face

1. A version of the video titled *fa'al al-ḥuwayṭī bilma'āniyah* was later uploaded to YouTube on the "alhwote" channel on May 12, 2013. It was still available as of June 2025: https://www.youtube.com/watch?v=l3CzyTzTAUQ.
2. Excerpts from the graphic video were included in a report that is available on the "CBC News—The National" YouTube channel in a video titled "Muath al-Kaseasbeh, ISIS hostage, purportedly burned alive."

Chapter 5. The Deep State

1. While the pardons gave the defendants "nearly everything they wanted" short of monetary compensation, as Mike Wendling (2025) of the BBC reported, they hardly make up for how their lives were upended in the interim.
2. For more on the tribal sensibilities underpinning the Abraham Accords, see Kaminer (2024), who seeks to take the genealogical conceit of the agreement's name seriously. As Kaminer notes, the naming of the accords refers to a common belief that Jews are descended from Abraham's son Isaac, while Arab-Muslims are descended from his other son Ishmael, making them "cousins" and therefore natural allies of sorts.
3. Among others, Bulos (2017) and Phillips and Hubbard (2017) wrote press accounts of the incident, the subsequent trial, and the reaction to the verdict.
4. The idea of "liquidation" (*taṣfiyya*) is used to refer to how those inconvenient to the powers that be are clandestinely eliminated. One particularly recurrent image associated with the term involves the hapless victim being injected with a poison by a fast-moving operative who then makes his escape as his victim appears to suddenly be taken violently ill and expire.
5. In fact, at least one American claimed to have survived the attack and provided an eyewitness account to US media sources (Phillips and Hubbard 2017).
6. A copy of Prince Hamzah's appeal titled "Jordan's Former Crown Prince Says He's Under House Arrest" can be found on the "Guardian News" YouTube Channel. It was still available as of June 2025: https://www.youtube.com/watch?v=92aNviCNUsg.

Chapter 6. Mercy

1. Although Jordan's oral history is replete with well-known episodes in which important figures were incarcerated by the Ottomans, the massive intensification of policing that coincided with the arrival of the British seems to have led many to not unreasonably associate the proliferation of the carceral paradigm with European modernity.

2. The shift from five generations of collective responsibility to three, which is discussed in greater detail in chapter 4 ("**Face**"), is most accepted in cases of unintentional homicide, but prominent figures have argued to me that it should be three in all cases (see also Shunnaq et al. 2025, 64–65). At the same time—especially in the wake of a particularly heinous crime—leaders may struggle to limit collective responsibility to merely five generations.

Epilogue. Locking Down

1. There has been sufficient chatter that specific Gazan tribes themselves have felt it necessary to deny the overtures to coordinate with Israel (Palestine Chronicle 2024).

Works Cited

Abdullah, R. 2013. *Mapping Digital Media: Egypt.* Open Society Foundation. https://www.opensocietyfoundations.org/publications/mapping-digital-media-egypt, accessed August 10, 2023.

Abrams, P. 1977 [1988]. "Notes on the Difficulty of Studying the State." *Journal of Historical Sociology* 1 (1): 58–89.

Abu Lughod, L. 1986. *Veiled Sentiments: Honor and Poetry in a Bedouin Society.* Berkeley: University of California Press.

Abu Lughod, L. 1989. "Zones of Theory in the Anthropology of the Arab World." *Annual Review of Anthropology* 18:267–306.

Abu Lughod, L. 2013. "Seductions of the 'Honor Crime.'" In *Do Muslim Women Need Saving?* Cambridge, MA: Harvard University Press, 113–142.

Abu-Rabia, A. 2005. "The Evil Eye and Cultural Beliefs among the Bedouin Tribes of the Negev, Middle East." *Folklore* 116:241–254.

Ahmed, Akbar. 2013. *The Thistle and the Drone: How America's War on Terror Became a Global War on Tribal Islam.* London: Bloomsbury.

Al-Abbadi, Ahmad Oweidi. 2006. *Bedouin Justice: The Customary Legal System of the Tribes and Its Integration into the Framework of State Polity from 1921–1982.* Amman, Jordan: Dar Jareer.

Al-Jahiz. 1997. *The Book of Misers.* R. B. Serjeant, trans. Reading, UK: Garnet Publishing.

Al-Khalidi, Suleiman. 2021. "Insight: The Sudden Visit to COVID Victims' Families That Sparked Jordan's Royal Rift." Reuters. https://www.reuters.com/world/middle-east/sudden-visit-covid-victims-families-that-sparked-jordans-royal-rift-2021–04–08/, accessed June 1, 2024.

Al-Marayat, Ghazi. 2012. *"wadi tha'lib wara' maqtal sa'iq Madaba* [*Valley of Wolves* Behind Killing of Madaba Driver]." *Al-Ra'i.* https://alrai.com/article/521261/%D9%85%D8%AD%D9%84%D9%8A%D8%A7%D8%AA/%D9%88%D8%A7%D8%AF%D9%8A-%D8%A7%D9%84%D8%B0%D8%A6%D8%A7%D8%A8-%D9%88%D8%B1%D8%A7%D8%A1-%D9%85%D9%82%D8%AA%D9%84-%D8%B3%D8%A7%D8%A6%D9%82-%D9%85%D8%A7%D8%AF%D8%A8%D8%A7, accessed June 1, 2024.

Al-‘oudat, M. A., and A. Alshboul. 2010. “‘Jordan First’: Tribalism, Nationalism and Legitimacy of Power in Jordan.” *Intellectual Discourse* 18 (1): 65–96.

Al-Saleh, M. 2016. “When Anti-Corruption Initiatives Meet the Culture of Wasta: The Case of Public Sector Reforms in Jordan.” PhD diss., University of Ottawa.

Alon, Y. 2007. *The Making of Jordan: Tribes, Colonialism and the Modern State.* London: Bloomsbury Publishing.

Althusser, L. 1971. *Lenin and Philosophy and Other Essays.* B. Brewster, trans. New York: Monthly Review Books.

Amar, P. 2013. *The Security Archipelago: Human-Security States, Sexuality Politics, and the End of Neoliberalism.* Durham, NC: Duke University Press.

Amos, D. 2013. “In a Rough Neighborhood, Jordan Clings to Its Stability.” National Public Radio. https://www.npr.org/sections/parallels/2013/07/01/196656296/stability-or-democracy-in-jordan-its-a-fragile-balance, accessed May 4, 2018.

Anderson, B. 1983 [2006]. *Imagined Communities: Reflections on the Origin and Spread of Nationalism.* New York: Verso.

Antoun, R. T. 2000. “Civil Society, Tribal Process, and Change in Jordan: An Anthropological View.” *International Journal of Middle East Studies* 32 (4): 441–463.

Aouragh, M. 2012. “Framing the Internet in the Arab Revolutions: Myth Meets Modernity.” *Cinema Journal* 52 (1): 148–156.

Appadurai, A. 1986. “Theory in Anthropology: Center and Periphery.” *Comparative Studies in Society and History* 28 (2): 356–361.

Arendt, Hannah. [1951] 1979. *The Origins of Totalitarianism.* New York: Harvest Books.

Armbrust, Walter. 1996. *Mass Culture and Modernism in Egypt.* Cambridge: Cambridge University Press.

Asad, Talal. 1973. *Anthropology and the Colonial Encounter.* London: Ithaca Press.

Asad, Talal. [1986] 2009. “The Idea of an Anthropology of Islam.” *Qui Parle?* 17 (2): 1–30.

Aslan, R. 2011. *No God but God: The Origins, Evolution and Future of Islam.* London: Arrow Books.

Assabeel. 2013. “Ma‘anis March on the Royal Court to Demand ‘Lifting the Blockade’ on Ma‘an.” *An-Nas Al-Akhbārī.* http://alnasnews.net/online/local/11150.html, accessed April 3, 2017.

Assi, S. 2018. *The History and Politics of the Bedouin: Reimagining Nomadism in Modern Palestine.* London: Routledge.

Ayalon, A. 1995. *The Press in the Arab Middle East: A History.* Oxford: Oxford University Press.

Ayish, M., and N. Mellor. 2015. *Reporting in the MENA Region: Cyber Engagement and Pan-Arab Social Media.* London: Rowman & Littlefield.

Azzeh, Laila. 2016. “Muslim Scholar Detained ‘Over Comments on Jordan’s Role in anti-Daesh War.’” *Jordan Times.* http://www.jordantimes.com/news/local/muslim-scholar-detained-over-comments-jordans-role-anti-daesh-war, accessed April 3, 2017.

Badarneh, Muhammad. 2023. “Self-Defence Discourse in Collectivist Cultures: The Case of Jordanian Tribes Defending Their Members Against Public Accusations of Corruption.” *Journal of Intercultural Communication Research* 52 (6): 607–628.

Baker, Aryn. 2011. "In Jordan, the King Decides It's the Right Time to Clean House." *Time.* http://content.time.com/time/specials/packages/article/0,28804,2045328_2045333_2045565,00.html, accessed May 4, 2018.

Barakat, N. 2023. *Bedouin Bureaucrats: Mobility and Property in the Ottoman Empire.* Stanford, CA: Stanford University Press.

Baram, A. 1997. "Neo-Tribalism in Iraq: Saddam Hussein's Tribal Policies 1991–96." *International Journal of Middle East Studies* 29 (1): 1–31.

Barr, J. 2008. *Setting the Desert on Fire: T. E. Lawrence and Britain's Secret War in Arabia, 1916–1918.* London: Bloomsbury Press.

Barr, J. 2011. *A Line in the Sand: Britain, France and the Struggle That Shaped the Middle East.* London: Simon and Schuster.

Barry, Ellen, Nicholas Bogel-Burroughs, and Dave Philipps. 2021. "Woman Killed in Capitol Embraced Trump and QAnon." *New York Times.* https://www.nytimes.com/2021/01/08/us/who-was-ashli-babbitt.html, accessed June 1, 2024.

Barth, Fredrik. 1968. *Ethnic Groups and Boundaries.* Boston: Little, Brown and Co.

Bataille, G. [1949] 1991. *The Accursed Share: An Essay on General Economy.* Robert Hurley, trans. New York: Zone Books.

Bateson, Gregory. 1935. "199. Culture Contact and Schismogenesis." *Man* 35: 178–183.

Bateson, Gregory. 1972. *Steps to an Ecology of Mind: Collected Essays in Anthropology, Psychiatry, Evolution, and Epistemology.* Northvale, NJ: Jason Aronson Inc.

Beatty, Andrew. 2005. "Emotions in the Field: What Are We Talking About?" *Journal of the Royal Anthropological Institute* 11(1): 17–37.

Ben Hounet, Y. 2021. *Crime and Compensation in North Africa: A Social Anthropology Essay.* London: Palgrave.

Benedict, R. 1935. "An Introduction to Zuni Mythology." In *An Anthropologist at Work, Writings of Ruth Benedict*, ed. Margaret Mead. New York: Equinox Books, 226–245.

Benedict, R. 1946. *The Chrysanthemum and the Sword: Patterns of Japanese Culture.* New York: Houghton Mifflin Harcourt.

Berger, John. 1972. *Ways of Seeing.* London: Penguin Books.

Birth, K. 2008. "The Creation of Coevalness and the Danger of Homochronism." *Journal of the Royal Anthropological Institute* 14 (1): 3–20.

Black-Michaud, J. 1975. *Cohesive Force: Feud in the Mediterranean and the Middle East.* New York: Blackwell.

Bloch, Maurice. 2013. *In and Out of Each Other's Bodies: Theory of Mind, Evolution, Truth, and the Nature of the Social.* London: Routledge.

Boehm, Christopher. 1984. *Blood Revenge: The Anthropology of Feuding in Montenegro and Other Tribal Societies.* Lawrence: University Press of Kansas.

Bourdieu, Pierre. 1977. *Outline of a Theory of Practice.* Cambridge: Cambridge University Press.

Brady, Anne-Marie. 2008. *Marketing Dictatorship: Propaganda and Thought Work in Contemporary China.* Plymouth, UK: Rowen and Littlefield.

Brady, Anne-Marie. 2012. *China's Thought Management.* London: Routledge.

Briggs, C. L. [1986] 2012. *Learning How to Ask: A Sociolinguistic Appraisal of the Role of the Interview in Social Science Research.* Cambridge: Cambridge University Press.

British Broadcasting Corporation. 2021. "Jordan's Prince Hamzah bin Hussein 'Under House Arrest.'" https://www.bbc.co.uk/news/world-middle-east-56626370, accessed May 5, 2025.

British Broadcasting Corporation. 2022. "Jordan's Prince Hamzah bin Hussein Renounces Title of Prince." https://www.bbc.co.uk/news/world-middle-east-60976314, accessed June 1, 2024.

Brodeur, J. 1982. "High Policing and Low Policing: Remarks about the Policing of Political Activities." *Social Problems* 30 (5): 507–520.

Brown, J. A. C. 2005. *Misquoting Muhammad: The Challenge and Choices of Interpreting the Prophet's Legacy*. London: Oneworld Publications.

Brown, Keith. 2008. "'All They Understand Is Force': Debating Culture in Operation Iraqi Freedom." *American Anthropologist* 110 (4): 443–453.

Bulos, Nabih. 2016. "Jordanian Journalist Shot to Death on Courthouse Steps after Posting Controversial Cartoon to Facebook." *Los Angeles Times*. http://www.latimes.com/world/middleeast/la-fg-jordan-journalist-killed-cartoon-20160925-snap-story.html, accessed April 3, 2017.

Bulos, Nabih. 2017. "Jordanian Soldier Sentenced to Life in Prison in Killing of Three U.S. Military Trainers." *Los Angeles Times*. http://www.latimes.com/world/middleeast/la-fg-jordan-us-soldiers-killed-20170717-story.html, accessed May 4, 2018.

Calhoun, Craig. 1992. *Habermas and the Public Sphere*. Cambridge, MA: MIT Press.

Candea, Matei. 2025. "French Law, Danish Cartoons, and the Anthropology of Free Speech." *Comparative Studies in Society and History* 67 (1): 5–32.

Carmody, P. 2012. "The Informationalization of Poverty in Africa? Mobile Phones and Economic Structure." *Information Technologies & International Development* 8 (3): 1–18.

Charrad, Mounira. 2001. *States and Women's Rights: The Making of Postcolonial Tunisia, Algeria, and Morocco*. Berkeley: University of California Press.

Chatterjee, P. 1993. *The Nation and Its Fragments: Colonial and Postcolonial Histories*. Princeton, NJ: Princeton University Press.

Chin, E. 2016. *My Life with Things: The Consumer Diaries*. Durham, NC: Duke University Press.

Chua, A. 2019. *Political Tribes: Group Instinct and the Fate of Nations*. New York: Penguin.

Chulov, Martin, and Michael Safi. 2021. "Phone Intercepts Shine More Light on Jordanian Prince's Alleged Coup Attempt." *The Guardian*. https://www.theguardian.com/world/2021/may/30/phone-intercepts-jordanian-prince-alleged-coup-attempt, accessed June 1, 2024.

Clastres, Pierre. 1974. *Society Against the State: Essays in Political Anthropology*. Princeton, NJ: Zone Books.

Cole, Juan. 2018. *Muhammad: Prophet of Peace Amid the Clash of Empires*. New York: Bold Type Books.

Coleman, E. G. 2010. "Ethnographic Approaches to Digital Media." *Annual Review of Anthropology* 39:487–505.

Davis, A. 2003. *Are Prisons Obsolete?* New York: Seven Stories Press.

Deeb, L., and J. Winegar. 2012. "Anthropologies of Arab-Majority Societies." *Annual Review of Anthropology* 41:537–558.

Delaney, Carol. 1991. *The Seed and the Soil: Gender and Cosmology in Turkish Village Society*. Berkeley: University of California Press.

Deleuze, Gilles. 1997. *Essays Critical and Clinical*. D. W. Smith and M. A. Greco, trans. Minneapolis: University of Minnesota Press.

Deloria, P. J. 1998. *Playing Indian*. New Haven, CT: Yale University Press.

Denbeaux, Mark, and Donna Crawley. 2023. "The January 6 Insurrectionists: Who They Are and What They Did." *Seton Hall Law School Legal Studies Research*. Forthcoming. https://papers.ssrn.com/sol3/papers.cfm?abstract_id=4512381, accessed June 1, 2024.

Department of the Prime Minister and Cabinet. 2019. "Australia-Israel Chamber of Commerce Speech." March 18. https://pmtranscripts.pmc.gov.au/release/transcript-42201.

Derrida, Jacques. 2000. *Of Hospitality: Anne Dufourmantelle Invites Jacques Derrida to Respond*. Rachel Bowbly, trans. Stanford, CA: Stanford University Press.

Dewey, John. 1927. *The Public and Its Problems*. New York: Henry Holt and Company.

Donzelot, J. 1977. *The Policing of Families*. R. Hurley, trans. New York: Pantheon Books.

Doucet, Lyse. 2025. "Trump's Meeting with Sharaa, Unthinkable Just Months Ago, Boosts Syrians' Hopes." *British Broadcasting Corporation*. May 14. https://www.bbc.co.uk/news/articles/c9dqp842nl8o, accessed May 26, 2025.

Doughan, Y. 2017. "Imaginaries of Space and Language: A Historical View of the Scalar Enregisterment of Jordanian Arabic." *International Journal of Arabic Linguistics* 3 (2): 77–109.

Doughan, Y. 2019. "The Reckoning of History: Young Activists, Tribal Elders, and the Uses of the Past in Jordan." *POMEPS Studies* 36:60–63.

Doughan, Y. 2024. "The Rule-of-Law as a Problem Space: Wāsṭa and the Paradox of Justice in Jordan." *Comparative Studies in Society and History* 66 (1): 131–154.

Dresch, Paul. 1987. "Placing the Blame: A Means of Enforcing Obligations in Upper Yemen." *Anthropos* 82 (4/6): 427–443.

Dresch, Paul. 1988. "Segmentation: Its Roots in Arabia and Its Flowering Elsewhere." *Cultural Anthropology* 3:50–67.

Dresch, Paul. 2000. "Wilderness of Mirrors: Truth and Vulnerability in Middle Eastern Fieldwork." In *Anthropologists in a Wider World: Essays in Field Research*, ed. Paul Dresch and Wendy James. New York: Berghahn Books.

Durkheim, E. [1893] 1984. *The Division of Labour in Society*. W. D. Halls, trans. New York: Free Press.

Durkheim, E. [1912] 1995. *The Elementary Forms of the Religious Life*. New York: Simon and Schuster.

Durot, Matt. 2022. "Saudi Prince Alwaleed Becomes Twitter's Second Largest Shareholder." *Forbes*. October 31.

Edwards, Paul. 1996. *The Closed World: Computers and the Politics of Discourse in Cold War America*. Cambridge, MA: MIT Press.

El-Ariss, T. 2019. *Leaks, Hacks and Scandals: Arab Culture in the Digital Age*. Princeton, NJ: Princeton University Press.

El-Haj, N. A. 2012. *The Genealogical Science: The Search for Jewish Origins and the Politics of Epistemology*. Chicago: University of Chicago Press.

El-Rayyes, Thoraya. 2015. "Controlling Online Media in Jordan: Censorship or Rule of Law." *7iber.com*. https://www.7iber.com/wireless_research/controlling-online-media-in-jordan-censorship-or-rule-of-law/, accessed April 3, 2017.

Ellul, J. 1964. *The Technological Society*. New York: Alfred A. Knopf.

Emad, M. M. 2021. "Tribal Customary Law in Contemporary Jordan: Conciliation and Security through Bedouin Justice." PhD diss., Western Sydney University. https://researchers-admin.westernsydney.edu.au/ws/portalfiles/portal/94904173/uws_68477.pdf, accessed June 11, 2025.

Engelke, M. 2017. *How to Think Like an Anthropologist*. Princeton, NJ: Princeton University Press.

Engels, Friedrich. [1884] 2001. *The Origin of the Family, Private Property and the State*. London: Wellred Books.

Evans-Pritchard, E. E. 1935. *Witchcraft, Oracles and Magic among the Azande*. Abridged ed. E. Gillies, ed. London: Oxford University Press.

Evans-Pritchard, E. E. 1949. *The Sanusi of Cyrenaica*. Oxford: Clarendon Press.

Evans-Pritchard, E. E. 1969. *The Nuer: A Description of the Modes of Livelihood and Political Institutions of a Nilotic People*. Oxford: Oxford University Press.

Ewing, K. 2008. *Stolen Honor: Stigmatizing Muslim Men in Berlin*. Stanford, CA: Stanford University Press.

Fabian, J. 1983. *Time and the Other: How Anthropology Makes Its Object*. New York: Columbia University Press.

Fair, H., and R. Walmsley. 2022. *World Prison Population List*. 13th ed. London: Institute for Crime and Justice Policy Research. https://www.prisonstudies.org/sites/default/files/resources/downloads/world_prison_population_list_13th_edition.pdf.

Faqir, Fadia. 2001. "Intrafamily Femicide in Defence of Honour: The Case of Jordan." *Third World Quarterly* 22 (1): 65–82.

Feighery, W. G. 2012. "Tourism and Self-Orientalism in Oman: A Critical Discourse Analysis." *Critical Discourse Studies* 9 (3): 269–284.

Fernández, B. 2011. *The Imperial Messenger: Thomas Friedman at Work*. London: Verso Books.

Fields, K., and B. Fields. 2014. *Racecraft: The Soul of Inequality in American Life*. London: Verso Books.

Fisk, R. 2005. *The Great War for Civilization: The Conquest of the Middle East*. New York: Alfred A. Knopf.

Fortune, Reo. [1932] 2013. *Sorcerers of Dobu: The Social Anthropology of the Dobu Islanders of the Western Pacific*. London: Routledge.

Foster, George. 1965. "Peasant Society and the Image of Limited Good." *American Anthropologist* 67 (2): 293–315.

Foster, George. 1972. "The Anatomy of Envy: A Study in Symbolic Behavior." *Current Anthropology* 13 (2): 165–202.

Foucault, M. [1977] 1995. *Discipline and Punish: The Birth of the Prison*. A. Sheridan, trans. New York: Vintage Books.

Foucault, M. 1991. "Governmentality." In *The Foucault Effect: Studies in Governmentality*, ed. G. Burchell, C. Gordon, and P. Miller. Chicago: University of Chicago Press.

Foucault, Michel. [1961] 2003. *Madness and Civilization*. London: Routledge.

Freeman, Derek. 1983. *Margaret Mead and Samoa: The Making and Unmaking of an Anthropological Myth*. Canberra: Australian National University Press.

Fried, Morton Herbert. 1967. *The Evolution of Political Society: An Essay in Political Anthropology*. New York: Random House.

Gade, C. B. 2013. "Restorative Justice and the South African Truth and Reconciliation Process." *South African Journal of Philosophy* 32 (1): 10–35.

Gao, E. 2016. "Tribal Mobilization, Fragmented Groups, and Public Goods Provision in Jordan." *Comparative Political Studies* 49 (10): 1372–1403.

Geertz, C. 1967. "The Integrative Revolution: Primordial Sentiments and Civil Politics in the New States." In *Old Societies and New States: A Quest for Modernity in Asia and Africa*. New York: Free Press of Glencoe, 105–157.

Gershon, I. 2010. *The Breakup 2.0: Disconnecting over New Media*. Ithaca, NY: Cornell University Press.

Ghosh, Amitav. 1983. "The Relations of Envy in an Egyptian Village." *Ethnology* 22 (3): 211–223.

Gilmore, R. W. 2022. *Abolition Geography: Essays Towards Liberation*. London: Verso Books.

Gilsenan, Michael. 1996. *Lords of the Lebanese Marches: Violence and Narrative in an Arab Society*. Berkeley: University of California Press.

Glennon, Michael. 2014. *National Security and Double Government*. Oxford: Oxford University Press.

Glubb, J. 1948. *The Story of the Arab Legion*. London: Hodder and Stoughton.

Gluckman, M. 1955. *The Judicial Process among the Barotse of Northern Rhodesia*. Manchester: Manchester University Press.

Goffman, Erving. 1967. "On Face-Work." In *Interaction Ritual: Essays on Face-to-Face Behavior*. New York: Doubleday, 5–45.

González, Roberto. 2009a. *Militarizing Culture: Essays on the Warfare State*. London: Routledge.

González, Roberto. 2009b. "On 'Tribes' and Bribes: 'Iraq Tribal Study,' al-Anbar's Awakening, and Social Science." *Focaal* 53:105–116.

Goody, Jack. 1999. "Anarchy Brown." *Cambridge Journal of Anthropology* 21 (3): 1–8.

Gough, Kathleen. 1971. "Nuer Kinship: A Re-examination." In *The Translation of Culture: Essays to E. E. Evans-Pritchard*, ed. Thomas O Beidelman. London: Tavistock, 78–121.

Graeber, David, and Marshall Sahlins. 2017. *On Kings*. Chicago: Hau Books.

Graeber, David, and David Wengrow. 2021. *The Dawn of Everything: A New History of Humanity*. London: Penguin UK.

Gramsci, A. 1971. *Selections from Prison Writings*. Q. Hoare and G. N. Smith, trans. London: Lawrence and Wishart.

Greaves, Andrew. 2007. *Lawrence of Arabia: Mirage of a Desert War*. London: Weidenfeld and Nicolson.

Greene, Joshua. 2014. *Moral Tribes: Emotion, Reason, and the Gap Between Us and Them*. London: Penguin.

Guha, Sumit. 2021. *Tribe and State in Asia through Twenty-Five Centuries*. New York: Columbia University Press.

Günel, G., S. Varma, and C. Watanabe. 2020. "A Manifesto for Patchwork Ethnography." Member Voices, *Fieldsights*, June 9. https://culanth.org/fieldsights/a-manifesto-for-patchwork-ethnography.

Habermas, Jurgen. 1989. *Structural Transformation of the Public Sphere*. Cambridge, MA: MIT Press.

Haddad, F. 2011. *Sectarian Visions in Iraq: Antagonistic Visions of Unity*. London: Hurst.

Haidt, Jonathan. 2012. *The Righteous Mind: Why Good People Are Divided by Politics and Religion*. London: Vintage.

Haidt, Jonathan. 2022. "Why the Past 10 Years of American Life Have Been Uniquely Stupid." *The Atlantic*. May.

Haidt, Jonathan, and Ravi Iyer. 2016. "How to Get Beyond Our Tribal Politics." *Wall Street Journal*. https://www.wsj.com/articles/how-to-get-beyond-our-tribal-politics-1478271810.

Hallaq, W. 2009. *Shariah: Theory, Practice and Transformations*. Cambridge: Cambridge University Press.

Hamed-Troyansky, Vladimir. 2024. *Empire of Refugees: North Caucasian Muslims and the Late Ottoman State*. Stanford, CA: Stanford University Press.

Hardt, Michael. 1999. "Affective Labor." *Boundary 2* 26 (2): 89–100.

Harris, Malcolm. 2023. *Palo Alto: A History of California, Capitalism and the World*. London: Little, Brown and Company.

Hasso, Frances. 2011. *Consuming Desires: Family Crisis and the State in the Middle East*. Stanford, CA: Stanford University Press.

He, Zhou. 2000. "Working with a Dying Ideology: Dissonance and Its Reduction in Chinese Journalism." *Journalism Studies* 1 (4): 599–616.

Hemmings, Clare. 2005. "Invoking Affect: Cultural Theory and the Ontological Turn." *Cultural Studies* 19 (5): 548–568.

Henderson, J. C. 2008. "Representations of Islam in Official Tourism Promotion." *Tourism Culture & Communication* 8 (3): 135–145.

Henrich, Joseph, Steven J. Heine, and Ara Norenzayan. 2010. "The Weirdest People in the World?" *Behavioral and Brain Sciences* 33 (2–3): 61–83.

Herzfeld, M. 1996 [2005]. *Cultural Intimacy: Social Poetics in the Nation-State*. London: Routledge.

Hirschkind, Charles. 2006. *The Ethical Soundscape: Cassette Sermons and Islamic Counterpublics*. New York: Columbia University Press.

Ho, Engseng. 2006. *The Graves of Tarim: Genealogy and Mobility across the Indian Ocean*. Berkeley: University of California Press.

Hocart, A. M. [1952] 1970. *The Life-Giving Myth and Other Essays*. London: Tavistock and Metheuen.

Hofstadter, Richard. [1963] 2012. *The Paranoid Style in American Politics*. New York: Vintage.

Horsley, Scott. 2016. "Obama at U.N.: Reject Tribalism Home and Abroad." *National Public Radio*. September 20. https://www.npr.org/2016/09/20/494751020/obama-at-u-n-reject-tribalism-home-and-abroad.

Hu, H. C. 1944. "The Chinese Concepts of 'Face.'" *American Anthropologist* 46 (1): 45–64.

Hughes, Geoffrey. 2015a. "Affection and Mercy: Kinship, State, and the Management of Marriage in Jordan." PhD diss., University of Michigan.

Hughes, Geoffrey. 2015b. "Infrastructures of Legitimacy: The Political Lives of Marriage Contracts in Jordan." *American Ethnologist* 42 (2): 279–294.

Hughes, Geoffrey. 2020a. "Envious Ethnography and the Ethnography of Envy in Anthropology's 'Orient': Towards a Theory of Envy." *Ethos* 48 (2): 192–211.

Hughes, Geoffrey. 2020b. "Introduction: Legal Regimes under Pandemic Conditions: A Comparative Anthropology." *Journal of Legal Anthropology* 4 (1): 71–75.

Hughes, Geoffrey. 2021. *Kinship, Islam, and the Politics of Marriage in Jordan: Affection and Mercy*. Bloomington: Indiana University Press.

Hughes, Geoffrey. 2022. "Engineering Gender, Engineering the Jordanian State: Beyond the Salvage Ethnography of Middle-Class Housewifery in the Middle East." *Critique of Anthropology* 42 (4): 359–380.

Hughes, Geoffrey, Megnaa Mehtta, Chiara Bresciani, and Stuart Strange. 2019. "Introduction: Ugly Emotions and the Politics of Accusation." *Cambridge Journal of Anthropology* 37 (2): 1–20.

Hughes, Geoffrey, and A. M. Walter. 2021. "Staying Tuned: Connections beyond 'the Field.'" *Social Analysis* 65 (1): 89–102.

Hutchinson, Sharon E. 1996. *Nuer Dilemmas: Coping with Money, War, and the State*. Berkeley: University of California Press.

ibn Al-Kalbi, Hisham. 1952. *The Book of Idols*. Nabih Amin Faris, ed. Princeton, NJ: Princeton University Press.

Ibn Kathir. [1372] 2000. *Tafsîr ibn kathîr*. Riyadh: Dar-us-Salam.

ibn Khaldun. [1377] 2015. *The Muqaddimah: An Introduction to History*. Franz Rosenthal, trans. Princeton, NJ: Princeton University Press.

Ibn Taymiyyah. [1262] 1989. *Diseases of the Hearts and Their Cures*. Abu Rumaysah, trans. Birmingham: Dar As-sunnah Press.

Jameson, Fredric. 1981. *The Political Unconscious: Narrative as a Socially Symbolic Act*. Ithica, NY: Cornell University Press.

Jones, M. O. 2022. *Digital Authoritarianism in the Middle East: Deception, Disinformation and Social Media*. London: Hurst Publishers.

Joseph, Suad. 1987. "Gender, Sexuality and Power in Arab Society: Arab Feminist Criticism of Discourse and Social Order." *Reviews in Anthropology* 14 (4): 298–304.

Joseph, Suad. 1999. *Intimate Selving in Arab Families: Gender, Self, and Identity*. Syracuse, NY: Syracuse University Press.

Juris, J. 2012. "Reflections on #Occupy Everywhere: Social Media, Public Space, and Emerging Logics of Aggregation." *American Ethnologist* 39 (2): 259–279.

Jusionyte, Ieva. 2016. "Crimecraft: Journalists, Police, and News Publics in an Argentine Town." *American Ethnologist* 43 (3): 451–464.

Kaba, M. 2021. *We Do This 'Til We Free Us: Abolitionist Organizing and Transforming Justice*. Chicago: Haymarket Books.

Kaminer, Matan. 2022. "Saving the Face of the Arabah: Thai Migrant Workers and the Asymmetries of Community in an Israeli Agricultural Settlement." *American Ethnologist* 49 (1): 118–131.

Kaminer, Matan. 2024. "The Abrahamic Ideology: Patrilineal Kinship and the Politics of Peacemaking in the Contemporary Middle East." *Millenium* 52 (2): 198–220.

Kandiyoti, Deniz. 1988. "Bargaining with Patriarchy." *Gender & Society* 2 (3): 274–290.

Kao, Kristen. 2012. "Jordan's Ongoing Election Law Battle." *Sada*. https://carnegieendowment.org/sada/48781.

Kao, Kristen. 2015. "Ethnicity, Electoral Institutions, and Clientelism: Authoritarianism in Jordan." PhD diss., University of California, Los Angeles.

Kao, Kristen. 2023. "Electoral Institutions and Identity Based Clientelism in Jordan." *Political Research Quarterly* 76 (3): 1235–1248.

Kaya, Serdar. 2009. "The Rise and Decline of the Turkish 'Deep State': The Ergenekon Case." *Insight Turkey* 11 (4): 99–113.

Keane, Webb. 2016. *Ethical Life: Its Natural and Social Histories.* Princeton, NJ: Princeton University Press.

Kenez, Peter. 1985. *The Birth of the Propaganda State: Soviet Methods of Mass Mobilization, 1917–1929.* Cambridge: Cambridge University Press.

Kenney, M., and J. Zysman. 2016. "The Rise of the Platform Economy." *Issues in Science and Technology* 32 (3): 61–69.

King, Gary, Jennifer Pan, and Margaret E. Roberts. 2013. "How Censorship in China Allows Government Criticism but Silences Collective Expression." *American Political Science Review* 111 (3): 484–501.

King, Gary, Jennifer Pan, and Margaret E. Roberts. 2017. "How the Chinese Government Fabricates Social Media Posts for Strategic Distraction, not Engaged Argument." *American Political Science Review* 107 (2): 326–343.

Kitayama, Shinobu, Hyekyung Park, A. Timur Sevincer, Mayumi Karasawa, and Ayse K. Uskul. 2009. "A Cultural Task Analysis of Implicit Independence: Comparing North America, Western Europe, and East Asia." *Journal of Personality and Social Psychology* 97 (2): 236–255.

Lawrence, T. E. 1922 [1997]. *The Seven Pillars of Wisdom.* London: Penguin.

Layne, Linda. 1989. "The Dialogics of Tribal Self-Representation in Jordan." *American Ethnologist* 16 (1): 24–39.

Layne, Linda. 1994. *Home and Homeland: The Dialogics of Tribal and National Identities in Jordan.* Princeton, NJ: Princeton University Press.

Leach, Edmund. 1954. *Political Systems of Highland Burma: A Study of Kachin Social Structure.* London: Athlone Press.

Leach, Edmund. 1986. "Tribal Ethnography: Past, Present, Future." *Cambridge Journal of Anthropology* 11 (2): 1–14.

Levi-Strauss, C. 1962. *Totemism.* Boston: Beacon Press.

Lewis, Oscar. 1960. "Some of My Best Friends Are Peasants." *Human Organization* 19 (4): 179–180.

Lie, John. 2001. "Ruth Benedict's Legacy of Shame: Orientalism and Occidentalism in the Study of Japan." *Asian Journal of Social Science* 29 (2): 249–261.

Lindholm, Charles. 1982. *Generosity and Jealousy: The Swat Pukhtun.* New York: Columbia University Press.

Lipmann, Walter. 1922 [1997]. *Public Opinion.* New York: Free Press.

Lutz, Catherine, and Lila Abu Lughod. 1990. *Language and the Politics of Emotion.* Cambridge: Cambridge University Press.

Lynch, Daniel. 1999. *After the Propaganda State: Media, Politics, and "Thought Management" in Reformed China.* Stanford, CA: Stanford University Press.

Lynch, Marc. 1999. *State Interests and Public Spheres: The International Politics of Jordan's Identity.* New York: Columbia University Press.

Lynch, Marc. 2005. *Voices of the New Arab Public: Iraq, Aljazeera, and Middle East Politics Today.* New York: Columbia University Press.

Macdougall, Susan. 2019. "Ugly Feelings of Greed: The Misuse of Friendship in Working-Class Amman." *Cambridge Journal of Anthropology* 37 (2): 74–89.

Macpherson, C. B. [1962] 2010. *The Political Theory of Possessive Individualism: From Hobbes to Locke*. Oxford: Oxford University Press.

Mahadeen, E. 2021. "Queer Counterpublics and LGBTQ Pop-Activism in Jordan." *British Journal of Middle Eastern Studies* 48 (1): 78–93.

Mahadeen, E. 2022. *Women and the Media in Jordan: Gender, Power, Resistance*. Singapore: Springer Singapore.

Malinowski, Bronislaw. [1927] 2003. *Sex and Repression in Savage Society*. London: Routledge.

Maloney, Clarence. 1976. *The Evil Eye*. New York: Columbia University Press.

Mamdani, Mahmood. 1996. "The Other Face of Tribalism: Peasant Movements in Equatorial Africa." In *Citizen and Subject: Contemporary Africa and the Legacy of Late Colonialism*. Princeton, NJ: Princeton University Press, 183–217.

Mann, M. 1984. "The Autonomous Power of the State: Its Origins, Mechanisms and Results." *European Journal of Sociology* 25 (2): 185–213.

Marcus, G. E. 1995. "Ethnography in/of the World System: The Emergence of Multi-Sited Ethnography." *Annual Review of Anthropology* 24 (1): 95–117.

Markus, Hazel R., and Shinobu Kitayama. 1991. "Cultural Variation in the Self-Concept." In *The Self: Interdisciplinary Approaches*. New York: Springer New York, 18–48.

Martin, Emily. 2013. "The Potentiality of Ethnography and the Limits of Affect Theory." *Current Anthropology* 54 (S7): S149–S158.

Martínez, José Ciro. 2022. *States of Subsistence: The Politics of Bread in Contemporary Jordan*. Stanford, CA: Stanford University Press.

Marx, K. [1867] 2004. *Capital: Volume I*. London: Penguin UK.

Masco, Joseph, and Lisa Wedeen. 2024. *Conspiracy/Theory*. Duke University Press.

Massad, J. 2001. *Colonial Effects: The Making of National Identity in Jordan*. New York: Columbia University Press.

Massumi, Brian. 1996. "The Autonomy of Affect." In *Deleuze: A Critical Reader*, ed. P. Patton. Oxford: Blackwell, 217–239.

Mawhinney, J. L. 1998. *Giving Up the Ghost: Disrupting the (Re) Production of White Privilege in Anti-Racist Pedagogy and Organizational Change*. Toronto: University of Toronto Press.

McFadden, T. J. 1953. *Daily Journalism in the Arab States*. Columbus: Ohio State University Press.

McKinnon, Susan. 2000. "Domestic Exceptions: Evans-Pritchard and the Creation of Nuer Patrilineality and Equality." *Cultural Anthropology* 15 (1): 35–83.

McLuhan, M. 1964 [2001]. *Understanding Media: The Extensions of Man*. New York: Routledge.

Mead, Margaret. 1928. *Coming of Age in Samoa: A Psychological Study of Primitive Youth for Western Civilization*. New York: William Morrow and Company.

Migdadi, Fathi, Muhammad Badarneh, and Kawakib Momani. 2010. "Divine Will and Its Extensions: Communicative Functions of maašaallah in Colloquial Jordanian Arabic." *Communication Monographs* 77 (4): 480–499.

Mikdashi, M. 2022. *Sextarianism: Sovereignty, Secularism, and the State in Lebanon*. Stanford, CA: Stanford University Press.

Miller, Daniel. 2011. *Tales from Facebook*. Cambridge: Polity Press.
Mingus, M. 2022. "Transformative Justice: A Brief Description." *Fellowship* 84 (2): 17–19.
Miqdadi, Fadia. 2017. "*'ashīra al-shiyāb tawaḍiḥ li-sawalīf asbāb 'bayān al-tha'r' alladhī ṣadar al-yūm*" [Shiyab tribe clarifies to Sawaleif the reasons for the "revenge statement" issued today]. *Sawaleif* https://www.sawaleif.com/%D8%B9%D8%B4%D9%8A%D8%B1%D8%A9-%D8%A7%D9%84%D8%B4%D9%8A%D8%A7%D8%A8-%D8%AA%D9%88%D8%B6%D8%AD-%D9%84%D8%B3%D9%88%D8%A7%D9%84%D9%8A%D9%81-%D8%A7%D8%B3%D8%A8%D8%A7%D8%A8-%D8%A8%D9%8A%D8%A7%D9%86-%D8%A7–242668/, accessed June 4, 2025.
Mitchell, Timothy. 1991. "The Limits of the State: Beyond Statist Approaches and Their Critics." *American Political Science Review* 85 (1): 77–96.
Mitchell, Timothy. 2013. *Carbon Democracy: Political Power in the Age of Oil*. New York: Verso Books.
Mookherjee, N. 2022. "Introduction: On Irreconciliation." *Journal of the Royal Anthropological Institute* 28 (SI1): 11–33.
Morgan, L. H. [1851] 1901. *League of the Ho-De'-No-Sau-Nee or Iroquois*. Vol. 1. New York: Burt Franklin.
Morgan, L. H. [1877] 1964. *Ancient Society*. Cambridge, MA: Harvard University Press.
Morgan, N., and A. Pritchard. 1998. *Tourism Promotion and Power: Creating Images, Creating Identities*. Chichester: John Wiley & Sons.
Mumford, J. 2020. *Vexed: Ethics beyond Political Tribes*. London: Bloomsbury Publishing.
Nader, L. 1969. "Up the Anthropologist: Perspectives Gained from 'Studying Up.'" In *Reinventing Anthropology*, ed. D. Hymes. New York: Random House, 284–311.
Nader, L. 1988. "The ADR Explosion: The Implications of Rhetoric in Legal Reform." *Windsor Yearbook of Access to Justice* 8:269–291.
Nader, L. 1990. *Harmony Ideology: Justice and Control in a Zapotec Mountain Village*. Stanford, CA: Stanford University Press.
Nagarajan, S. 2020. "Saudi Arabia's $300 Billion Wealth Fund Ditched Facebook, Disney, and Boeing Stocks, and Poured Billions into ETFs in the Second Quarter." *Business Insider*. August 17.
Neiburg, Federico, Marcio Goldman, and Peter Gow. 1998. "Anthropology and Politics in Studies of National Character." *Cultural Anthropology* 13 (1): 56–81.
Ngai, S. 2005. *Ugly Feelings*. Cambridge, MA: Harvard University Press.
Niehaus, I. 2021. "Savages Have No Crime! Radcliffe-Brown on Social Sanctions and the Law." *Journal of Legal Anthropology* 5 (1): 135–162.
Ortner, S. 1972. "Is Female to Male as Nature Is to Culture?" *Feminist Anthropology* 1 (2): 5–31.
Osanloo, A. 2020. *Forgiveness Work: Mercy, Law and Victim's Rights in Iran*. Oxford: Oxford University Press.
Ottaway, M., and A. Hamzawy. 2011. *Protest Movements and Political Change in the Arab World*. Vol. 28. Washington, DC: Carnegie Endowment for International Peace.

Our World in Data. 2024. "Excess Mortality: Cumulative Deaths from All Causes Compared to Projection Based on Previous Years, per Million People." https://ourworldindata.org/grapher/cumulative-excess-deaths-per-million-covid?tab=table, accessed July 16, 2024.

Palestine Chronicle. 2024. "'Not an Alternative'—Coalition Rejects Israel's Attempts at Tribal Rule in Gaza." *Palestine Chronicle.* March 11. https://www.palestinechronicle.com/not-an-alternative-coalition-rejects-israels-attempts-at-tribal-rule-in-gaza/, accessed 26 May 2025.

Patai, R. [1973] 2006. *The Arab Mind.* New York: Scribner.

Peake, F. G. 1934. *A History of Trans-Jordan and Its Tribes.* Amman, Jordan: Arab Legion.

Peake, F. G. 1942. *Arab Command. The Biography of Lieutenant-Colonel F. G. Peake Pasha C.M.G., C.B.E.* London: Hutchinson & Co.

Peletz, Michael. 1994. "Neither Reasonable nor Responsible: Contrasting Representations of Masculinity in a Malay Society." *Cultural Anthropology* 9 (2): 135–178.

Pely, D. 2016. *Muslim/Arab Mediation and Conflict Resolution: Understanding Sulha.* New York: Routledge.

Peters, Emyrs. 1967. "Some Structural Aspects of the Feud among the Camel-Herding Bedouin of Cyrenaica." *Journal of the International African Institute* 37 (3): 261–282.

Philips, Dave, and Ben Hubbard. 2017. "Soldier Who Survived Shootout in Jordan Tells His Story." *New York Times.* https://www.nytimes.com/2017/07/25/world/middleeast/special-forces-jordan-shootout-survivor.html, accessed June 1, 2024.

Pitt-Rivers, Julian. 2017. *From Hospitality to Grace: a Pitt-Rivers Omnibus.* Damien Bright and Matthew Carey, trans. Giovanni da Col and Andrew Shryock, eds. Chicago: Hau Books.

Poulantzas, N. 1973. *Political Power and Social Classes.* London: New Left Books.

Pratt, Mary Louise. 1986. "Fieldwork in Common Places." In *Writing Culture: The Poetics and Politics of Ethnography*, ed. James Clifford and George E. Marcus. Berkeley: University of California Press, 27–50.

Price, D. H. 2011. *Weaponizing Anthropology: Social Science in Service of the Militarized State.* New York: AK Press.

Price, Monroe, Andrei Richter, and Peter Yu. 2002. *Russian Media Law and Policy in the Yeltsin Decade: Essays and Documents.* The Hague: Kluwer Law.

Qutb, S. 1970. *Social Justice in Islam.* John Hardie and Hamid Algar, trans. New York: Octagon Books.

Rachdi, H. 2024. "#Queer_Revolution_Morocco: A Disoriented Moroccan (Counter-) Archive from the Eyes of Its Queers." In *Global LGBTQ Activism: Social Media, Digital Technologies, and Protest Mechanisms*, ed. Paromita Pain. London: Routledge, 20–142.

Radcliffe-Brown, A. R. 1931. *The Social Organisation of Australian Tribes.* Melbourne: Macmillan.

Radcliffe-Brown, A. R. 1947. "Evolution, Social or Cultural." *American Anthropologist* 49 (1): 78–83.

Raines, T., M. Goodwin, and D. Cutts. 2017. "Europe's Political Tribes." Chatham House. United Kingdom. https://policycommons.net/artifacts/1423262/europes-political-tribes/2037524/, CID: 20.500.12592/7dqdm0, accessed June 30, 2023.

Richards, Audrey. 1941. "A Problem of Anthropological Approach." *Bantu Studies* 15 (1): 45–52.

Robins, Philip. 2004. *A History of Jordan*. Cambridge: Cambridge University Press.

Rogan, E. L. 2002. *Frontiers of the State in the Late Ottoman Empire: Transjordan, 1850–1921*. Cambridge: Cambridge University Press.

Ryan, Curtis R. 1998. "Peace, Bread and Riots: Jordan and the International Monetary Fund." *Middle East Policy* 6 (2): 54–66.

Said, E. 1978. *Orientalism: Western Concepts of the Orient*. New York: Pantheon.

Said, Edward. 1994. *Culture and Imperialism*. New York: Vintage Books.

Sangren, K. 2022. "Processual Recognition in Chinese Traffic Disputes." *PoLAR: Political and Legal Anthropology Review* 45 (1): 26–41.

Schapera, I. 1938. *A Handbook of Tswana Law and Custom*. Oxford: Oxford University Press.

Schechter, S. 1982. *Women and Male Violence: The Visions and Struggles of the Battered Women's Movement*. London: Pluto Press.

Scheele, Judith. 2021. "State-Like and State Dislike in the Anthropological Margins." *Journal of the Royal Anthropological Institute* 27 (4): 909–927.

Scheele, Judith, and Andrew Shryock. 2019. *The Scandal of Continuity in Middle East Anthropology: Form, Duration, Difference*. Bloomington: Indiana University Press.

Schoeck, Helmut. 1969. *Envy: A Theory of Social Behavior*. London: Secker and Warburg.

Schraube, Ernst, and Ute Osterkamp. 2013. *Psychology from the Standpoint of the Subject: Selected Writings of Klaus Holzkamp*. London: Palgrave Macmillan UK.

Schwedler, J. 2022. *Protesting Jordan: Geographies of Power and Dissent*. Stanford, CA: Stanford University Press.

Scott, J. B. 2019. "Death on Repeat: Violence, Viral Images and Questioning the Rule of Law in Brazilian Favelas." *Journal of Legal Anthropology* 3 (1): 21–40.

Scott, James C. 2009. *The Art of Not Being Governed: An Anarchist History of Upland Southeast Asia*. New Haven, CT: Yale University Press.

Sedgwick, Eve. 2002. *Touching Feeling: Affect, Pedagogy, Performativity*. Durham, NC: Duke University Press.

Sedgwick, Eve, and Adam Frank. 1995. "Shame in the Cybernetic Fold: Reading Silvan Tomkins." *Critical Inquiry* 21 (2): 496–522.

Shepard, William. 2003. "Sayyid Qutb's Doctrine of 'Jāhiliyya.'" *International Journal of Middle East Studies* 35 (1): 521–545.

Shryock, A. 1997. *Nationalism and the Genealogical Imagination: Oral History and Textual Authority in Tribal Jordan*. Berkeley: University of California Press.

Shryock, Andrew. 1999. "Dynastic Modernism and Its Contradictions: Testing the Limits of Pluralism, Tribalism, and King Hussein's Example in Hashemite Jordan." *Arab Studies Quarterly* 22 (3): 57–79.

Shryock, Andrew. 2004. *Off Stage/On Display: Intimacy and Ethnography in the Age of Public Culture*. Stanford, CA: Stanford University Press.

Shryock, Andrew, and Sally Howell. 2001. "'Ever a Guest in Our House': The Emir Abdullah, Shaykh Majid al-Adwan, and the Practice of Jordanian House Politics, as Remembered by Umm Sultan, the Widow of Majid." *International Journal of Middle East Studies* 33 (2): 247–269.

Shunnaq, M., S. Ramadan, M. Na'amneh, K. Al-Otum, J. A. Dizard, H. A. Al-Dajah, and W. Sekhaneh. 2025. "The Paradox of Conformity and Resistance: Socio-Political Transformation and the Persistence of Tribal Customary Law in Modern Jordan." *Contemporary Levant* 10 (1): 57–75.

Silliman, Stephen W. 2008. "The 'Old West' in the Middle East: US Military Metaphors in Real and Imagined Indian Country." *American Anthropologist* 110 (2): 237–247.

Simon, Andrew. 2022. *Media of the Masses: Cassette Culture in Modern Egypt*. Stanford, CA: Stanford University Press.

Skillen, Daphne. 2016. *Freedom of Speech in Russia: Politics and Media from Gorbachev to Putin*. London: Routledge.

Skocpol, Theda. 1985. "Bringing the State Back In: Strategies of Analysis in Current Research." In *Bringing the State Back In*, ed. Peter B. Evans, Dietrich Rueschemeyer, and Theda Skocpol. Cambridge: Cambridge University Press, 3–38.

Smith, Richard. 2008. *Envy: Theory and Research*. Oxford: Oxford University Press.

Smith, William Robertson. 1885. *Kinship and Marriage in Early Arabia*. Cambridge: Cambridge University Press.

Sneath, David. 2007. *The Headless State: Aristocratic Orders, Kinship Society, and Misrepresentations of Nomadic Inner Asia*. New York: Columbia University Press.

Sneath, David. 2009. "Tribe, *Ethnos*, Nation: Rethinking Evolutionist Social Theory and Representations of Nomadic Inner Asia." *Ab Imperio* 4:80–109.

Sooyler, Mehtap. 2015. *The Turkish Deep State: State Consolidation, Civil-Military Relations and Democracy*. London: Routledge.

Sparks, Colin. 2008. "Media Systems in Transition: Poland, Russia, China." *Chinese Journal of Communication* 1 (1): 7–24.

Spooner, Brian. 1970. "The Evil Eye in the Middle East." In *Witchcraft Confessions and Accusations*, ed. Mary Douglas. London: Routledge, 310–321.

Steinhaus, Hugo. 1948. "The Problem of Fair Division." *Econometrica* 16: 101–104.

Stewart, Desmond. 1977. *T. E. Lawrence*. New York: Harper Row.

Strathern, M. 1992. *After Nature: English Kinship in the Late Twentieth Century*. Cambridge: Cambridge University Press.

Strathern, M. 1996. "Cutting the Network." *Journal of the Royal Anthropological Institute* 2 (3): 517–535.

Strathern, M. 2018. "Persons and Partible Persons." In *Schools and Styles of Anthropological Theory*, ed. M. Candea. London: Routledge, 236–246.

Swedenburg, Ted. 2003. *Memories of Revolt: The 1936–1939 Rebellion and the Palestinian National Past*. Fayetteville: University of Arkansas Press.

Sweis, Rana. 2013. "Tribal Clashes at Universities Add to Tensions in Jordan." *New York Times*. http://www.nytimes.com/2013/04/25/world/middleeast/tribal-clashes-at-universities-add-to-tensions-in-jordan.html, accessed March 16, 2018.

Sweis, Rana. 2015. "Jordan Gives Prison Term for Criticism on Facebook." *New York Times*. https://www.nytimes.com/2015/02/16/world/middleeast/jordan-sentences-muslim-brotherhood-leader-for-facebook-post.html, accessed April 3, 2017.

Sweis, Rana, Adam Rasgon, and Patrick Kingsley. 2021. "Divided Kingdom: Jordan Shaken by Split Between King and Ex-Crown Prince." *New York Times*. https://www.nytimes.com/2021/04/04/world/middleeast/jordan-king-abdullah-royal-dispute.html?partner=slack&smid=sl-share, accessed June 1, 2024.

Táíwò, O. O. 2022. *Elite Capture: How the Powerful Took Over Identity Politics (and Everything Else)*. Chicago: Haymarket Books.

Tobin, S. A. 2016. *Everyday Piety: Islam and Economy in Jordan*. Ithaca, NY: Cornell University Press.

Tomkins, Silvan. 1963. *Affect, Imagery, Consciousness*. Vol. II: *The Negative Affects*. New York: Springer.

Trouillot, M. R. 2003. *Global Transformations*. New York: Palgrave Macmillan.

Tufekci, Z. 2017. *Twitter and Teargas: The Power and Fragility of Networked Protest*. New Haven, CT: Yale University Press.

Ünver, H. Akin. 2009. "Turkey's 'Deep-State' and the Ergenekon Conundrum." *Middle East Institute Policy Brief* 23. https://www.files.ethz.ch/isn/99724/No_23_Turkey%27s_Deep-State.pdf.

Verdery, Katherine. 2018. *My Life as a Spy: Investigations in a Secret Police File*. Durham, NC: Duke University Press.

Vinea, Ana. 2018. "An Emerging Affliction: Islamic Healing, the Psy Sciences, and What Lies In-Between." *Medicine Anthropology Theory* 5 (1): 50–77.

Wacquant, L. 2009. *Punishing the Poor: The Neoliberal Governance of Social Insecurity*. Durham, NC: Duke University Press.

Wagner, Roy. 1975 [2016]. *The Invention of Culture*. Chicago: University of Chicago Press.

Wallace, Anthony F. C. [1961] 1970. *Culture and Personality*. 2nd ed. New York: Random House.

Wamsley, Laurel. 2017. "When Harry Met Barack: Obama Tells Prince About Life After White House." December 27. https://www.npr.org/sections/thetwo-way/2017/12/27/573774407/in-bbc-interview-obama-tells-prince-harry-about-post-presidency-life.

Ward, Alex. 2021. "Jordan's Royal Family Feud and Alleged Coup Plot, Explained." *Vox*. https://www.vox.com/22367819/jordan-coup-attempt-arrest-abdullah-hamzah, accessed June 1, 2024.

Ward, Ian. 2024. "The Seven Thinkers and Groups That Have Shaped JD Vance's Unusual Worldview." *Poltico*. July 18. https://www.politico.com/news/magazine/2024/07/18/jd-vance-world-view-sources-00168984.

Warner, M. 2002. "Publics and Counterpublics." *Public Culture* 14 (1): 49–90.

Watkins, J. 2022. *Creating Consent in an Illiberal Order: Policing Disputes in Jordan*. Cambridge University Press.

Weber, Eugene. 1976. *Peasants into Frenchmen: The Modernization of Rural France, 1870–1914*. Stanford, CA: Stanford University Press.

Weber, Max. 1978. In *Economy and Society*, ed. Guenther Roth and Claus Wittich. Berkeley: University of California Press.

Wekker, G. 2016. *White Innocence: Paradoxes of Colonialism and Race*. Duke University Press.

Wendling, Mark. 2025. "Trump Pardons Give Jan 6 Defendants Nearly Everything They Wanted." *British Broadcasting Corporation*. https://www.bbc.co.uk/news/articles/cjw4vjvlgxpo, accessed May 5, 2025.

Westermarck, Edward. 1926. "The Evil Eye." In *Ritual and Belief in Morocco*. London: Macmillan and Co., 414–478.

The White House. 2016. "Address by President Obama to the 71st Session of the United Nations General Assembly." September 20. https://obamawhitehouse.archives.gov/the-press-office/2016/09/20/address-president-obama-71st-session-united-nations-general-assembly.

Wien, Peter. 2021. "Tribes and Tribalism in the Modern Middle East: Introduction." *International Journal of Middle East Studies* 53 (3): 471–472.

Wiktorowicz, Q. 1999. "Islamists, the State, and Cooperation in Jordan." *Arab Studies Quarterly* 21 (4): 1–17.

Williams, Kristian. 2011. "The Other Side of the COIN: Counterinsurgency and Community Policing." *Interface: A Journal for and About Social Movements* 3 (1): 81–117.

Williams, Maren. 2016. "Nahed Hattar Assassinated Before Start of Cartoon Blasphemy Trial in Jordan." *Comic Book Legal Defense Fund.* /nahed-hattar-assassinated-before-start-of-cartoon-blasphemy-trial-in-jordan/.

Wilson, M. C. 1987. *King Abdullah, Britain and the Making of Jordan.* Cambridge: Cambridge University Press.

Wilson, R. A. 2000. "Reconciliation and Revenge in Post-Apartheid South Africa: Rethinking Legal Pluralism and Human Rights." *Current Anthropology* 41 (1): 75–98.

Winner, L. 1980. "Do Artifacts Have Politics?" *Daedalus,* 121–136.

Wojnarowski, Frederick. 2021. *Unsettling Times: Land, Political Economy and Protest in the Bedouin Villages of Central Jordan.* PhD diss., University of Cambridge.

Wojnarowski, Frederick. 2023. "Settling Land, Unsettling People: Living with and Contesting Land, Social Change and Grand Schemes in Rural Central Jordan." *History and Anthropology,* 1–26.

Wolf, Bleek. 1979. "Envy and Inequality in Fieldwork: An Example from Ghana." *Human Organization* 38 (2): 200–205.

Yom, S. L. 2009. "Jordan: Ten More Years of Autocracy." *Journal of Democracy* 20 (4): 151–166.

Yom, S. L. 2013. "Jordan: The Ruse of Reform." *Journal of Democracy* 24 (3): 127–139.

Yom, S. L. 2014. "Tribal Politics in Contemporary Jordan: The Case of the Hirak Movement." *Middle East Journal* 68 (1): 229–247.

Zehr, H. 1990. *Changing Lenses: A New Focus for Crime and Justice.* Scottdale, PA: Herald Press.

Zhao, Yuezhi. 1998. *Media, Market, and Democracy in China: Between the Party Line and the Bottom Line.* Champaign: University of Illinois Press.

Zhu, Ying. 2012. *Two Billion Eyes: The Story of China Central Television.* New York: New Press.

Index

www.ingramcontent.com/pod-product-compliance
Lightning Source LLC
LaVergne TN
LVHW092138190926
847825LV00034B/118